States of Exception

This book addresses the relevance of the state of exception for the analysis of law, while reflecting on the deeper symbolic and jurisprudential significance of the coalescence between law and force.

The concept of the state of exception has become a central topos in political and legal philosophy as well as in critical theory. The theoretical apparatus of the state of exception sharply captures the uneasy relationship between law, life and politics in the contemporary global setting, while also challenging the comforting narratives that uncritically connect democracy with the tradition of the rule of law. Drawing on critical legal theory, continental jurisprudence, political philosophy and history, this book explores the genealogy of the concept of the state of exception and reflects on its legal embodiment in past and present contexts – including Weimar and Nazi Germany, contemporary Europe and Turkey. In doing so, it explores the disruptive force of the exception for legal and political thought, as it recuperates its contemporary critical potential.

The book will be of interest to students and scholars in the field of jurisprudence, philosophy and critical legal theory.

Dr **Cosmin Cercel** is Associate Professor in Law at the University of Nottingham. He is the author of *Towards a Jurisprudence of State Communism: Law and the Failure of Revolution* (Routledge: 2017).

Dr **Gian Giacomo Fusco** is Lecturer in Law at the University of Kent and associate professor at Uczelnia Łazarskiego.

Dr **Simon Lavis** is Lecturer in Law at the Open University.

Part of the

LAW AND POLITICS: CONTINENTAL PERSPECTIVES
series

series editors

Mariano Croce, *Sapienza University of Rome, Italy*
Marco Goldoni, *University of Glasgow, UK*

for information about the series and details of previous and forthcoming titles, see https://www.routledge.com/law/series/LPCP

States of Exception

Law, History, Theory

Edited by
Cosmin Cercel, Gian Giacomo Fusco
and Simon Lavis

Routledge
Taylor & Francis Group
a GlassHouse book

First published 2021
by Routledge
2 Park Square, Milton Park, Abingdon, Oxon OX14 4RN

and by Routledge
52 Vanderbilt Avenue, New York, NY 10017

Routledge is an imprint of the Taylor & Francis Group, an informa business

A Glasshouse book

British Library Cataloguing-in-Publication Data
A catalogue record for this book is available from the British Library

Library of Congress Cataloging-in-Publication Data
A catalog record has been requested for this book

ISBN: 978-0-367-07716-7 (hbk)
ISBN: 978-0-429-02229-6 (ebk)

Typeset in Times New Roman
by Taylor & Francis Books

Contents

Contributors

Cosmin Sebastian Cercel is Associate Professor in Law at the University of Nottingham. His research focuses on genealogies of law and politics with specific reference to twentieth-century continental legal history. He is the author of *Towards a Jurisprudence of State-Communism: Law and the Failure of Revolution* (London: Routledge, 2017), a monograph analyzing the jurisprudential aspects of state communism. Recent publications include "The Law of Blood: Totalitarianism, Criminal Law and the Body Politic of World War Two Romania" in Stephen Skinner (ed.), *Ideology and Criminal Law: Fascist, National Socialist and Authoritarian Regimes* (Oxford: Hart, 2019), 345-68. 'Law's Disappearance: the State of Exception and the Destruction of Experience', in Fabien Girard and Simone Glanert (eds), *Law's Hermeneutics: Other Investigations* (London: Routledge, 2017). He has co-edited with Rafał Mańko and Adam Sulikowski, *Law and Critique in Central Europe* (Oxford: Counterpress, 2016).

Gian Giacomo Fusco is a Lecturer in Law at Kent Law School (University of Kent) and associate professor in Law at Uczelnia Łazarskiego (Warsaw). He has obtained his doctoral degree in Law at the Univesity of Kent. His research interests include jurisprudence, critical theory, history of ideas and urban studies. He is currently working on a book on the notion of 'form of life' in Giorgio Agamben.

Tormod Otter Johansen (LLD, LLM, MA) is a researcher at the University of Gothenburg. His research interests are in public law, especially the relationship between constitutional issues and administrative issues, legal theory, both in the public law field and in general legal philosophy. He has published in these fields and in the field of procedural law. Together with three other scholars in law and theology in Gothenburg and Lund he is currently working on an interdisciplinary project – 'End of law', for the period 2020–2024. The group is led by Mårten Björk, Lund University.

Dimitrios Kivotidis is a Lecturer in Law at the University of East London. His research interests revolve around questions of sovereignty, the state of exception, democracy and the relation between constitutional processes and crisis, with a specific emphasis on the relevance of Marxist philosophy in approaching these topics.

Simon Lavis is a Lecturer in Law at the Open University. His research focuses on the nexus between law, history and theory in relation to Nazi Germany; including the history and theory of Nazi law, the historiographical and jurisprudential representation of the Third Reich, and the role of law in the transition to authoritarianism. His recent publications include 'Nazi Law as Non-Law in Academic Discourse' in Stephen Skinner (ed.), *Ideology and Criminal Law: Fascist, National Socialist and Authoritarian Regimes* (Oxford: Hart, 2019), 59-76; and 'The Distorted Jurisprudential Discourse of Nazi Law: Uncovering the "Rupture Thesis" in the Anglo-American Legal Academy', (2018) 31(4) *International Journal for the Semiotics of Law* 745–770.

Rafał Mańko is Fellow at the Amsterdam Centre for Transformative Private Law, University of Amsterdam. He received a master's degree in law from the University of Warsaw (2003), followed by a PhD in law from the University of Amsterdam (2014) and a Doctor *habilitatus* degree in law (*venia legendi*) from the University of Wrocław (2019). His research focuses on the socio-legal aspects of the transformation from actually existing socialism to capitalism, as well as on critical legal theory, with a particular emphasis on the critical theory of adjudication, law and ideology, and critique of legal form. He has co-edited (with Cosmin Cercel and Adam Sulikowski) *Law and Critique in Central Europe: Questioning the Past, Resisting the Present* (2016). His most recent publication is 'Artur Kozak's Juriscentrist Concept of Law: A Central European Legal Innovation' (2020) 45 *Review of Central and East European Law* 334.

Sara Raimondi is a Lecturer in Politics & International Relations at the New College of the Humanities, London. Her research is situated in political theory and contemporary political philosophy. She completed her doctoral thesis at the Department of Politics and International Relations at the University of Westminster, with a doctoral project around the relationship between biopolitical and neo-vitalist approaches in debates on the politics of life in contemporary political theory. Her further research interests cover humanism, political ontology, and theories of states of exception. Sara has published research outputs in journals such as *Democratic Theory and Contemporary Political Theory.*

Przemysław Tacik is Assistant Professor at the Institute of European Studies, Jagiellonian University of Krakow. He holds PhDs in philosophy and law. His interests include contemporary continental philosophy, Jewish philosophy and political philosophy, as well as international law and critical legal studies. Apart from papers in English and in Polish, as well as translations from French, he has authored three monographies: *Sociology of Zygmunt Bauman* (2012, in Polish),

The Accession of the European Union to the European Convention on Human Rights (2017, in Polish) and *Freedom of Lights: Edmond Jabès and Jewish Philosophy* of Modernity (2015, in Polish; English translation – 2019).

Ceylan Begüm Yıldız is a PhD candidate at Birkbeck College, School of Law. Her research areas include political and legal violence, gendered and racialised subjectivities, social movements, performative theory and critical theory.

David Fraser, FAcSS, is Professor of Law and Social Theory at the University of Nottingham. His research focuses on the role of law and legal professionals in the Shoah and on modern Jewish legal history. His current project examines Jewish legal self-defense against Nazi/fascist antisemitism in the 1930s in Canada, South Africa, the United Kingdom, and the United States.

Introduction

Untimely considerations on the state of exception

Gian Giacomo Fusco, Cosmin Cercel and Simon Lavis

I.

State of exception is one of those concepts in the politico-juridical vocabulary whose established popularity is not affected by their evident terminological uncertainty. Since the beginning of the twenty-first century, with the emergence of what has been defined as the war on terror, academic production on the subject has been literally flooded by an imponent stream of contributions. However, at this historical juncture, when exceptional measures have become a stable part of the seemingly decadent life of liberal democracies, the problem of the state of exception seems to have lost its appeal. Indeed, one of the reviewers of the early version of the proposal for this book noted that interest in the state of exception is somehow declining.[1] The thousands of pages on the legal and political reactions to emergencies that have filled up books, academic journals and newspapers at the beginning of the new millennium seem to have buried the state of exception under a blanket of obsolescence. The interest in such an important doctrine of Western jurisprudence seems to belong to the past, the remoteness of which, however, has not yet been fully determined. What is more, despite the debates fuelled by the implementation of the legal-governmental measures that have created the global framework for the war on terror, from the standpoint of liberal legalism emergencies remain a paradox.

In the face of the hyper-normalisation of emergencies, to sustain that the question of the state of exception is not compelling or appealing anymore is, for us, symptomatic of both a specific academic and legal myopia in the face of blatant evidence, which we aim to challenge throughout this volume, and a dependence of scientific focus on trends and fashion.

Yet, in this rather polemic introduction, there is a further and more disturbing factor that must be taken into account to explain why the state of exception turns out to be an obsolete question. It might be the case that the high tolerance of the use of emergency powers and to the exuberance of executive powers, with the subsequent erosion of basic rights as well as the emergence of authoritarian drives at

1 The explosion of interest in emergency law in response to the COVID-19 coronavirus crisis illustrates the risk of writing the exception out of contemporary jurisprudential discourse.

the core of liberal democracy, has become so normal as to make exceptions uninteresting. What makes the state of exception important is indeed its exceptionality, and when this feature wanes, exceptions logically lose their appeal. Our considerations, thus, can only be untimely: 'that is to say, acting counter to our time and thereby acting on our time and, let us hope, for the benefit of a time to come'.[2]

2.

The shock and awe that has engulfed the liberal legal establishment in the wake of the authoritarian turn, the surge of nationalism and identarian politics, bewildering as it may be, is indicative of the theoretical scarcity of the existing conceptual paradigms that have fashioned the legal canon since the time of the fall of the Berlin Wall, if not from the very early years of the post-war period. Faced with the return of the repressed historical experience of authoritarianism, constitutional theorists, jurisprudents, human rights lawyers and global governance theorists have fallen prey to a moment of anxiety. In the presence of the repudiation of liberal legality, the defenders of the existing ideological superstructure have sought comfort either in the core of legality or within models from political theory and political science. As such, the ominous veer towards overt authoritarian practices – from challenges to judicial independence[3] and academic freedom[4] to racism[5] and the questioning of legal certainty[6] – has been read through the lens of populism.[7] Concepts such as populist constitutionalism[8], autocratic legalism[9] and stealth authoritarianism[10] have become the new symbolic veil that covers a present marked by conflict, tension, struggle and repression. What is left unchallenged is, unsurprisingly, the place and function of legal normativity within this very dynamic. As this strand of literature emphasises, even in the wake of all the current devaluation of the democratic form: 'liberalism is … a constitutive precondition for

2 Friedrich Nietzsche, *Untimely Meditation*, R. J. Hollingdale transl. (Cambridge: Cambridge University Press, 1997), 60.
3 Commission v Poland (Indépendence de la Cour suprême), ECJ 2019.
4 Andras L. Pap, *Democratic Decline in Hungary: Law and Society in an Illiberal Democracy* (Abingdon: Routledge, 2018).
5 Commission takes next step in infringement procedure against Hungary for criminalising activities in support of asylum applicants (http://europa.eu/rapid/press-release_IP-19-469_en.htm).
6 European Commission for Democracy Through Law, 'Romania: Opinion on the Emergency Ordinances GEO No.7 and GEO No. 12 Amending the Laws of Justice', 24 June 2019.
7 Jan-Werner Müller, *What is Populism?* (Philadelphia: University of Pennsylvania Press, 2016), 19–20.
8 David Landau, 'Populist Constitutions', (2018) 85 *Chicago Law Review* 521; Paul Blokker, 'Varieties of Populist Constitutionalism: The Transnational Dimension', (2019) 20 *German Law Journal* 332.
9 Kim Lane Scheppele, 'Authoritarian Legalism', (2018) 85 *Chicago Law Review* 545.
10 Ozan O. Varol, 'Stealth Authoritarianism', (2015) 100 *Iowa Law Review* 1673.

democracy, which provides for the rule of law, checks and balances, and guaranteed fundamental rights.'[11]

From this point on, we are brought back from where it all started, namely the illusion surrounding law's ability to institute democracy,[12] if not its necessary connection to the liberal form.[13] As it has been observed in a rather different context, 'to each problem it appears to be a solution and the solution is almost always law'.[14] The models circulated so far in an attempt to make sense of the present shift in politics and constitutional practice within the legal field not only offer a limited and somewhat distorted image of what the present crisis entails but function as a stop-gap, positively preventing us from addressing the current status of legality and inquiring into the features of authoritarianism in power. Authoritarian rulers of the day, from Erdoğan to Bolsonaro and Trump, from Putin to Orbán and Kaczyński, are lumped together in a haphazard manner[15] with little attention being paid to their historical trajectories; as in a theatrics of anti-legality, they are portrayed as omnipotent subjects cynically manipulating the law to pursue their goals.[16]

For its part, the people, as the constitutional subject, is reduced to a silent bystander of this profanation of legality, deprived of agency. In the background the law is simply an inert instrument, subjected to reframing; insofar as the new authoritarians 'don't destroy state institutions; they repurpose rather than abolish the institutions they inherited'.[17] At the antipodes, in celebrating the return of the political,[18] the critical field positively ignores the historical sources of the present predicament[19] while satisfying itself in forgetting the structural character of the law, its resilient stickiness and its binding force in commanding and detouring political trajectories. The common features of this quandary, shared by both defenders and critics of the emerging regimes of legality, in approaching the actual threat to the existing politico-legal order find their source in a shared oblivion to law's historical connivance with the authoritarian projects. What has been forgotten in this process is law's inscription and construction in relation to a

11 Gábor Halmai, 'Populism, Authoritarianism and Constitutionalism', (2019) 20 *German Law Journal* 296, 311.
12 Hans Kelsen, *The Essence and Value of Democracy*, Brian Graf transl. (Lanham: Rowman & Littlefield, 2013 [1929]).
13 Maria Paula Saffon and Nadia Urbinati, 'Procedural Democracy, the Bulwark of Equal Liberty', (2013) 41 *Political Theory* 441.
14 Pierre Legrand, 'Antivonbar', (2006) 1 *Journal of Comparative Law* 13, 14.
15 Scheppele, 'Authoritarian Legalism', 550–58; Landau, 'Populist Constitutions', 522–31; see also, Blokker, 'Varieties of Populist Constitutionalism', 346, where Yanis Varoufakis is also added to the list.
16 Scheppele, 'Authoritarian Legalism', 571–77.
17 Ibid., 573.
18 Enzo Traverso, *The New Faces of Fascism*, David Boder transl. (London: Verso, 2019) 27.
19 Ibid., 25.

history of violence,[20] as well as of its function as an archive[21] that is able to register and actively support the movements within polities. But ignorance of the law excuses no one, and the substance of what is repressed is likely to catch up with a subject's historical becoming.

In order to overcome these theoretical limitations, which entail obvious political and constitutional consequences – in terms of both framing legality and building strategies for responding to the authoritarian onslaught against the traces of the emancipatory potential that our polities still retain – we need to turn towards the law and its exception. This is because what has been positively excluded from the ambit of the current debates related to the shifting status of liberal democracy, the threat or the lure of populism, the rise of nationalism, xenophobia or the revision of the status-quo is the very infrastructure that supports the present – that is, the deeper layers of extra-legality embedded in legal concepts and practices. Ultimately, the key to understanding the catastrophe befalling the present, or grasping the regenerative potential of new ways of being-together, seems to revolve around the mystery of the legal form and its instrumental function.

3.

In the last two decades, the succession of multiple and diversified emergencies have had a decisive impact in Western governmental systems and societies, which unsurprisingly reacted by strengthening their securitarian drives. In a rather disturbing fashion, liberal democracies tended increasingly to challenge the pressure brought by global crisis – from international terrorism to the current waves of migration – through the hardening of police measures and the consequent limitation of civil and political liberties. We are assisting an unprecedented proliferation of non-ordinary legislative procedures, a growing role of executives and of technocratic administrative bodies, to the detriment of the functioning of legislative institutions that necessarily determines the restriction of areas of political participation. Once more, emergencies are showing their fundamental transformative potential. Indeed, the instruments and procedures, which are typically activated to challenge periods of profound crisis, are gradually turned into stable elements of government. Since the turn of the new millennium, emergencies have triggered a drive towards a reactionary mutation of liberal democratic institutions, disguised as a necessary response to tensions and threats, whose reality is often spectacular rather than substantial.

Democratic regimes are traditionally equipped with emergency constitutional measures, such as the state of siege (or war) and martial law, which maintain an

20 Walter Benjamin, 'Critique of Violence', in Marcus Bullock and Michael W. Jennings (eds), *Walter Benjamin: Selected Writings, 1: 1913–1926* (Cambridge, MA: Harvard University Press, 1996 [1921]), 250.

21 Renisa Mawani, 'Law's Archive', (2012) 8 *Annual Review of Law and Social Science* 337.

essential exceptional meaning. However, referring to the extreme of social and political crisis that is war, they remain (often) in latency as unsuited to tackling the fragmented nature of the multiplicity of emergencies populating the current global scenario. As Ferejohn and Pasquino noted, 'an explanation for the disuse of constitutional emergency powers must lie, in part, in the development of a new legal model for dealing with emergencies', which they define as being a 'legislative model'.[22] This model, which has become common usage in the more stable democratic regimes, 'handles emergencies by enacting ordinary statutes that delegate special and temporary powers to the executive'.[23] Central to this practice is the idea of emergency as an exception to the normal legislative operation of the law, which – once the emergency has been resolved – will be restored.

However, as the authors suggested, this model – albeit quite functional in the social and political context of Western democracies – is not immune to risks: 'the laws made to deal with the emergency may become embedded in the normal legal system, essentially enacting permanent changes in that system under colour of the emergency'.[24] And of course this could have a substantial impact on liberties and on the structural balance of powers upon which liberal democracies are built.

It is safe to say that with the emergence of a legislative model the state of exception assumed a rather insidious form. It has been able to legitimise itself more effectively through the integration and no longer the suspension of the constitution, transforming itself into stable and permanent law. In certain cases it is no longer possible to determine what legal normality consists of, since there was never a suspension or break away but only the hybridization of several legal registers (especially criminal, legislative and administrative), leading to an inextricable tangle that no longer permits solutions. The introduction of extraordinary measures, whose justification assumed a complex legal form, masked the breaking of the norm: as the exception can no longer be eliminated, the law has increasingly sought to assimilate and normalise it. Therefore, it can be argued, as Mark Neocleous does, that 'far from being outside the rule of law, emergency powers emerge from within it'.[25]

As the unfolding of historical events, at least from the interwar period onwards, has shown, the state of exception calls into question law's ability to establish itself as a coherent self-sufficient instrument of signification for political communities. Modern law, with its call to founding values such as formal equality and the protection of individual freedoms, derives its authority from the ability to institute communal life by separating itself from the imposition of substantiated morals. However, in pursuing a supposed neutrality, the law has

22 J. Ferejohn and P. Pasquino, 'The Law of the Exception: A Typology of Emergency Powers', (2004) 2 *International Journal of Constitutional Law* 216.

23 Ibid., 217.

24 Ibid., 219.

25 Mark Neocleous, 'The Problem with Normality: Taking Exception to "Permanent Emergency"', (2006) *31 Alternatives* 207.

proven to be a double-edged technique of regulation and administration of power, which couples a liberating dimension with a more authoritarian (and inhuman) side. Law's normativity, as grounded in the idea of legality, cannot guarantee the principles underpinning its supposed function: it cannot exclude the exception. But this seems to be the fate of the law as a human artefact: it is because of its substantial neutrality and inertia that positive law is prone to be used for whatever scope, even if this means undermining itself.

4.

The starting point of our work is the recognition that the theoretical apparatus of the state of exception sharply captures the uneasy relationship between law, life and politics while at the same time challenging the comforting narratives that uncritically connect democracy with the tradition of the rule of law. As such, the exception exposes a caesura within the very structure of the law (understood as a system of signification), which opposes the normative legal content to the unarticulated force of law. The state of siege, uses of martial law, the recourse to expedient legal procedures during and beyond times of crises, the rise of military and administrative powers, and the confusion between legal, administrative and military categories all seem to document and embody the essential fracture between form and force fostered by our legal systems functioning under the aegis of the exception. Yet the exception is not reducible to these historical instantiations, but also arguably seizes on an important, yet thoroughly overlooked, aspect of modern societies, namely the fact that 'confronted with an excess, the system interiorizes what exceeds it through an interdiction and in this way "designates itself as exterior to itself"'.[26]

Embodied in the figure of a socio-political standoff – as *stasis*, or civil war – or in the recurrent use of emergency decrees, the exception represents an abnormal course of the law, a limit-experience emerging at the point of encounter between the legal order and the contingency of the social and the political. The liminality of the exception, its peculiar position (or place), as a limit or threshold, renders such a concept a privileged *heuristic* sign for approaching the normal functioning of law in its intimate relation with the other spheres of social life. As Lon Fuller perspicuously observed:

> When all goes well and established legal rules encompass neatly the social life they are intended to regulate … the law … proceeds with a transparent simplicity suggesting no need for reflective scrutiny. Only in illness, we are told, does the body reveal its complexity. Only when legal reasoning falters and reaches out clumsily for help do we realize what a complex undertaking the law is.[27]

26 Giorgio Agamben, *Homo Sacer: Sovereign Power and Bare Life*, Daniel Heller-Roazen transl. (Stanford: Stanford University Press, 1998 [1995]), 18.
27 Lon Fuller, *Legal Fictions* (Stanford: Stanford University Press, 1967), viii.

The exception thus appears as a paradigmatic practice whose analysis can at least provisionally be usefully applied to other spheres than the law by opening new paths for reflection on the limits of the dominant political discourse. Hence, the exception has occupied an important place in a variety of fields, including aesthetics, linguistics, political theory, international relations and more generally cultural studies, being applied to a manifold series of contexts ranging from analyses of sovereign power and the production of *homines sacri* to colonialism, literary criticism and film studies. Yet this proliferation of the signifier exception seems to obscure the initial critical thrust of the concept, which is none the less jurisprudential. Accordingly, one of the tasks that we aim to set out for this book is to reflect critically on the legal dimension of the state of exception.

Indeed, our intention is to recuperate this initial critical potential of the exception and to render it useful as a conceptual framework for a historical and genealogical understanding of the law within the Western tradition. As such, we intend to further and critically examine the state of exception by focusing on two interconnected lines of inquiry.

First, we are interested in reflecting on the specific politico-legal impact of the theory of the exception in relation to the status of modern legality and its structural inability to ground the rule of law coherently. Within this context, we aim to explore the implicit jurisprudential stand (intended as a line of enquiry that connects Schmitt's thought to Agamben and the contemporary reading of the state of exception) informing the conceptual framework in which the idea of state of exception operates. The exception recalls explicitly the question of the coherence and the consistency of legal orders, in their tangled relationship with the contingency of events. According to its canonical definition, the exception refers to all those unpredictable cases, which cannot (and must not) be provided for by law's text; otherwise they would not be exceptions. In front of the exception, the law has generally two options: its negation or its regulation. In both cases, the exception represents a crack in the certainty of legal reasoning. Indeed, on the one hand the negation of the legality of the state of exception is nothing other than turning a blind eye on a specific legal doctrine that has accompanied law since time immemorial. On the other hand, the regulation of the exceptions turns out to be unable to frame and neutralise the excesses that the exception by definition entails.

Second, we acknowledge that the state of exception is situated both as a concept building on a complex network of political and legal philosophical legacies and a praxis revealing a no less complex material history in its own right. In this sense, we would like to address the latent dialogue that the state of exception opens between the intellectual legacy of the Weimar Republic and the interwar period and more recent political experiences. The state of exception builds on a very specific reading of history as well as on a genealogy of political thought explicitly linked to the theory of totalitarianism inasmuch as it is linked to an understanding of the emergence of the modern democratic-revolutionary tradition. The tendency of political and legal systems to regulate emergency powers – producing a sort of self-immunisation through the incorporation of the possibility of acting against or outside the rules – and allow for a manipulability of such powers emerged explicitly with the revolutionary movements that have characterised modern European history. The state of exception, we maintain, should be considered as the *fil rouge* that connects the liberal democratic tradition with authoritarianism.

Thus, its significant historical element is another 'untimely' feature of this collection, which addressed the historical theory and practice of the exception in conjunction with the history and theory of law's contribution to authoritarianism. Reopening the constitution of the state of exception in various historical contexts and re-exposing it to interrogation in light of the philosophical development of the exception provides the means to uncover and scrutinise the threads that join traditions and regimes otherwise treated as discrete and often in opposition. Exemplary among the historical contexts discussed is the Third Reich, with its strong links to relevant strands of legal thought and practice. Some of the figures identified in the following section as key reference points in this collection – Giorgio Agamben, Carl Schmitt, Walter Benjamin – have important connections to Weimar and/or Nazi Germany, via either their lives or their writings, or both.

Furthermore, perhaps the paradigmatic lesson absorbed for law from the Nazi regime and the Holocaust was to have more of it, in ways that have fundamentally shaped the modern, Western – and to a degree, world – legal order: more international law to explicitly outlaw, deter and (ultimately) prosecute similar genocidal acts; more well-regulated exception provisions in state constitutions to prevent sovereign exploitation such as occurred in the Weimar-Nazi transition; and more law enumerating and safeguarding individual rights to preclude their being undermined. In the post-war period, these developments were informed by a narrative that located Nazi rule as an exception outside of not only 'normal' law but also 'normal' historical development; a 12-year legal and historical aberration, which severed law's complicity in the Nazi project, and therefore in the ghastly potential of the exception realised by the Holocaust.

In contrast to this, this volume's interrogation of the authoritarian past of the exception, whether in relation to the Third Reich or elsewhere, reinforces the correspondence of norm and exception at a fundamental level through the layers of extra-legality entrenched within the law – and in doing so, problematises the tendency to treat law perpetually as the solution. As such it raises the possibility that extermination does not simply represent the potential of the exception, but of law itself.

5.

This volume contains nine essays and an afterword. The contributions provide a panoply of different perspectives on the question of the state of exception in theory and practice. As editors, we did not pursue homogeneity of vision or uniformity in the style of presentation of arguments. Rather than dictators acting on a commission aiming to prevent catastrophes or towards imposing a regime of truth, we consider our role more akin to that of silent and technical co-ordinators. The authors, thus, were left free to enquire into the core questions of this collection (summarised in this introduction) in the way they deemed more in line with their individual sensitivities. There is, however, a measure of coherence and community that goes beyond the mere structural and conceptual articulation of the book. It is undeniable and perhaps inescapable that the subject matter of the book is going to be at least haunted by the presence of the thought of Giorgio Agamben, whose rereading of the concept in recent decades has left an indelible trace on its philosophical articulation. Behind this imprint lies the other unavoidable dualism marking the Weimar era of catastrophes – Walter Benjamin and Carl Schmitt are part of the intellectual references that have ostensibly moulded our understanding of exception.

This sense of harmony is not accidental. As a matter of fact, most of the contributors of this book have participated in a series of panels that the editors have organised within the 'Critical Legal Conference' starting with Brighton in 2014 and continuing until the convention in Milton Keynes in 2018. The discussions held there continued both at other venues, such as the 'Critical Juridical Symposia' in Opole (2018) and Cracow (2019), as well as within the virtual clouds surrounding our being-in-the-law, before being materialised in this present form. Therefore, this book is a document of a collaborative, if not collective, exploration undertaken both under and against the precarious conditions and limitations of our neoliberal academic world, with its staunch disdain for authentic thought and critical thinking. It is also, alas, a document of times out of joint, that as critical lawyers and theorists we were perhaps able to grasp before their unfolding. Conceived and written with a sense of impending catastrophe, the substance of this book is certainly marked by a dissatisfaction with the ways in which law, the exception 'in which we live' and, for that matter, all core politico-legal issues that have become the texture of our present are discussed, analysed and reflected within our contemporary established jurisprudential and constitutional law theoretical circles.

Accordingly, this collection has a contrapuntal – if not contrarian – thrust in terms of its style, scope and content. Drawing on the 'courage of hopelessness' that the contributors undeniably share, our aim was to move beyond the existing limits of understanding the exception and to save its politico-legal potential from purely antiquarian uses. Its aim is to re-think and redeploy the conceptual inventory of the *state of exception* beyond its already devalued status, thus opening new venues for critical inquiry of both past and present, as well as by bringing the theory of the exception before the materiality of its praxis and historical origins. In this sense, by being untimely we strive to be contemporary. As Agamben put it in his reading of Osip Mandelstam, 'to be contemporary is (…) a matter of courage, because it means being able not to firmly fix one's gaze on the darkness of the epoch, but to perceive in this darkness a light that (...) infinitely distances itself from us'.[28] However, it is not only this temporal dimension, which imbues our projects, but also a shared consciousness of the need to reflect on the exception through local contexts, and historical settings that have shaped its global articulation. While Weimar and Nazi Germany remain reference points for such investigations, critical histories of the exception in Turkey, socialist Poland and putatively liberal Italy are other starting points for uncovering the operation of the exception.

Following this path, this book is as much an exercise in thinking the exception with, against and beyond the authors who have apposed their signature on its contemporary theorisation, an act that takes on a perhaps sacrificial dimension. Such a refusal of the 'name of the Father' is a reaction to the very unfolding of the state of exception, which continues to grow before our eyes. This brings us to a last element of commonality marking this collection, that is its relative generational homogeneity: as critical lawyers and theorists socialised and marked by the perpetual presence of the exception, we are wary both of its conceptual limits in describing the antinomies of contemporary legality, as well as its constant deployment in the politico-legal realm. The contributions are, each in its own way, attempts at moving beyond the exception, either by unravelling its conceptual limits or by exposing its historical roots.

The essays are grouped in two parts. The first, 'Law, theory and the logic of the exception', includes five essays focusing on some of the more thorny theoretical aspects raised by the state of exception as a jurisprudential object. The second part, 'histories of the exception', instead, is composed of four essays, which investigate the theory and practice of the administration of emergency powers, with direct reference to historical events. In organising the volume in such a way, we intended the first part as laying down the theoretical framework for the second part. And of course, in a dialectical fashion, the more historical interpretations included in the second part are meant to offer a confirmation of some of the hypotheses advanced in the first. However, given the varied nature and the scope of the contributions constituting the book, it is ultimately up to the readers to find connections and contrasts between the two parts.

The volume opens with Gian Giacomo Fusco's 'Exception, fiction, performativity', which addresses in a genealogical fashion the state of exception as a legal object. By looking to what has been defined as the 'fictitious state of exception', this chapter argues that the modern legal provisions for the administration of emergency powers should be considered as specific legal techniques whose inner logic is akin to that of legal fictions. Therefore, the state of exception, which is generally interpreted as a reaction to a given factual situation, should be better understood in terms of performativity.

28 Giorgio Agamben, *Nudities*, David Kishik and Stefan Pedatella transl. (Stanford: Stanford University Press, 2011), 14–15.

The second essay is Cosmin Cercel's '"Through a glass, darkly": Law, history and the frontispiece of the exception', which tackles critically the state of exception in its relation to the status of legal normativity and the legal form. This chapter maintains that in order to understand the political confusion of the present status of legality, perpetually used as a powerful tool to legitimise a transformation of liberal democratic regimes into quasi-authoritarian executive-driven government, it is necessary to enquire into the theory and practice of the state of exception in its tension with legal form and practice.

Cercel's study is followed by Przemysław Tacik's 'The other side of exception: Sovereignty, modernity and international law'. This chapter, by focusing on Agamben's theory of the exception, aims at exploring the relationship between sovereignty, international law and modernity that is nearly absent in Agamben's writings due to the aforementioned interrelated omissions. The concept of the state of exception, originally pertaining to the field reigned by sovereignty, might be well adapted to international law, where they take up the position of the obverse side of national sovereigns. In this view, the notorious conflation of fact and law in the international order appears not as a contingent flaw, but an immanent feature of this order, correlative to the mechanism of exception under sovereign power. Finally, Agamben's analyses of the phenomenon of camps will be used to explore the link between sovereignty, bare life and international law.

In Tormod Otter Johansen 'Minor law: Notes towards a revolutionary jurisprudence', Agamben's critique of the state of exception and of sovereign violence is coupled with Pashukanis' Marxian theory of law. By scrutinising the basic assumption that sees the self-standing of legal orders as necessarily connected to the force of coercive violence, this chapter tries to think law as a form of non-coercive social organisation. However, this implies a radical shift from the 'traditional' hegemonic conception of law as regulation based on given forms of obligation, towards a 'minor law', which in normativity is sustained without any form of authority.

The final essay of Part I is Simon Lavis' 'The exception of the norm in the Third Reich: (Re)reading the Nazi constitutional state of exception', which focuses on the vexed question of the legal status of 'Nazi Law'. Through a close engagement with the 'dual' character of the state's law under Hitler's regime, this chapter investigates how the theory of the state of exception could be used to interrogate and understand the mobile limits of the two sides of the law – the informal/authoritarian; and the use of formal rule of law-driven regulation – in the Third Reich. More specifically, this contribution seeks to establish Agamben's work on the state of exception as a useful tool to read critically the legal *aporia* of the Third Reich.

Part 2 commences with Dimitrios Kivotidis' '"Norm" and "exception": From the Weimar Republic to the Nazi state form'. In this chapter, Kivotidis examines the unity between 'norm' and 'exception' as different forms of exercise of public power. According to this reading, both 'norm' and 'exception' are essential forms for the reproduction of bourgeois rule and the change from one form to the other is contingent upon the intensification of socio-economic antagonisms. This argument is pursued on the basis of an examination of the transition from the Weimar Republic to the Nazi state form, as reflected in the work of Carl Schmitt.

This is followed by Rafał Mańko's '"Our Fatherland has found itself on the verge of an abyss": Poland's 1981 martial law, or the unexpected appearance of the state of exception under actually existing socialism', which offers a unique in its genre interpretation of the uses and consequences of the martial law implemented in Poland in early 1980s. Such event represents a rare example of the use of exceptional power in a socialist country, where the working class is nominally sovereign, and where legality does not take the 'liberal' form of Western democracies. In this chapter, Mańko, by retracing the legal foundation of the Polish martial law and specific jurisprudential meaning of the General's dictatorship, exposes how, paradoxically, the state of exception in the context of really existing socialism served as an instrument to the transition to a more liberal democracy and capitalism.

Ceylan Begum Yildiz's chapter, 'A state in anomie: An analysis of modern Turkey's states of exception' considers the transformation of exceptional measures from a historical perspective while exposing the pattern of states of exceptions in Turkey. Her chapter follows Agamben's lead in investigating Turkey as an anomic state, while introducing a subject-oriented perspective to unfold the particular pattern of states of exception upon which the Turkish nation state was built and continues to exist.

In the final chapter of Part II, Sara Raimondi's 'Beyond "the most serious suspension of rights" of Genoa: Violence, anomie and force (of law)' demonstrates that the taxonomy of the exception stretches beyond the instances commonly found in the existing literature and opens up the question of the function of exceptional measures within the context of contemporary democracies. In this regard, the analysis highlights how, across multiple contexts, the exception operates at the intersection and blurring point of the juridical and the political, right and violence, inside and outside, legal and physical status of those who are victims of exceptional practices, and of citizenship and bare life. The case of abuses and law-suspension in Genoa offers an example of exception beyond its factual declaring and demonstrates that exceptional instances are used by states also in the context of democratic life, and, potentially, against their own citizens whenever state institutions feel threatened.

Part I

Law, theory and the logic of the exception

Chapter 1

Exception, fiction, performativity

Gian Giacomo Fusco

Introduction

A few days after the terrorist attacks in Paris of 13 November 2015, the French president François Hollande spoke before a joint session of parliament in this way:

> France is at war. The acts committed in Paris and near the Stade de France on Friday evening are acts of war. They left at least 129 dead and many injured. They are an act of aggression against our country, against its values, against its young people, and against its way of life. They were carried out by a jihadist army, by Daesh, which is fighting us because France is a country of freedom, because we are the birthplace of human rights. At this exceptionally solemn moment, I wanted to address a joint session of Parliament to demonstrate our national unity in the face of such an abomination and to respond with the cool determination that this vile attack against our country calls for [...] I shall marshal the full strength of the State to defend the safety of its people. I know I can count on the dedication of police officers, gendarmes, service personnel, and you yourselves, our national representatives.[1]

This speech followed a declaration of state of emergency (*état d'urgence*) for the whole of France announced on the same evening of the attacks, which entered into force the next morning. Introduced into the French legal order with the law n. 55–385 of 3 April 1955, the state of emergency was devised at that time to contain the sabotage activities and armed actions conducted during the Algerian war by the liberation front (FLN).[2] This law is

1 'Speech by the President of the Republic before a joint session of Parliament', 16 November 2015, available at https://onu.delegfrance.org/Francois-Hollande-s-Speech-Before-a-Joint-Session-of-Parliament

2 It is worth noting that the *état d'urgence* is one of the three provisions for the administration of exceptional powers in times of emergency. The other two are the state of siege (art. 36 of the constitution) and the regulation of extraordinary

configured properly as a state of exception, which gives the executive the powers to implement restrictive measures in relation to the freedom of movement, residence and assembly, and to limit certain civil liberties. And as is nowadays usual, the state of emergency declared in November 2015 lasted approximately two years, and ended with the promulgation of new anti-terror legislation[3] that integrated into French law some of the exceptional measures granted by the state of emergency.[4]

What France has been experiencing in recent years should come as no surprise. Indeed, it is now common to many Western jurisdictions involved in the so-called war on terror that they live in a state of war without a war actually existing or being formally declared. As a matter of fact, and of law, terrorism cannot be classified as a war. Hence, the characterisation of an event (no matter how serious and threatening) that does not satisfy the necessary conditions to be defined as war, as a war, must be taken for what it is: a useful narrative giving legitimacy to the declaration of state of emergency. The use of a vocabulary of war by President Holland is blatantly functional to the implementation of legal measures intended for an 'actual' war.[5] And although legally rather problematic, this strategy is paradigmatic of the state of exception as a 'normal' form of government, according to

powers of the president in the case of severe crisis (regulated by art. 16 of the constitution).

3 "Loi n° 2017–1510 du 30 octobre 2017 renforçant la sécurité intérieure et la lutte contre le terrorism", see: www.legifrance.gouv.fr/affichTexte.do?cidTexte=JORFTEXT000035932811&dateTexte=&categorieLien=id

4 On the integration and normalisation of emergency laws into democratic regimes, see: Jean-Claude Paye, *Global War on Liberty*, James H. Membrez transl. (New York: Telos Press, 2007); Günter Frankenberg, *Political Technology and the Erosion of the Rule of Law: Normalizing the State of Exception*, H. Bauer, G. Frankenberg transl. (Cheltenham: Edward Elgar, 2014); Ryan Patrick Alford, *Permanent State of Emergency: Unchecked Executive Power and the Demise of the Rule of Law* (Montreal: McGill-Queen's University Press, 2017); Alan Greene, *Permanent States of Emergency and the Rule of Law: Constitutions in an Age of Crisis* (London: Bloomsbury, 2018).

5 President Hollande was fully aware of this. Indeed, he stated that 'the law which governs the state of emergency of 3 April 1955 cannot really match the kind of technologies and threats we face today' and 'Our Constitution currently has two specific schemes that are not appropriate for the situation we are in. The first scheme involves Article 16 of the Constitution. It specifies that the regular functioning of public authorities be suspended. The president will then take such measures as warranted by the circumstances, overriding the distribution of the constitutional powers. And then there's Article 36 of the Constitution, which relates to the state of siege. And this isn't appropriate either. A state of siege is decreed in situations of imminent peril resulting from a foreign war or an armed insurrection. In this situation, various powers are then transferred from the civil to the military authorities'. See 'Speech by the President of the Republic before a joint session of Parliament'.

which 'a state of peace itself can at the same time be a state of emergency',[6] on the grounds of a decision of a legitimate authority.

In its canonical definition, the state of exception consists of a partial or complete temporary suspension of a normative order to safeguard its survival in a critical situation, which usually entails the restriction of certain rights and constitutional guarantees and a variable infringement of the principle of separation of powers, through the delegation of special powers to the executive. As such, the state of exception finds its (onto)logical presupposition, and its only *raison d'être*, in the presence of determinate exceptional facts constituting a threat for the state. As has been observed, an 'emergency is a state of fact; however, as the brocard fittingly says, *e facto oritur ius* [law arises from fact]'.[7] But the widespread use and abuse of emergency powers that we are witnessing teaches us that the relation of determination between the exception as a fact and the exception as a legal response is not as strict as it might seem at a theoretical level. The use of the state of emergency and more generally of exceptional laws is now so common that their relation to a factual necessity seems lost. In this regard, Kim Lane Scheppele maintains that emergency powers, in contemporary constitutional regimes when used, are 'never the sort of total emergencies [...] as one might imagine from theory'[8]; they are implemented partially, discreetly and pervasively, altering the substance of the law but leaving a semblance of legality intact, often on the ground of 'rhetorical' threats.

When the exception becomes a regulated and normalised technique of government, the verification of its legality or illegality – a central trope of past and present jurisprudence[9] – becomes a trivial enterprise. More

6 Slavoj Žižek, *Welcome To The Desert of The Real! Five Essays on September 11 and Related Dates* (London: Verso, 2002), 107.

7 Gaetano Arangio-Ruiz, *Istituzioni di diritto costituzionale italiano* (Milan: Bocca, 1972 [1913]), 528.

8 Kim Lan Scheppele, 'Legal and Extra-Legal Emergencies', in K. E. Whittington and G. A. Caldeira (eds), *Oxford Handbook of Law and Politics* (Oxford: Oxford University Press, 2008), 174.

9 From the first half of the twentieth century, with the so-called debate on constitutional dictatorship, to the more recent legal analysis of the emergencies within the war on terror, scholars in challenging the issues of exceptional powers divided themselves into legalist and extra-legalist; those 'who seek to include the state of exception within the sphere of the juridical order and those who consider it something external, that is, an essentially political, or in any case extra-juridical, phenomenon'. These models are 'defined via a spatial metaphor of law as a container', assuming the form of a discourse over the limits and the places of law and exception. For the legalists, exceptional measures have to be considered as part of the legal system, and emergencies must be met legally recurring to them. The extra-legalists instead consider the state of exception as something irreducible to the legal form, something that is and must remain outside the limits of the law; thus, serious crisis must be challenged without the formal-procedural

important, instead, would be calling into question the very nature of the exception as a 'legal object', which 'lies squarely within the field of public law'.[10] To this end, in this chapter, taking inspiration from some arguments advanced by Carl Schmitt and Giorgio Agamben, I will examine what has been termed as *fictitious* (or *political*) state of exception. Emerging in the context of the French Revolution in relation to the doctrine of the state of siege, the idea of a fictitious state of exception – as opposed to a real one – represents a kind of prototype for all the contemporary forms of regulated emergency powers. As we will see, a state of exception is 'fictitious' inasmuch as it allows for a suspension of the normal course of the law on the base of a 'subjective' decision (usually made according to the loose criteria of emergency, security, danger, imminent threat, etc.); for this reason, crucial to the regulation of the state of emergency is *who* has the authority to decide it. And because of its rather peculiar relation with facts, in what follows I will argue that the state of exception should be considered as a specific legal technique whose function and logic is akin to those of legal fictions. Consequently, the possibility of abusing emergency powers simply to obtain a certain goal, and not as a reaction to a chain of perilous events, will appear as inscribed in the very nature of the exception as a legal object. But this raises a further crucial philosophical and jurisprudential point. Generally, the state of exception has been interpreted as a reaction to a given situation of danger; in this chapter, I will argue instead that the exception must be better understood in terms of performativity.

Fictional state of exception

In the volume *Political Technology and the Erosion of the Rule of Law: Normalizing the State of Exception*, Günter Frankenberg claims that the 'Machiavellian' moment of the preservation and defence of order, necessitates a 'pseudo-democratic or pseudo-legalist masquerade',[11] which adopts the semantics of the doctrine of the exception. While it might seem rather unfair to dismiss one of the central and most debated doctrine in law's history as a pseudo-legalistic masquerade, Frankenberg's comments are revealing of some

limits of the law. Moreover, for the extra-legalists, the inclusion of the exception into the realm of law accounts for a proper contamination of law itself by perverting the central principles of the rule of law. See: G. Agamben, *State of Exception* (Chicago: University of Chicago Press, 2005); Scheppele, 'Legal and Extra-Legal Emergencies'; and William E. Scheuerman, 'Survey Article: Emergency Powers and the Rule of Law After 9/11', (2006) 14(1) *Journal of Political Philosophy* 61.

10 Martin Loughlin, *Foundations of Public Law* (Oxford: Oxford University Press, 2010), 402.

11 Frankenberg, *Political Technology and the Erosion of the Rule of Law: Normalizing the State of Exception*, 12–13.

theoretical aspects central to the definition of the exception. As Carl Schmitt explained on different occasions, the regulation of sovereign exceptional powers is to a certain extent pointless. It is not possible to pre-define limits to the action of the agent entitled to make decisions in the state of the exception because, very simply, an emergency is by definition not predictable in all its extension. Even when the norms guiding a government in a time of emergency are included in the formal structure of the legal order (i.e. in constitutional emergency measures), it is not possible to subsume emergency powers totally within the system of norms. Indeed, to confer (legally) a certain extra-legal discretion is the ultimate trademark of the state of exception. In this sense the state of exception, as a legal doctrine, amounts properly to a masquerade, which allows derogation from the law while pretending to do it legally.

But the term masquerade is also telling in another sense – the one that pertains to the sphere of the 'fictional'. From the point of view of legal history, the modern (and contemporary) doctrine of the state of exception finds its paradigmatic ancestor in what has been termed the 'fictitious state of siege' (*état de siège fictif*). As Schmitt has explained in concluding his book on *Dictatorship*, in its fictional-political version the French doctrine of the state of siege represented a sort of prototype for the emergency provisions of contemporary constitutional regimes. In Schmitt's view, what it is currently understood as 'state of exception' is the last step in the evolution of the institution of the dictatorship. And the establishment of the state of siege, in its fictional-political form, is exemplary of a more general tendency: the gradual regulation and normalisation of what was once the special legal institution of the dictatorship.

The doctrine of the state of siege emerged during the French Revolution when the question of the suspension and preservation of rights during political crisis became an issue. For the *ancient regime* the regulation of crisis government could not amount to a problem, since it was 'unnecessary to suspend rights that do not exist or augment powers that are already absolute'.[12] Established with a decree of the National Assembly on 8 July 1791, the state of siege was a purely military institution, concerning the 'status' of fortified areas. This law concerned technical-military issues related to the maintenance and classification of military posts. More specifically, this decree regulated in detail 'the policing of the fortifications; terms and conditions for the employment of officers; and accommodation for troops, construction of fortifications, compensation for the private property that was of necessity confiscated as a result'.[13] This law meticulously established the relationship between the military forces and civilians by distinguishing three states [*états*]: "state of peace" [*état de paix*], in which the military officials had power and

12 Ibid., 80.
13 Carl Schmitt, *Dictatorship*, Michael Hoelzl and Graham Ward transl. (Cambridge: Polity, 2014 [1921]), 158.

responsibility only over the army and military affairs; the 'state of war' [*état de guerre*], in which policing responsibility remained in the hands of civilian bodies but the military commanders were entitled to assume police powers when necessary for the military security of the area; and the 'state of siege' [*état de siege*], where all the legal functions of civilian authorities concerning the maintenance of order and police force passed to the military commander, who exercised them personally.[14]

As Schmitt argued, the concept of the state of siege underwent a radical mutation when 'the actual state of siege was replaced by a declaration of state of siege'.[15] During the turmoil that preceded the birth of the Second Republic, a decree of the Constituent Assembly issued on 24 June 1848 placed the city of Paris in a state of siege. The 'commendable performance' of the commissar, and the success of the measures taken, led to the constitutionalising of the state of siege with the law of 9 August 1849.[16] This provision was updated and amended in 1878, in conformity with new constitutional arrangements. With the reduction of the state of siege to a constitutional doctrine, Schmitt maintains, the government acquired the power to determine the 'state of siege whenever it deemed it necessary. The formal act of the government's declaration supplanted the real state of emergency. The concept gained a political meaning; the technical-military procedure was employed in the service of domestic politics'.[17] In this moment, the *state of siege* has undergone a radical mutation: it has lost its factual character as reflecting an actual situation (état *de siege*), and has become a formal act of a government (état *de siege fictive*), depending on a decision of a governing (sovereign) agent.

It is worth looking at the words of the constitutional provisions for the state of siege, as included in the law of 1878:

> 1. The state of siege can only be declared in the event of imminent danger resulting from a foreign war or an armed insurrection. Only a law can declare the state of siege. This law will designate the communes, arrondissements, and departments to which it is to apply. It will fix the period of its duration. At the expiration of this period, the state of siege ceases automatically, unless a new law shall prolong its effects [...] 7. As soon as the state of siege has been declared, the powers of police and those others with which the civil authority has been clothed for the maintenance of order pass in their entirety to the military authority [...]

14 Ibid. Schmitt's reconstruction of the development of the doctrine of the state of siege is largely based on Theodor Reinach, *De l'etat de siege: Étude historique et juridique* (Paris: Pichon, 1885).

15 Ibid., 160.

16 Clinton Rossiter, *Constitutional Dictatorship: Crisis Government in the Modern Democracies* (Princeton: Princeton University Press, 1948), 81.

17 Schmitt, *Dictatorship*, 161.

> 9. The military authority has the power, (1) to conduct searches by day or night in the homes of citizens; (2) to deport liberated convicts and persons who do not have residence in the areas placed in the state of siege; (3) to direct the surrender of arms and munitions, and to proceed to search for and remove them; (4) to forbid publications and meetings which it judges to be of a nature to incite or sustain disorder. 11 Despite the state of siege, citizens continue to exercise the rights guaranteed by the Constitution whose enjoyment is not suspended by the preceding articles.[18]

Essential to the fictional state of siege, Schmitt points out, is that 'the authorization to take an action that the given situation necessitates has been replaced by a number of limited functions'.[19] In the modern constitutional state, he goes on, 'the solid unity of the state had finally been secured. Tumults and riots could disturb the security, but the homogeneity of the state would not be seriously threatened by social factions within it'; and in a stable situation 'the execution can be regulated according to legal procedure, as long as the enemy is not a power that throws into question this unity'.[20] The state of siege, in its fictional-political version, represents the general paradigmatic-model for constitutional provision regulating emergency powers; as Rossiter suggested, 'the state of siege was the model for similar instruments [...] in almost all [...] civil law countries, and even in Anthony Hope's mythical Ruritania'.[21]

The development of the doctrine of the state of siege, from a pure military to a fictive-political form, represented a substantial turning point for the legal conception of crisis management. As Schmitt noted, the fictional state of siege became the nodal point of a legal fiction[22] since the 'siege' was no longer dependent on the presence of factual conditions but became determined by a decision. Indeed, the evolution of the doctrine of the state of siege

> involved the gradual conversion of this purely military institution to one that was political in character, one in which the state of siege became *fictif*, a term to indicate that an open, civil area menaced by invasion or rebellion was to be regarded in law as 'besieged'[23]

in order to allow certain legal/political consequences to take place. The history of state of exception, thus, is the 'history of its gradual emancipation

18 Rossiter, *Constitutional Dictatorship*, 82.
19 Ibid., 173.
20 Ibid., 178.
21 Rossiter, *Constitutional Dictatorship*, 77.
22 Schmitt, *Dictatorship*, 160
23 Rossiter, *Constitutional Dictatorship*, 80.

from the wartime situation [...] to be used as an extraordinary police measure' to deal with internal turmoil and disorders of different nature.[24] And every suspension of the normal course of the law resulting from a decision of an authority (the limits and content of which are regulated by law) finds its prototype in the fictional state of siege; and like this one, must be considered as rooted in the peculiar status of the law during wartime.

Dictatorship, *Iustitium*

In his strenuous critique of liberal legality and of the pretence of the principle of the 'rule of law', Schmitt defines as 'fictitious' a state of exception that is regulated by law, with the scope of preserving some individual rights and liberties. This is very briefly the conclusion he reaches in the last chapters of the book on *Dictatorship*, where he suggests that with the regulation of 'dictatorial' powers typical of modern constitutional regimes, what was determined de facto – as a logical reaction to a determined situation of danger – has been transformed into something that must be 'decided on'. It seems, though, that for Schmitt the very transformation of dictatorial powers into a legal doctrine makes of the exception something fictional.

The idea of the state of exception as essentially 'fictitious' (if not properly a legal fiction) is a central tenet of Agamben's *State of Exception*. In this book he criticises Schmitt's genealogy of the exception (while admittedly accepting its substantial arguments). For Agamben, the ancestor of the modern state of exception must not be identified in the figure of the 'dictatorship', but in another institute of Roman law: the *iustitium*. Along with the more popular dictatorship, in fact, the *iustitium* represented a further instrument for the administration and solution of crisis. While the first envisaged a specific magistrate that assumed full powers for no longer than six months, the latter did not concern the election of a single figure and the definition of a specific mandate but materialised itself in a generalised suspension and alteration of the legal system.

In the first centuries of the Roman Republican history, the *iustitium* was declared in particularly serious situations. This was usually followed by a temporally limited suspension of judicial and legal activities, decreed by a magistrate to respond to a particular need (usually the recruitment of soldiers). Confronted with a situation that endangered the Republic, the Senate had the possibility of emanating a *senatus consultum ultimum* [final decree of the senate] by which the consuls, the praetor and the tribunes of the people and in extreme cases, all citizens, are called to take whatever measures they deem necessary for the salvation of the state. This special '*consultum*' was based upon a decree declaring a *tumultus* [tumult] (an emergency resulting from a foreign war, insurrection or civil war), which usually led to the proclamation of the *iustitium*.

24 Agamben, *State of Exception*, 5.

The key element in this legal procedure is the *tumultus*, which is not a term designating a war or a specific form of emergency but a general term designating the *magna trepidatio*, the general state of agitation. Agamben notes that the tumult represents the key element, the necessary presupposition, for the *iustitium* to be declared. Much like in a state of emergency, the tumult is something that must be determined and defined before the necessary legal consequences ensue. The senate had the authority to decide on the presence of an emergency situation, such as the imminent threat of enemy aggression or disorder or the danger of the rise of a civil war, and in all these situations it can declare a *tumultum* to be in place; this procedure is already in itself a system of alert for the population, necessary to speed up and streamline the otherwise rigid formalities of the decision-making process.

But what exactly is a *tumultus*? In the Philippics, Cicero states the 'canonic' definition of tumult by distinguishing it from a war: 'for there can be war without a tumult, there can be no tumult without a war. For what else is a tumult than a confusion so great that greater fear arises from it?' For Cicero, the tumult must be distinguished as different from both war and all other specific states of crisis. Agamben in this regard claims that a tumult is not a war, 'but technically designates the state of disorder and unrest'. Much like the modern idea of an emergency, the term 'tumult' constitutes for Roman law 'the caesura by means of which, from the point of view of public law, exceptional measures may be taken'. 'The relation between bellum and *tumultus*', Agamben concludes, 'is the same one that exists between war and military state of siege on the one hand and state of exception and political state of siege on the other'.[25] Hence, Agamben concludes, the state of exception as a general alteration of a normative order has its paradigmatic ancestor not in the dictatorship – as Schmitt seems to suggest – but in the *iustitium*.

Despite this divergence, Agamben agrees with Schmitt on a crucial point: the modern state of exception, as a regulated technical form of government, by definition involves what is to a certain extent a work of fiction. Given its dependence on the decision of a sovereign authority, the state of exception becomes an effective instrument to be turned on or off at will, even when a threat has not yet materialised or its being a menace is not explicitly evident. Indeed, already in imperial Rome the use of the state of exception – in the form of the *iustitium* – had become 'nothing other than the sovereign's attempt to appropriate the state of exception by transforming it into a family affair'.[26] For this reason, in Agamben, the legal production of the state of exception assumes the guise of an instrument that allows a body to act legally in derogation of the law; it is the specific fiction through which the law finds

25 Giorgio Agamben, *State of Exception*, Kevin Attell transl. (Chicago: University of Chicago Press, 2005 [2003]), 41.

26 Ibid., 68

an anchorage to the outside by opening up a space in which a legal transgression of legality becomes possible.[27]

The indeterminacy of the language of the exception

The histories of the evolution of the doctrine of the state of siege and of the Roman law institute of the *iustitium* show that the definition of the state of exception as a reaction to a critical situation is not totally accurate. The exception is grounded not on facts but on a decision of what certain facts are. The difference between an 'emergency' and a 'state of emergency' is of the same order of the difference between a fact and a judgment over what a fact is – which is an interpretation, if not an opinion. And as with every interpretative act, a decision on the exception relies on categories, coordinates and key words. Due to its historical and normative evolution (which has we have seen saw the conversion of a military institution into a political and legal one), the state of exception is justified by (the often hyperbolic) reference to a war lexicon. Indeed, the legal provisions for the management of crisis in different jurisdictions share some common characteristics. They refer, for instance, to events that are threatening the life of nations – such as war, insurrection and invasion – and entail measures designed for situations of open conflict.

But this is a rather problematic aspect. In most cases emergencies do not take the form of war or armed conflict. Therefore, constitutional regimes find themselves equipped with obsolete legal instruments that are not efficient in challenging emergencies other than war. In this respect, Bruce Ackerman, astounded by the responses of the Bush administration to the 9/11 attacks, detected a peculiar insufficiency of the law in dealing with the current forms of terrorism. The law, he claims, provides two fundamental concepts for fighting and challenging terror, *war* and *crime*, neither of which is fit for the purpose of fighting terror.[28] The war on terror, according to Ackerman, is neither a war nor a crime, so the 'sweeping incursion on fundamental liberties'[29] stated by legislation on war and the 'normal' provision for the management of crime do not fit the actual configuration of the terrorist threat.

27 The attempt at defining the state of exception in terms of immunitary reaction, elaborated by Roberto Esposito, reveals here all its insufficiency. It is true as he claims that 'to be able to immunize the existence of the community from threats coming from the outside [...] the law needs to protect itself first. But according to the immunitary dialectic [...], it may do so only by relying on the same principle it seeks to dominate, on the same force it must keep at bay.' In Roberto Esposito, *Immunitas. The Protection and Negation of Life*, Z. Hanafi transl. (Malden: Polity Press, 2015), 26. The immune reaction presupposes actual exposure to a threat; while for the state of exception this is not a necessary condition.

28 Bruce Ackerman, 'The Emergency Constitutions', (2004) 113 *Yale Law Journal* 1029, 1032.

29 Ibid.

Perhaps the most controversial aspect of the state of exception – and of emergency more generally – is the indeterminacy of the legal language regulating it. Categories such as serious and immediate threat,[30] alarm,[31] case of necessity and urgency,[32] and state of tension[33] but also national security, public order and invasion are rather flexible and subject to different interpretation, uses and abuses. There is no standard definition of what an emergency is, and the legal vocabulary is not helpful in determining it. Potentially, the same acts (with their legal consequences) might be taken to both challenge an emergency due to internal disorders and respond to a natural disaster. But this is, in a way, the logical consequence of what emergency powers are thought to be for. As Alexander Hamilton rightly observed, the circumstances that may endanger national safety are infinite and unpredictable; and for this reason, no constitutional mechanism is able to frame and provide for it, since

> it is impossible to foresee or to define the extent and variety of national exigencies, and the correspondent extent and variety of the means which may be necessary to satisfy them. The circumstances that endanger the safety of nations are infinite, and for this reason, no constitutional shackles can wisely be imposed on the power to which the care of it is committed. This power ought to be coextensive with all the possible combinations of such circumstances; and ought to be under the direction of the same councils, which are appointed to preside over the common defense.[34]

It might be argued that the indeterminacy of the legal language of exceptional powers reflects on the one hand the impossibility of grasping contingency at a denotative level and on the other hand the necessity for the law to allow a certain flexibility in dealing with the unpredictable. Needless to say, this linguistic elasticity permits for emergency powers to be used in relation to very different situations almost irrespective of the 'severity' or type of the threats.[35]

30 French Constitution art. 16.
31 Spanish Constitution, art. 116.
32 Italian Constitution art. 77.
33 German Constitution, art. 80 a – 1.
34 Alexander Hamilton et al., *The Federalist Papers* (Oxford: Oxford University Press, 2008), 114.
35 The Italian case is in this regard particularly instructive. The troubled period of the 'anni di piombo' saw the emergence of a legislative practice that, according to jurists and scholars, has changed – legally – the nature of the Italian constitutional asset. Since then, in fact, the use of law decree by governments has become the norm. Art. 77 of the Republican Constitution established that 'in extraordinary situations of necessity and emergency' the government could adopt 'provisional measures having force of law' (law-decrees), which had to be presented the same day to parliament and which went out of effect if not converted into law within sixty days of their issuance. Most of the normative apparatus of

Paraphrasing Schmitt, the state of exception is always something that must be decided on, and therefore determined *ex auctoritate propria*. But in this sense the modern state of exception, whose history we have seen began with the emergence of the doctrine of the fictional state of siege, overturn the 'classical' interpretation of exceptional powers, according to which emergency is a state of fact out of which the law arises. Hence the banal but necessary consideration that states of emergency are not always and not wholly emergency. And it is its ephemeral relations with facts that led Schmitt to conclude that the state of exception has become the 'nodal point of a legal fiction with the help of which certain legal consequences are supposed to have come about'[36] and Agamben to claim resolutely that the state of exception is the '*fictio iuris* par excellence, which claims to maintain the law in its very suspension'.[37]

The logic of legal fictions

Although the juxtaposition of the concepts of state of exception and legal fictions is theoretically hazardous (especially since the first pertains to the field of public law, while the latter is traditionally tied to the linguistic practice of court procedure), drawing analogically between the two is indeed a useful strategy to understand the 'nature' of the state of exception as a legal phenomenon. In its ordinary definition, a legal fiction is a statement that 'a judge, a scholar or a lawyer tells, while simultaneously being aware that the statement is not a fact'.[38] As Yan Thomas defines it, a fiction is a 'method (process) [...] that belongs to the pragmatic of law. It consists in disguise the facts, to declare them other than they are, and in taking from the same adulteration and false supposition, the legal consequences'.[39] In other words,

the 'special law' has been enacted through the use of decree-law; and it was starting from the experience of the 1970's that in Italy the use of such a normative tool became common practice. Some defined such misuse of executive emergency power a pathology, others highlighted the blatant unconstitutionality of it; in any case, law-decrees now constitute the normal form of legislation to such a degree that they have been described as 'bills strengthened by guaranteed emergency'. This implies, however, that the democratic principle of the separation of powers has been altered and that the executive power has in fact, at least partially, absorbed the legislative power. See: Carlo Fresa, *Provvisorietà con forza di legge e gestione degli stati di crisi* (Padova: CEDAM, 1981); Pietro Pinna, *L'emergenza nell'ordinamento costituzionale italiano* (Milano: Giuffrè, 1988); Andrea Cardone, *La 'normalizzazione' dell'emergenza: Contributo allo studio del potere extra ordinem del Governo* (Torino: Giappichelli, 2011); Giovanna Pistorio, *La Decretazione d'urgenza* (Roma:Tre-Press, 2016).

36 Schmitt, *Dictatorship*, 160.

37 Agamben, *State of Exception*, 59.

38 Annelise Riles, 'Is the Law Hopeful?', *Cornell Law Faculty Working Papers*, 2010, 68.

39 Yan Thomas, 'FictioLegis', in *Les Opérations du droit* (Paris: Le Seuil, 2011), 133.

we are in presence of a legal fiction when in a specific situation actors involved in making legal decisions agree on a description of the real world but decide to act as if in the presence of a different state of affairs to attain a specific goal.

Law's practice and history is populated by fictions of very different kinds. From the legal personality of corporations to the adulteration of facts in court proceedings, the creation of specific fictional objects or expedients has been part of the law from time immemorial. As Michael Quinn points out, legal fictions can be grouped in three broad categories: (i) legal/moral fictitious entities – such as obligation and power; (ii) procedural or linguistic expedients used by legal actors attain a certain particular outcome or to bring cases within their remit – the rule of Roman law which considered foreigner 'as if' they were Roman citizens, or the decision of a London court that Minorca was in London in order to acquire jurisdiction over a case are classic examples of this type of fictions; (iii) theoretical fictions – like the assertion that common law judges do not make law but merely apply law that always existed.[40] What all these types of legal fiction have in common is their being 'to a certain extent' false, construed facts that nevertheless have concrete real effects in the reality of legal practice.

In his *Ancient Law* Henry Maine includes legal fictions, along with equity and legislations, among the instruments through which law is 'brought into harmony with society'.[41] Legal fictions, he claims, are 'invaluable expedients for overcoming the rigidity of law',[42] which however should be considered as belonging to early stages of legal civilisation. Leaving aside the historical positioning of legal fictions in the evolution of the form of law, Maine's argument exposes clearly the practical function of this peculiar tool. A legal fiction allows for the determination of the 'factual' ground for the implementation of the law. It is, therefore, a practice which permits an adaptation of the law to unprecedented circumstances, by creating the factual conditions upon which law applies. Lon Fuller – who nevertheless defined legal fictions as a pathology of law – claimed in this regard that fictions are 'generally the product of the law's struggles with new problems'; since 'we cannot foresee what changes are destined to take place in our social and economic structure',[43] the legal fiction will remain a useful tool for adapting the law to renewed conditions.

40 Michael Quinn, 'Fuller on Legal Fictions: A Benthamic Perspective', in Maksymilian Del Mar and Wiliam Twining (eds), *Legal Fictions in Theory and Practice*, (London: Springer, 2015), 65.

41 Henry Maine, *Ancient Law* (New York: Henry Holt & Co.), 24.

42 Ibid., 25.

43 Lon Fuller, *Legal Fictions* (Stanford, CA: Stanford University Press, 1967), 94.

The operative logic of legal fictions consists of the creation of specific fictitious facts that allow the law to apply to circumstances in which it could not normally be applied. In this sense, fictions are a useful technical tool for the adaptation of an order of norms to unforeseen circumstances while remaining unchanged. As Maine puts it, a legal fiction 'conceals, or affects to conceal, the fact that a rule of law has undergone alteration, its letter remaining unchanged, its operation being modified'.[44] The implementation of legal fictions involves an actual change in the law while maintaining the fiction that it remained the same.[45] The underlying logic of the state of exception, thus, could be consider as analogous to the one of legal fiction: in both cases an alteration of the normal rule of law is the outcome of a non-objective determination of facts, while supposedly keeping the text of the law intact in its punctual suspension/modification. The early formulation of the fictitious state of siege is in this respect particularly instructive. In this case, the suspension of certain rights protected by the law is the outcome of the 'fiction', according to which a specific area under threat as to be regarded in law *as if* besieged. But this implies logically that the law remains unchanged while its application is modified.

So, it might be argued that the doctrine of the exception shares with the legal fiction the peculiarity of being an instrument for the modification or alteration of the law with the pretence of maintaining its continuity. Indeed, they are both considered in legal theory as techniques implemented to preserve the letter of the law in the face of new, unpredicted facts. Therefore, it might be argued that the state of exception and legal fictions share the same nature: they are both technical instruments allowing, in different ways, the preservation of the law through its substantial modification. Both the state of exception and legal fictions involve a non-objective determination of facts; however, for the latter, legal consequences are decided on the base of false premises, while for the former the partial or total suspension of a normative order could be the outcome of a 'real' emergency. Moreover, a further distinction must be made: if the legal fiction is aimed to create specific (fictional and false) facts for the application of a limited set of rules, the exception's purpose is to create the concrete possibility of the suspension and non-application of the law – with all the risks this enterprise brings. In both cases, however, the law calls – legally – to exceed its dictates in order to gain the condition of its possibility, guaranteeing for itself the ability to act on the outside. Indeed, both legal fictions and the exception are essentially illegal; but it is this illegality that allows the law to preserve its integrity.

44 Maine, *Ancient Law*, 25.
45 G. Leung, 'Illegal Fiction', in Benjamin Hutchens (ed.), *Jean-Luc Nancy: Justice, Legality and World*, (London, New York: Continuum, 2012), 82.

Performativity

In a compelling passage on the significance of emergency powers as a paradigm of government, Agamben argues that 'the state of exception appears as the opening of a fictitious lacuna in the order for the purpose of safeguarding the existence of the norm and its applicability to the normal situation'; this lacuna, he continues, 'is not within the law [la legge], but concerns its relation to reality'.[46] Indeed, the exception, according to what has been argued so far, calls into question law's relation to reality in a twofold way. First, being configured as a reaction to a determined critical situation it exposes the rather feeble link that ties law's normative integrity to the contingency of events. Second, as with all legal principles and categories, the state of exception is a paradigm of the peculiar modality in which the language of law relates and inform reality. For the law, facts are not simply things placed in the outside world waiting to be discovered. On the contrary, as Geoffrey Samuels explains:

> The idea that legal science is a discourse that has its object in actual factual situations is to misunderstand, fundamentally, legal thought. … [Law] functions as much within the world of fact as within the world of law and it is this dual role that endows it with its capacity to create virtual facts. Lawyers, like scientists, do not work directly on reality but construct rationalized models of this reality, and it is these models that become the 'objects' of legal discourse. The models of fact upon which the […] lawyers work are as 'virtual'.[47]

In this sense, the concept of state of exception and the whole terminological arsenal of emergency laws are the specific virtual facts (or legal patterns) through which the law apprehends its relationship with the contingency of social and political (but also economic) events. And as we have seen previously through the words of Alexander Hamilton, it is the difficulty for the law to 'grasp' what will happen next that makes the legal language of emergency powers necessarily indeterminate (or virtual).

But, as is always the case with the law, legal objects and decisions, no matter how virtual or fictional, have 'real' consequences. To paraphrase Hans Vaihinger, for the law 'the world of the "unreal" is just as important as the world of the so-called real or actual (in the ordinary sense of the word); indeed it is far more important'.[48] Its ritual formality and functional systemic

46 Agamben, *State of Exception*, 31.
47 Geoffrey Samuels, 'Is Law a Fiction?', in *Legal Fictions in Theory and Practice*, 74.
48 Hans Vaihinger, *The Philosophy of 'As If': A System of the Theoretical, Practical, and Religious Fictions of Mankind*, C. K. Ogden transl. (New York: Harcourt Brace, 1935 [1911]), xlvii.

closure makes the law capable of creating 'new worlds out of old ones in a process which one could describe […] as *fact from fiction*'.[49] However, legal objects – the world the law concurs in creating – are not something the reality of which must be doubted. It is difficult to deny the existence binding relations and subjectivities, created by law's words. The law is indeed nothing other than a linguistic practice capable of creating its own reference in the outside world: or as Agamben maintains, the law is 'the realm in which all language tends to assume a performative value'.[50]

The idea of performativity has proven to be particularly instructive for characterising the constructive link between law's language and reality. To put it bluntly, the paradigm of performativity in law, while addressing the unavoidable bond that ties the spheres of legal normativity and the outside world, presupposes the neat distinction between the plane of norms and command and the reality they are called to regulate. In this light, legal objects can have a real effect on the world as long as they are not facts. What constitutes law's performative essence is the capacity to produce a reality, which stands apart from the factual world but at the same time has an effect on it. Indeed, it could be argued that the law is a discursive practice in which dwells the same creational potentiality of language. A fact, an event or a thing becomes part of the (legal) world only when is translated into the language of law: '*quod non est in actis non est in mundo*'.[51]

The poignancy of the paradigm of performativity for jurisprudence is acknowledged by John L. Austin, the author who first developed it into a theory. As he claimed, not without a certain sarcasm, the dismissal of the question of performativity of legal utterances, and the 'widespread obsession that the utterances of the law … *must* somehow be statements true or false, has prevented many lawyers from getting this whole matter much straighter'.[52] Austin's theory is as simple as it is enigmatic: there are some linguistic elements, the *speech acts*, the meaning of which refers to a reality that their own enunciation creates. The examples are well known (to declare, to promise, to command, etc.) and an explanation here is not required for the purposes of this paper. What is important to take into account is that performative speech acts require conditions that, if not met, make them to fail in their function. A speech act takes place only when is uttered according to

49 C. Messner, '"Living" Law: Performative, Not Discursive', (2012) 25(4) *International Journal for the Semiotics of Law* 544; here Messner refers to Nelson Goodman, *Ways of Worldmaking* (Indianapolis: Hackett, 1978).

50 Giorgio Agamben, *The Time that Remains: A Commentary on the Letter to the Romans*, Patricia Dailey transl. (Stanford, CA: Stanford University Press, 2005), 132.

51 Michele Spanò, 'Le Parole e le Cose (del Diritto)', in Yan Thomas, *Il Valore delle Cose* (Macerata: Quodlibet, 2015), 91.

52 John L Austin, *How to Do Things with Words* (London: Oxford University Press, 1962), 19.

precise circumstances, which authorise and guarantee its validity. Austin listed four necessary conditions for a performative utterance to succeed:

> A1. There must exist an accepted conventional procedure having a certain conventional effect, that procedure to include the uttering of certain words by certain persons in certain circumstances, and further, A2. the particular persons and circumstances in a given case must be appropriate for the invocation of the particular procedure invoked. B1. The procedure must be executed by all participants both correctly and B2. completely.[53]

This list of necessary conditions could be grouped in two sets: on the one hand we have what might be termed *procedural* rules that must be followed (accepted conventional procedure that must be executed correctly and completely); on the other hand we find the *authoritative* aspect of the act, according to which a performative utterance will have the desired effect only when pronounced by the 'appropriate' author-person. If the conditions are not met, Austin claims, we are in presence of *infelicities* – that is, acts the performativity of which 'misfires'. When a person already married utters a marriage vow – or when the marriage is celebrated without the necessary ritual-normative procedure – the act proffered simply does not take place, and no marriage occurs. And by the same token, anyone can shout in a public square, 'I declare the state of national emergency', and 'as it cannot be an act because the requisite authority is lacking, such an utterance is no more than words; it reduces itself to futile clamour, childishness, or lunacy'.[54]

As has been observed, the 'necessary conditions' that Austin placed as vital to a speech act are rather close to the "validating conditions" of obligations, contracts and covenants more generally.[55] For the law, a statement assumes legal force only when pronounced or validated by a person whose position gives her the appropriate authority, as decreed by a certain accepted conventional procedure. The coincidence between the law's practice and the validating conditions of a performative act is here glaring: the sentence of a judge – to legislate, to stipulate a contract, etc. – needs, like a speech act, the presence of both a procedural (formal-normative) and an authoritative (personal) element. These two elements must work in synergy to make law's statements legally valid.

From this point of view, the state of exception appears as a legal performance (carried out according to an established 'accepted conventional

53 Ibid., 14–15.

54 Émile Benveniste, *Problems in General Linguistic* (Miami: University of Miami Press, 1971), 236.

55 Elaine Scarry, 'The Declaration of War: Constitutional and Unconstitutional Violence', in Austin Sarat and Thomas R. Kearns (eds), *Law's Violence* (Ann Arbor: University of Michigan Press, 2009), 29. See also: Howard Warrender, *The Political Philosophy of Hobbes: His Theory of Obligation* (Oxford: Clarendon Press, 1957).

procedure' by the right person), but of a special kind. By suspending the normal framework of the law, the exception produces a peculiar distortion of law's performativity since it 'performs' legally a specific change in the operativity of law, according to which a set of norms and rights, while still in existence, do not have legal effects. In the exception the normal-procedural element of law is altered or, to use Schmitt's words, recedes, while the personal authoritative element emerges as the primary guarantee of law's existence. Indeed, one of the most common traits of emergency administration is the concentration of powers in the hands of a single authority (usually the executive). With the state of exception, we assist a (partial if not total) reunification of the different forms of powers – usually separated and balanced – in a single deciding body that, because of the crisis, generally has the authority of acting with a degree of discretion – infringing in certain cases basic rights protected by the law. The alteration of the established legal-decision-making procedure and the re-joining of the powers in the hands of a single governmental body illuminate the authentic fullness of sovereign authority. For this reason, every declaration of state of exception must be considered *authoritarian*.

Conclusion

The modern doctrine of the state of exception as a fictitious or political technique of government is rooted in the experience of being besieged, which is in the most perilous situation for the survivorship of the integrity of the state. And this is visible in the language of emergency laws. From a strictly legal point of view, the state of exception consists of a crisis reaction mechanism that delegates to a single body exceptional powers in order to restore a condition of normality as quickly as possible. The state of exception is thus intended as a tool to protect a given constituted order in times of crisis. But by providing the authority to declare a 'state' of emergency as being in place, the doctrine of the exception allows a legitimate authority to make 'real' what it is not, or what it is not yet real. Such a decision, as has been argued, must be considered a work of fiction – with, however, very real consequences, the most important of which is the obfuscation of the classic categories of 'war' and 'peace'.

The recognition that the fictional state of exception, as a form of administration of emergency regulated by law, might offer a vehicle for abusive state action has always been clear. The risk is that the increased concentration of governmental powers, along with an alteration of the constitutional checks and balances, could foster the emergence of an authoritarian system out of a democratic one. Already Rossiter in his seminal work on constitutional dictatorship maintained that emergencies tend to perpetuate themselves, despite all the control mechanisms typically present in constitutions. As he claimed, the impression that the delegation of legislative powers, the making of law by decree and in general the state of emergency are purely transitory and temporary solutions is just misleading. On the contrary, he goes on, 'the instruments of government depicted here as temporary "crisis" arrangements have in some countries, and may eventually in all countries, become lasting peacetime institutions'.[56] And recent developments are further proof of this trend.

It thus seems as if the possibility of being abused is inscribed in the very nature of the state of exception as a legal object – and this is a belief shared by many.[57] In order to improve our position in the struggle against an exception that has become the rule and given the incessant failures of jurisprudence to find a way out of this, the task before us is to move towards thinking of legal normality with no exceptions – even if this means going beyond the law as we know it.

56 Rossiter, *Constitutional Dictatorship*, 313.
57 Oren Gross, 'Chaos and Rules: Should Responses to Violent Crisis Always Be Constitutional?', (2003) 112 *Yale Law Journal* 1011, 1021.

Chapter 2

'Through a glass, darkly'

Law, history and the frontispiece of the exception

Cosmin Cercel[1]

Nemo censetur ignorare exceptionem

What, if anything, is the paradigm of the exception able to offer to a critical understanding of our politico-legal present? How – that is, through which conceptual framework and by reference to which procedure of truth – are we to address the disruption produced in our polities by the maelstrom of crises affecting the world during the past decade? Last and not least, how are lawyers able to make sense of the shifting grounds of legality and the cracks within the symbolic order of liberal democracy?

The argument that I advance here is a simple one: there are two interconnected ways in which we can make sense of the substance of our legal present. They both are within the reach of lawyers, and they have been present within various traditions of legal and political theory for a while. Continuing to ignore them is not only a matter of intellectual responsibility but tantamount to connivance to law's unfolding history of self-erasure. To dispel the mystery surrounding this panacea, I hasten to add that on one hand there is the very concept of the state of exception, with both its intellectual genealogy and its material history of practices. On the other, there is nothing else than the status of the law as a field of knowledge and as a praxis moulded by historical experience. By bringing both together we can develop a powerful theoretical apparatus able to cut through the mist of jurisprudential obscurity, intellectual quietism and political confusion that surrounds the present status of legality.

The starting point of this analysis rests with the jurisprudential core of the concept of the state of exception. In its amphiboly – as both a politico-legal practice of suspending the law and a theoretical paradigm of modern law and politics – the state of exception embodies our *Zeitgeist*. Martial law, expedite administrative measures, secret courts, indefinite administrative

1 Research for this chapter was undertaken in the context of the research project entitled 'Heads of State (Princes, Kings and Presidents) and the Authoritarian Dynamic of Political Power in Romanian Constitutional History', funded by the Romanian Research Funding Agency (UEFISCDI), PN-III-P4-ID-PCE-2016–0013.

detention, temporary suspension of constitutional guarantees are all part of the humdrum of daily legality, constituting what was euphemistically coined as the 'preventive state'.[2] At the time I am writing this chapter, President Trump has declared a National Emergency Concerning the Southern Border of the United States.[3] Last year, faced with the yellow vest protests, the French minister of the interior was flirting with the idea of declaring a state of emergency[4] only a year after it has been lifted and three years since its initial declaration in the wake of the terrorist attacks in Paris of November 2015.[5] Now, these are surely extreme measures emerging in a particular context and not the same as practices as questionable and stealthy[6] as packing courts and other institutional bodies, as taking control of the judiciary and the press, as curtailing academic freedoms. Yet there is an undeniable discursive link between the suspension of the constitutional process and the minute sapping and dismantling of putative rational legal institutions, just as there is an underlying ideological conflation between the discourse of exception and the public displays of ultranationalism. The recent marches in Warsaw[7] and Sofia,[8] the affirmation of the far right and the overall return of nationalist rhetoric bear witness for this overlapping between security and identitarian concerns. We are indeed living within a time of exception.

No matter how worrying these practices appear to be at a first glance, they become even more so if placed in their proper historical context. As signifying practices they point back explicitly to the interwar period and the alternative

2 András Sajó and Renáta Uitz, *The Constitution of Freedom: An Introduction to Legal Constitutionalism* (Oxford: Oxford University Press, 2017), 440–444.
3 Proclamation 9844 of 15 February 2019 Declaring a National Emergency Concerning the Southern Border of the United States, 84 Federal Register No. 34, 20 February 2019.
4 'Instaurer l'état d'urgence? Castaner dit ne pas avoir de "tabou"', *L'Obs*, 1 December 2018, available at: www.nouvelobs.com/politique/20181201.AFP9398/instaurer-l-etat-d-urgence-castaner-dit-ne-pas-avoir-de-tabou.html; 'Le recours à l'état d'urgence, une option face aux débordements des "gilets jaunes"?', *Le Monde*, 3 December 2018, available at: www.lemonde.fr/les-decodeurs/article/2018/12/03/le-recours-a-l-etat-d-urgence-une-option-face-aux-debordements-des-gilets-jaunes_5392147_4355770.html.
5 Decree No. 1475 of 14 November 2015 concerning the application of Statute 55–883 of 3 April 1955, JORF No. 264, 14 November 2015, p. 21297; Statute No. 1501 of 20 November 2015 extending the application of the Statute 55–883 of 3 April 1955 on the state of emergency and reinforcing the efficacy of its provisions, JORF No. 271, 21 November 2015, p. 21665.
6 Landau, 'Populist Constitutions', 534–5.
7 '"White Europe": 60,000 nationalists march on Poland's independence day', *The Guardian*, 12 November 2017, available at: www.theguardian.com/world/2017/nov/12/white-europe-60000-nationalists-march-on-polands-independence-day.
8 'Far-right activists stage torchlit march in Bulgarian capital', *Reuters*, 16 February 2019, available at: www.reuters.com/article/us-bulgaria-farright-march/far-right-activists-stage-torchlit-march-in-bulgarian-capital-idUSKCN1Q50PG.

projects of modernity[9] that that era has fostered. In doing so, they reconstruct the law according to new ideological lines and expose the 'unworked through', resistant past within the contemporary imaginaries of the Western legal traditions. This is not simply a case of reconnecting to past experience, of mimicking or reproducing modes of political takeover in an attempt to seizing power; rather it is an affirmation of what has always already been part of the constitutional and political horizon of our polities. From the standpoint of a *longue durée* history of the law, we are now witnessing yet another moment in a process of increasing affirmation of the powers of the executive,[10] sweeping constitutional guarantees and securing control over the legal apparatus.[11] It is from within this line of inquiry that the continuity with the past politico-legal practices is not simply a rhetorical and ideological trope raised in order to provoke, soothe or shock our political sensitivities but a historical nexus that can be documented through an analysis of the regimes of legality in place in Europe and beyond.[12]

The antinomies of the legal form

Given that the law's structure finds itself at the borders of material practices and conceptual representation and that law is an ideological apparatus[13] with a material inscription[14] and a conceptual body, its history knows very few moments of rupture. The memorial, symbolic and ultimately legal practices through which postwar liberalism, state-communism or post-communist transitions have tried to address this resistant material discursive dimension within the body of the law have been extremely scarce and generally inaccurate. Central concepts for constitutional law and theory, such as sovereignty, legality and belonging, have continued to be thought, taught and professed with very little – if any – attention paid to their historical construction,

9 David D. Roberts, *The Totalitarian Experiment in Twentieth Century Europe* (London: Routledge, 2006), 412–452.
10 Karl Loewenstein, 'The Balance between Legislative and Executive Power: A Study in Comparative Constitutional Law', (1938) 5 *Chicago Law Review* 566.
11 Even mainstream constitutional lawyers would agree to this assessment, without drawing the otherwise obvious historical conclusion. See Sajó and Uitz, *The Constitution of Freedom*, 440–445.
12 Christian Joerges and Navraj Singh Ghaleigh (eds), *Darker Legacies of Law in Europe: The Shadow of National Socialism and Fascism Over Europe and Its Legal Traditions* (Oxford: Hart, 2003); David Fraser, *Law after Auschwitz: Towards a Jurisprudence of the Holocaust* (Durham, NC: Carolina Academic Press, 2005); Stephen Skinner (ed.), *Fascism and Criminal Law: History, Theory, Continuity* (Oxford: Hart, 2015); Stephen Skinner, (ed.), *Ideology and Criminal Law: Fascist, National Socialist and Authoritarian Regimes* (Oxford: Hart, 2019).
13 Louis Althusser, *Sur la reproduction* (Paris: Presses Universitaires de France, 1996 [1970]), 106–111.
14 Warren Montag, 'The Soul Is the Prison of the Body: Althusser and Foucault 1970–1975', (1995) 88 *Yale French Studies* 53, 63.

ideological weight and semantic luggage. As Peter Sloterdijk aptly put it in his scathing, yet misdirected criticism of German revolutionary communism, the idea of 'another state, once again a state'[15] seems to have been the horizon limiting the reconstruction of polities at the end of wars and in the wake of major social reshuffling. Now, this reconstruction was both wanting in scope and obscure in its ideology and structure – from the wilful and informed limited prosecution of fascist executioners and collaborationists[16] in both the West[17] and the East[18] to the ambiguous preservation of ideological tropes such as anticommunism in the West[19] and nationalism clothed as patriotism in the East.[20] Beyond these trends affecting the 'general' ideology of the polities lie also the minute history of constitutional reforms, transitional justice processes, as well as the daily life of academic production and legal training which by and large continued to function on the continent as much as in common law jurisdictions as if nothing had happened. And indeed, from a legal standpoint, informed by the formalist paradigms, nothing had happened with the substance and practice of the law. 'Law continued while six million died',[21] and indeed law through its agents continued to entertain the illusion of a unitary body of rules able to structure the life of the polities and knit communities under its rule, unexposed to historical upheaval.

This trend was irrespective and at times contrary to the ideological pledges of the regimes in place, and certainly irrespective of the contingent ideological content of the particular norms at either constitutional or infra-constitutional level. Law was there to stay, even in the midst of purportedly revolutionary transformations, of political reforms and in its explicit or implicit disapplication.[22] Yet, the resilience and survival of the legal form is not a matter of securing formally or substantially freedoms or rights in an

15 Peter Sloterdijk, *Critique of Cynical Reason* Michael Eldred transl (Minneapolis: University of Minnesota Press, 1987), 68.
16 Jerome S. Legge, 'Collaboration, Intelligence and the Holocaust: Ferdinand Ďurčanský, Slovak Nationalism, and the Gehlen Organisation', (2018) 32 *Holocaust and Genocide Studies* 224.
17 David Fraser, '(De) Constructing the Nazi State: Criminal Organizations and the Constitutional Theory of the International Military Tribunal', (2017) 39 *Loyola of Los Angeles International & Comparative Law Review* 117.
18 Francine Hirsch, 'The Soviets at Nuremberg: International Law, Propaganda, and the Making of the Postwar Order', (2008) 113 *American Historical Review* 701; Michael J. Bazyler and Kellyanne Rose Gold, 'The Judicialization of International Atrocity Crimes: The Kharkov Trial of 1943', (2012) 80 *San Diego International Law Journal* 77.
19 Traverso, *The New Faces of Fascism*, 116–118.
20 Cosmin Cercel, *Towards a Jurisprudence of State Communism: Law and the Failure of Revolution* (Abingdon: Routledge, 2018), 146–150.
21 Fraser, *Law after Auschwitz*, 145.
22 Cosmin Cercel, 'The Other Otherwise: Law, Historical Trauma and the Severed Gardens of Justice', (2014) 8 *Pólemos: Journal of Law, Literature and Culture* 275.

attempt to articulate and limit the foundational violence of the law. Rather, the opposite seems to be true. Through its very operation, the legal form secures the survival of the exercise of unlimited sovereign power. Let us rest on this point further: since the end of the First World War, an unprecedented growth of expedient measures situated at the limits of the legal system, yet within its boundaries, can be attested against the background of (and against the) mechanisms meant to supplant and limit the arbitrary exercise of power.[23] This took the form of mechanisms such as the institution of martial law, of emergency measures of a military, security and financial nature, of explicit suspensions of fundamental rights,[24] as well as diffuse powers that escape the scrutiny of courts. Sometimes these provisions found a place even within the very texture of codified legislation, such as in the case of criminal legislation, continuing to act at the level of principles informing the legal grammar of polities.[25] Last, but not least, it nested within the very formulation of the mechanisms pledging protection of human rights but at the same time the primacy of the protection of the legal order and state sovereignty.[26] However, this is not a mere case of a conflict of values that can make the object a balancing of rights but a fundamental limit of the normativity in grounding itself.

At this stage the peculiar historical context in which the affirmation of the primacy of the legal form occurred as well as the subsequent paradoxes it entails should be emphasised. If the most rigorous theory articulating the law as a normative category pertaining to the realm of ought is indeed Kelsen's *Pure Theory of Law*,[27] one of its often disregarded features in relation to its intellectual and material origins is its inscription within the same historical trajectory that has produced the growth of executive power and the series of suspension of the law. Let us note not only that the *pure theory* is not only implicitly connected to the debates related to the application of the infamous article 48 in the Weimar constitution[28] but written within a historical

23 Karl Loewenstein, 'Autocracy Versus Democracy in Contemporary Europe I', (1935) 29 *American Political Science Review* 571.

24 Karl Loewenstein, 'Militant Democracy and Fundamental Rights I', (1937) 31 *American Political Science Review* 417.

25 Cosmin Cercel, 'The Enemy Within: Criminal Law and Ideology in Interwar Romania', in Stephen Skinner (ed.), *Fascism and Criminal Law: History, Theory, Continuity* (Oxford: Hart, 2015), 101–126.

26 Cosmin Cercel, 'The Law of Blood: Totalitarianism, Criminal Law and the Body Politic of World War Two Romania, in Stephen Skinner (ed.), *Ideology and Criminal Law: Fascist, National Socialist and Authoritarian Regimes* (Oxford: Hart, 2019).

27 Hans Kelsen, *Introduction to the Problems of Legal Theory*, Bonnie Litschewski Paulson and Stanley Paulson transl. (Oxford: Oxford University Press, 1992 [1934]).

28 Lars Vinx, *The Guardian of the Constitution: Hans Kelsen and Carl Schmitt on the Limits of Constitutional Law* (Cambridge: Cambridge University Press, 2015).

sequence that starts with the fall of the Austro-Hungarian Empire and the reconstruction of state sovereignty in both Western and Central European polities. The Kelsenian affirmation of law as a system of norms, and of the pure theory as a way of describing their relation from a standpoint that is value-free and 'clean' from moral, sociological or historical taint,[29] appears thus as a theoretical attempt at preserving the status of legality outside the interplay of historical forces and political struggles. The peculiar explanation of the interplay between validity and efficacy of the *Grundnorm*[30] within the context of revolution is indicative of not only the limits of such a project but also a specific regime of historicity that marks legal thought. To put it simply, in a case of a revolution – and Central Europe had witnessed a few in the wake of the Great War – the *Grundnorm* has to entertain at least a certain relation to factual reality.[31] As Kelsen writes,

> the validity of a legal system governing the behaviour of particular human beings depends in a certain way, then, on the fact that their real behaviour corresponds to the legal system – depends in a certain way … on the efficacy of the system.[32]

Put otherwise, in order to be valid, the law has to be effective. It is precisely this scarcely explained relation between efficacy and validity that is both the Achille's heel in the liberal concept of law and an important indicator of the common epistemological assumptions that have connected and informed opposing camps within the analysis of legality. Carl Schmitt's insistence on the importance of the sovereign decision within the pages of *Political Theology*,[33] following his analysis developed in both *Dictatorship*[34] and the *Value of the State and the Signification of the Individual*,[35] is part of an *episteme* that had structured the basic frames of the legal mind in a time of crisis. Schmitt's insistence on the connection between the exercise of sovereign power and the exception[36] and the distinction between normalcy and disorder[37] is not a mere affirmation of the primacy of politics or of the political over the law. Read within the intellectual trajectory of his core concepts – state, sovereignty and the law – the state of exception is the space that opens the affirmation of

29 Kelsen, *Introduction*, 4–7.
30 Ibid., 58.
31 Ibid., 59.
32 Ibid., 60.
33 Carl Schmitt, *Political Theology*: Four Chapters on the Concept of Sovereignty, George Schwab transl. London, MIT Press, 1985 [1922]).
34 Carl Schmitt, *Dictatorship*, Michael Hoelzl and Graham Ward transl. (Cambridge, Polity, 2014 [1921]).
35 Carl Schmitt, *La valeur de l'Etat et la signification de l'individu*, Sandrine Baume transl. (Geneva: Librairie Droz, 2003 [1914]).
36 Schmitt, *Political Theology*, 5.
37 Ibid., 13.

the sovereign body through the operation of the law: 'The exception reveals most clearly the essence of state's authority. The decision parts here from the legal norm and (...) authority proves that to produce law it need not be based on law'.[38]

As such, the apparent liminal character of the exception and of exceptional measures within the constitutional body of rules[39] is brought to the fore as the authentic site of sovereign power – that is, indissociably connected to the law and state.[40] Let us recall here the medial place of the state within Schmitt's initial writings – as the institution able to connect the ideal realm of normativity to the moving social reality. Accordingly, the state is 'a formation within the legal sphere whose meaning nests exclusively in the task of realizing the law'.[41] In so far as the sovereign is the one who decides over the exception, the sovereign is also the one who decides on the normality, insofar as 'for a legal order to make sense, a normal situation must exist and he is sovereign who decides whether this normal situation actually exists'.[42] The exception is thus the operation that is able to sustain the normal ordering of society, as 'the state suspends the law in the exception on the basis of its right to self-preservation'.[43]

There should be no uncertainty with regard to the common intellectual imaginary shared by both Schmitt and Kelsen, which goes beyond their personal socialisation within the German-language world of legal theory. References to Kelsen are not only a constant presence within the writings of the *Crownjurist* but the neo-Kantian sources supporting an understanding of the law as a normative category – that is, as a matter of form – are the background against which both the idea of the state as mediation[44] and later on the state of exception as the point of reference of sovereignty are built. As Schmitt writes, echoing Kelsen's unresolved nexus between validity and efficacy: 'there exists no norm that is applicable to chaos'.[45]

According to Schmitt, the legal form is the background and the map that enables one to grasp the remnants of authentic sovereignty under the historical veils raised by the liberal misadventure. One should note at this point not only the political and theological implications of Schmitt's writings in the early years of the interwar period but also their relation to the legal historical thread followed within the pages of the *Dictatorship*. Indeed, it is useful to emphasise how much the conceptualisation of the 'exception' owes not only to a criticism of the liberal categories of legality but also to a historical thesis

38 Ibid.
39 Ibid., 5.
40 Ibid.
41 Schmitt, *La valeur de l'Etat*, 100.
42 Schmitt, *Political Theology*, 13.
43 Ibid., 12.
44 Schmitt, *La valeur de l'Etat*, 119.
45 Schmitt, *Political Theology*, 13.

of the debasement of the true meaning of sovereignty under the conditions of the rise of liberalism. That is because, according to Schmitt, what created the unity of the state was the monarchical absolutism of the 17th and 18th centuries.[46] Dictatorship, not unlike the state of exception, was both the trace of this historical thread – the remnant within the texture of the modern state – and its ultimate defence against the perceived dissolution grown in the shadows of liberal neutralisation.[47] The operation of the exception is thus the answer to both a political and a jurisprudential conundrum. As Schmitt writes, 'dictatorship is a problem of concrete reality without ceasing to be a legal problem'.[48] Dictatorship is thus the locus of sovereignty, as it is the nexus between Schmitt's theory and the historical context of the early inter-war period. To be sure, this defence of sovereignty is written in the echo of the German revolution[49] and the effective state of civil war that had engulfed the transition from the Empire to the Weimar Republic.[50] Let us note at this stage the similar and connected historical thread that unites both Kelsen's and Schmitt's respective contexts, to which they offer ostensibly different answers.

Deposing the legal form

But not only the Great War and the exceptional civil war context determines historically the content and form of this intellectual debate. Another source – even if less discussed in relation to the either the pure theory or the state of exception, is the 1917 revolution and the emergence of the first proletarian state, itself contending with the consequences of the war. It is thus at the antipodes of Schmitt and Kelsen that a third and a fourth possible answer to the question of the relation between law, politics and social reality are constructed. Sharing conceptual and intellectual baggage by writing from within the margins of the post-Kantian tradition – not unlike Kelsen and Schmitt – and flirting more with Marxism than either of them, Walter Benjamin seeks neither to ground legality in an ahistorical realm nor to save sovereignty from within the disapplying forces of the revolution.[51] Rather, his project is to secure the purity of revolution and violence from the taints of both law and sovereignty. The implications of this stand lie within the realms of political

46 Schmitt, *Dictatorship*, 53–67; Schmitt, *Political Theology*, 47–49.
47 Schmitt, *Political Theology*, 37–39.
48 Schmitt, *Dictatorship*, 118.
49 Gopal Balakrishnan, *The Enemy: An Intellectual Portrait of Carl Schmitt* (London: Verso, 2000), 28–47; Pierre Broué, *The German Revolution*, John Archer transl. (Leiden: Brill, 2005 [1971]), 89–260.
50 Enzo Traverso, *Fire and Blood: The European Civil War 1914–1945*, David Fernbach transl. (London: Verso, 2017 [2007]), 48.
51 Walter Benjamin, 'Critique of Violence', in Marcus Bullock and Michael W. Jennings (eds), *Walter Benjamin: Selected Writings. Vol. 1, 1913–1926* (Cambridge: Harvard University Press, 1996 [1921]), 236–252.

theory, jurisprudence and theology – as indeed the heterodox Marxism he is defending finds its sources within both a reconstruction of historical materialism and a re-reading of Jewish messianism.[52] Accordingly, Benjamin's jurisprudential stand takes the particular form of a legal scepticism – in so far as law is conceived as 'a prerogative of the kings and nobles, in short of the mighty; and that, mutatis mutandis, will remain so as long as it exists'.[53]

While this position finds its roots in a Marxist tradition unearthing the ways in which the legal form is obscuring the reality of oppression, exploitation and domination, it also goes beyond it by signalling a structural – and seemingly ahistorical – connivance between the legal form and violence, and more specifically 'mythical' violence – that is, the violence built on the powers of myth and which necessarily 'demands sacrifice'.[54] In Benjamin's words, '[m]ythical violence is bloody power over mere life for its own sake'.[55] Insofar as 'lawmaking is power making and, to that extent, an immediate manifestation of violence',[56] law finds itself on the side of mythical violence,[57] a violence that imposes the law and existing order of things, and which can be deposed only by divine violence. As the 'the highest manifestation of violence unalloyed by man',[58] divine violence is the one able to overcome the continual restatement of the law.

Evgeny's Pashukanis' defence of a dissolution of the legal form and system as the conclusion of the revolutionary transformation[59] echoes this legal scepticism. For him, the site of the legal relationship – a form which operates like commodity does in the realm of economy[60] – is to be found in the realm of private law, constructing from within the grammar and the ideological framework of bourgeois legality. As he writes, '[T]he subject as the bearer and addressee of all possible demands, and the chain of subjects bound by demands addressed to one another, is the basic juridic fabric corresponding to the economic fabric'.[61] Constitutional law and public law, conceived as areas of mere ideology that function according to the principle of expediency,[62] are

52 Jacob Taubes, 'Walter Benjamin: A Modern Marcionite? Scholem's Benjamin Interpretation Reexamined' in Colby Dickinson and Stéphane Symons (eds) *Walter Benjamin and Theology* (New York: Fordham University Press, 2016), 164–178.
53 Benjamin, 'Critique of Violence', 249.
54 Ibid., 250.
55 Ibid.
56 Ibid., 249.
57 Ibid., 250.
58 Ibid., 252.
59 Evgeny Bronislavovich Pashukanis, 'The General Theory of Law and Marxism', in Piers Beirne and Robert Sharlet (eds), *Pashukanis: Selected Writings on Law and Marxism*, Peter B. Maggs transl., (London: Academic Press, 1980), 37–131.
60 Ibid., 69.
61 Ibid., 71.
62 Ibid., 112.

not the place where legal relationships are produced, but the place where the state is simply imagined as a legal superstructure.[63] Accordingly, '[t]he state apparatus actually realizes itself as an impersonal "general will", as "the authority of law" etc., to the extent that society appears as a market'.[64] What is indeed able to produce a significant change within the operation of the law, is a radical transformation at the level of economy, and of the concepts supporting the view of a society as a market and the individual as a legal person. It is only such a reshuffling that would be able to finally depose the law and bring about its withering away, thus fulfilling the dictatorship of the proletariat: 'Liberation (…) would only occur when the general withering away of the legal superstructure begins'.[65]

What is important in these theoretical positions developed on the left side of the political spectrum and within the path opened by the Russian Revolution, is the insistence on law's ability to taint the content of a revolutionary transformation – that is, the resilience of the legal form as well as its necessary relation to other spheres, such as economy and politics. In other words, a mere 'takeover' of the sites of power is never enough in changing the law, nor is it the final point of its deposition. More importantly, the legal form emerges as being supported by a wider array of relations – moulded by history and economy – that keep it articulated and alive within the structure of the polities, regardless of, if not in opposition to, the figure or the body of the sovereign.[66]

These theoretical interventions that provided the substance of the jurisprudential debates of the interwar period did not disappear either with Hitler's rise to power in Germany or with Stalin's rise to the helm of the Communist Party of the Soviet Union. To begin with, Schmitt's state of exception grounding the sovereign decision was redeemed by historical experience, both in the eventual application of Article 48 and in the effective suspension of the Weimar Constitution. His contribution to the legal drama of the Reichstag fire as well as his theoretical insights from *Political Theology* found echo in his damning *The Führer Protects the Law.*[67] Yet this final contribution to the theory of exception and authoritarianism was perhaps part of a wider trend of exceptional measures and emergencies engulfing the world at the time.[68] For its part, Benjamin's search for a revolutionary violence able to depose the law would remain only a sublime objective – neither the reality of

63 Ibid., 73.
64 Ibid., 95.
65 Ibid., 125.
66 Cercel, *Towards a Jurisprudence of State Communism*, 96.
67 Carl Schmitt, 'Der Führer schützt das Recht,' *Deutsche Juristen-Zeitung* 39, 1 August 1934, 945–950.
68 For the reception of Carl Schmitt's work in wartime Romania, see Marius Cişmigiu, *Regimul constituţional român: constituţia de criză şi ordinea politică* (Bucharest: Curentul, 1943).

Soviet Russia nor the revolution and Civil War in Spain would be able to break the deadlock between law, revolution and violence. On the contrary, the fascist onslaught with its long thread of security measures, as well as the Stalinist betrayal, indefinitely postponed both divine justice and the withering away of law and state. Pashukanis' death in the purges, as well as the purge of his work from the theoretical legal canon,[69] left no room for a different relation between law and sovereign power than the one already present in the structure of imperial states. Last but not least, Kelsen's *Pure Theory* might not have had a great career in the final interwar years, yet it thoroughly influenced the political theoretical stand of some of the postwar debates, before becoming the default theoretical position for constitutional lawyers on the continent. While indeed the conundrum between validity and efficacy might not have been answered from the standpoint of a pure theory, Kelsen's embrace of a liberal democratic stand[70] and his advocacy for a connection between legal form and democracy continues to influence the understanding of law and politics to this day, while his formalism found quarters in the work of practical lawyers from both sides of the Iron Curtain.

The paradigm of exception

At the time when Agamben published his first rendition of the state of exception, within the pages of *Homo Sacer*,[71] the concept of exception seemed to have disappeared from the ambit of both political theory and, especially, legal studies. Either relegated to a practice of somewhat antiquarian interest – regardless of the uses of exceptional measures from Northern Ireland to Ceauşescu's Romania – or to a confusion with the derogatory meaning of dictatorship, the coalescence between law and state violence was effaced under the new democratic pledges of the law understood as a neutral medium founded on reason. The end of communism enveloped the violent history of law within a 'white mythology'[72] as if it 'has effaced in itself that fabulous scene which brought it into being, and yet remains, active',[73] This eschatological illusion of a now radically different form of politics from the past had found its opposition in the vague resuscitation of the Schmittian and Benjaminian tropes that served the critical project of deconstruction.[74] With it, however, the authority of the law was still left within the realm of mystical

69 Piers Beirne and Robert Sharlet, 'Editors' introduction', in Beirne and Sharlet (eds), *Pashukanis* 1.

70 See, for instance, Hans Kelsen, 'Foundations of Democracy', (1955) 66 *Ethics* 1.

71 Giorgio Agamben, *Homo Sacer: Sovereign Power and Bare Life*, Daniel Heller-Roazen transl. (Stanford: Stanford University Press, 1998 [1995]).

72 Jacques Derrida, *Marges de la philosophie* (Paris: Minuit, 1972), 254.

73 Ibid.

74 Jacques Derrida, *Force de loi* (Paris: Galilée, 1994).

foundations,[75] which prevented a full-fledged critique that would take into account what is '"rotten" in the law'.[76]

For Agamben the law takes an important place in his project of revisiting the nexus that ties bare life and politics. On the path opened by Foucault's insights into the historical rise of biopolitics and Arendt's reading of the dislocation of the public sphere by the irruption of biological life within the political realm,[77] Agamben sought to move beyond the metaphysical structure that commands such an articulation between the otherwise distinct spheres of life and politics.[78] On this path, the law, understood as essentially an operation of exception,[79] is the structure able to connect the life devoid of attribute to the machinery of politics:

> The 'sovereign' structure of the law, its peculiar and original 'force', has the form of a state of exception in which fact and law are indistinguishable (…). Life, which is thus obliged, can in the last instance be implicated in the sphere of the law only through the presupposition of its inclusive exclusion, only in an *exceptio.*[80]

By exploring the mysterious figure of the *homo sacer*, what the Agambenian project aims at is to identify the secret quilting point between the juridico-political institutional model of analysing sovereign power and the biopolitical one, from which the normativity of the law has been evacuated. The *homo sacer*, an ancient institution of Roman law defining those found guilty of crimes and whose life could have been lawfully taken away, without being sacrificial, exposes a long series of paradoxes inherent in the structure of the Roman law.[81] It unveils the nexus between crime, punishment and sovereign power as well as the obscure connection between legal thought and the sphere of religion.[82] The sacrality of the *homo sacer* marks of a zone of indistinction between sacred and profane, between politics, law and religion representing an originary political structure through which sovereign power – in its dual religious and profane guises – invests the individual body of the subjects. As Agamben writes, '[l]ife that cannot be sacrificed and yet may be killed is sacred life'.[83]

This paradox is indeed structural, and it reveals law's core feature – that of being a system of signification – a *langue.*[84] In its application, the law is

75 Ibid., 84–98.
76 Ibid., 95.
77 Agamben, *Homo Sacer*, 10.
78 Ibid., 11.
79 Ibid., 19.
80 Ibid., 22.
81 Ibid., 47.
82 Ibid., 47–51.
83 Ibid., 52.
84 Ibid., 22.

always a form of exception, just as the word presupposes a suspension of language.[85] Moreover, each instantiation of the law is a form of exception. Within this structure of the state of exception, literally of taking-law-from-the-outside, lies the paradox of the necessary presupposition of an outside-of-the-law: '[l]anguage is the sovereign who, in a permanent state of exception, declares that there is nothing outside language and that language is *always beyond itself*'.[86] Thus, law, as language, presupposes the non-linguistic, the unarticulated, and perhaps the violence of the 'real', in order to institute itself as a part of the symbolic order. By this presupposition and inclusion of the excess, the distinction between institution and destitution of the law is supressed. Accordingly, within the exception there is no meaningful distinction to be made between lawlessness and legality.

The paradoxes of sovereignty seized within this context are initially obscured by the philosophical thread that is at the core of this stage of the Agambenian project. Neither constitutional theory nor legal theory capture Agamben's writing within the pages of the first rendition of *Homo Sacer*, but the status of the human subject as subject of rights that are emerging within the conditions of the exception and their undoing operated by the shadowy presence of biopolitics.[87] In this sense, the analysis of the operation of the exception is itself suspended, and the core of his inquiry is taken on by the relation between life and sovereign power. Perhaps unsurprisingly, as the Heideggerian roots of this project would suggest, Agamben is primarily interested in seizing the philosophical origins and the intellectual traces left within the unfolding of the history of thought by the nexus between unarticulated life and sovereign power.

The exception, as a part of the operation of the law is thus only one of the forms of this encounter – important as it might be – but not a paradigmatic one for the history of the Western political subject. Rather, what he proposes as a paradigm is the camp, as an unmediated locus of production of a life that is immediately and directly inscribed in the production of sovereignty.[88] In his words, 'the camp – as the pure, absolute, and impassable biopolitical space (insofar as it is founded solely on the state of exception) – will appear as the hidden paradigm of the political space of modernity'.[89]

From this point on, law and exception, as forms of opening and founding of the camp, are sidelined by an unrelenting engagement with the breach and undoing of rights under the encroachment of biopolitics on political thought.[90] Of course, references to either the canonical legal texts enacting

85 Ibid., 20.
86 Ibid.
87 Ibid., 68.
88 Ibid., 72–73.
89 Ibid.
90 Ibid., 75–79.

human rights[91] or to constitutional arrangements and theory continue to sign the argument, yet the law is subsumed to the waves of biopolitics, and it has become a zone of indistinction between life, nature, history and politics to the point of being rendered inoperative in the functioning of totalitarian states – for Agamben, 'the dimension in which the extermination took place is neither religion nor law, but biopolitics'.[92]

Almost ten years later, *State of Exception*[93] revisits the structure of this legal paradox in an attempt to bring to the fore the normative and structural operation of the law that is indissolubly linked to the articulation between *zoé* and *bíos*,[94] insofar as the state of exception has an 'immediate biopolitical significance'.[95] At this time, Agamben returns to the historical and jurisprudential sources of the conundrum entailed by law's suspension. If Carl Schmitt plays a central role in approaching the concept of exception in its politico-legal guise, Walter Benjamin is also invoked, in order to reconstruct the full thrust of the interwar debate.[96] Kelsen – implicitly[97] – and Pashukanis[98] also make a marginal appearance within the analysis of the edges of the exception in marking the limits of understanding the law as pure normativity and the status of law after its revolutionary deposition. From this point of view, the second instalment of *Homo Sacer* is supposed to be a form of denouement, not only by tying together important legal theoretical questions that have made the substance of the interwar legal theory but also by sketching a philosophical stand able to overcome the structural entanglement between law and violence. However, this denouement is at best postponed, if not effectively sapped from within, by a gesture that forgets the materiality of the exception and by an ahistorical position that forces one to disregard law's history of violence.

The starting point within this instance is the present unfolding exception that was already legible for Agamben and other astute observers on the trail left by the war on terror.[99] The parallel with the interwar period, although not marked at that time by the particular ideological inflections that sign our contemporary unfolding of the exception, was present at the level of the operation of the law: the constitutional protections offered by liberal democracies were effectively suspended when faced with the excess of anti-legal violence.[100] It is this thread that prompts and marks the style and substance

91 Ibid., 73–78.
92 Ibid., 68.
93 Giorgio Agamben, *State of Exception*, Kevin Attell transl. (Chicago: University of Chicago Press, 2005 [2003]).
94 Ibid., 4.
95 Ibid.
96 Ibid., 32–39; 52–64.
97 Ibid., 33–34.
98 Ibid., 63.
99 Ibid., 3–4.
100 Ibid., 4.

of Agamben's investigation. By means of a historical excursus going back to the late 18th century,[101] we are able to seize the proliferation of the exception during the interwar years as well as the secret nexus connecting it to the debasement of the law.

Yet, this excursus takes place from within the postulation of the existence of the exception at the level of material – that is formless, unarticulated – constitution of the various legal systems of the Western tradition.[102] This existence of the exception – that becomes readable at the end of the Great War – is curiously no longer dependent on the exception's formalisation within the legal apparatus. Accordingly, the exception is somewhat autonomous of the process of legal operation as 'the history of the institution, at least since World War One, shows that its development is *independent* of its constitutional or legislative formalisation'.[103] The uncertain place occupied by the exception within the law cannot be disputed, and Agamben takes his time to explain the extent to which the problem of the exception cannot be reduced to a matter of necessity, and cannot be simply be ascribed to a strict topographical distinction as an outside of the law.[104] The exception is necessarily nested within the law. However, the slight autonomy of the exception with regards to the form of law and its presence at the level of functions enables Agamben to move a step further beyond what historians would generally credit and describe as modernity.[105] The exception is thus connected to other figures of the law, and legal institutions – such as *Decretum Gratiani*[106] and the practice of *justitium*.[107] At the same time, the investigation slips through the railings of the law and history and moves towards the interstices of theology and anthropology, in a zone of indistinction where the pre-juridical encounters modernity.[108] Looked from the standpoint of its operation, the exception, in its materiality, effectively discloses law's finitude that renders its *force*. In other words, '[i]t is as if the suspension of law freed a force or a mystical element, a sort of legal *mana* (…), that both the ruling power and its adversaries, the constituted power as well as the constituent power, seek to appropriate'.[109]

Law, understood as exception, is always already haunted by its inconsistency drawing itself towards its uncertain margins that seem not to have any discernible historical bounds. Thus, *justitium*, the suspension of the law

101 Ibid., 5–6; 11–22.
102 Ibid., 10.
103 Ibid. [emphasis added].
104 Ibid., 23–25.
105 Mark Mazower, 'Foucault, Agamben: Theory and the Nazis', (2008) 2 *Boundary* 23, 27.
106 Agamben, *State of Exception*, 24–25.
107 Ibid., 41–49.
108 Ibid., 65–69.
109 Ibid., 51.

declared 'usually'[110] as a reaction to internal strife (*tumultus*), is 'the archetype of the modern state of exception'.[111] As a standstill of the law, it emphasises not only the hold that the non-juridical has over legality but also the inner void at the core of the exception.[112] The isolation of such a void is the unlikely quilting point able to tie the knots between Schmitt's political theology and Benjamin's *pure violence*. While Schmitt aims to inscribe violence within the function of the law[113] – a task that is perhaps not difficult as it is only a matter of recuperating and rendering visible law's historical and mythical foundations – Benjamin aims at keeping revolutionary violence out of the reach of the law. As a violence that 'is lethal without spilling blood',[114] divine violence is the one able to overcome the law. While this reading is correct, and one can agree with Agamben's diagnosis on the terms of the debate,[115] less attention seems to be paid by him to the reasons for which Benjamin's divine violence should be freed from the shackles of legality. It is, of course, the question of mediation of violence, but also the very history of law that taints its becoming.[116] In this last instance we can most likely find within Benjamin's project the traces of a historical materialism that even within the midst of the anomie is able to conceive history as a history of class struggle. Perhaps, at the end of the day, the gigantomachy is not around a void as Agamben would have it, but around a very specific meaning of the void at the core of the exception: on one side is the excess of power, while on the other the very destitution of power. While one could speculate over the 'metaphysical stakes'[117] of this debate, the historical and intellectual horizon of this debate should not be forgotten. In other words, one should not simply conflate exception and revolution under the neutralising gaze of an 'onto-theo-logical strategy aimed at capturing pure being into the meshes of the *logos*',[118] insofar as the 'white eschatology' of the exception is still unable to cover the ideological dividing line traversing these theoretical stands.

Within the exception, what becomes apparent is not only that secret link that connects legality to its opposite lawlessness and anarchy but also the lack of grounding of any attempt at instituting legality. Through its operation, the exception also marks a threshold in which the possibility of a law that is not applied but only studied[119] can be grasped. Such a position of the law, arguably an answer to the question tormenting both early Christians and Marxists

110 Ibid., 41.
111 Ibid.
112 Ibid., 51.
113 Ibid., 54.
114 Benjamin, 'Critique of Violence', 250.
115 Agamben, *State of Exception*, 59.
116 Benjamin, 'Critique of Violence', 249.
117 Agamben, State of Exception, 59.
118 Ibid., 60.
119 Ibid., 64.

as to the status of law after its deposition,[120] is that of an inoperative legality.[121] Through a play of knowledge, what is brought to the fore as a form of redeeming the legal form and of overcoming its conundrum, is presumably a law that is valid without being efficient, the pure normativity that Kelsen was able to identify beyond the paradox of efficacy[122]: 'One day humanity will play with law just as children play with disused objects, not in order to restore them to their canonical use but free them from it for good.'[123]

Such a messianic undertone supporting the possibility of overcoming the exception and liberating politics from the forces of the law[124] – that is, of its historical ties with sovereign power and violence – is not only obscure in terms of performance but also unrelentingly optimistic. The *study* of law as a disused object able to be freed from its historical ties is neither a new practice nor an entirely pure one. If one was to be polemical about the nature of this play, we would perhaps ask whether it is the *casuistry* and the purely formal analysis of law in its study within our schools of law from times immemorial (that go back precisely to the Roman law tradition) to this very day is not what generates the exception? Put another way, isn't it the lawyer's very inability to think law historically that produces the exception?

The frontispiece of the exception

Something can and should be saved from this project of thinking the exception as a core feature of modern legality. As such, *State of Exception*, in its very failure or suspension of finding a denouement to the legal conundrum of validity and efficacy – and to the intellectual thread that had become pregnantly visible within the interwar period – is able to rightly identify the topoi of the debate. That is to say, together with Agamben, that the law *as such* is in no way safe from the corosive forces of history, and a state of law[125] – or a rule of law – is no longer able to be secured at this historical juncture, if it ever was. Yet, what is left outside the scope of this inquiry is the material history of the exception, as well as the historical inscription of the intellectual genealogy scrutinising its unfolding. That is because, just like the law, the exception does not take place in a vacuum, but it is part of a history that is not easily reducible to an interplay between sovereign power, normative structures and *zoe*. Such a history includes and cannot be disentangled from the material history of class struggle in which the legal state of exception occurs. If the exception, as the inner core of the theory of the state, is indeed 'the reef on which the revolutions of the twentieth century have been

120 Ibid., 63.
121 Ibid., 64.
122 Ibid. 64; 87.
123 Ibid., 64.
124 Ibid., 88.
125 Ibid., 87.

shipwrecked',[126] and the theory of the state and law was the blind spot of the Marxist analysis, there is yet the very starting point in Agamben's project which has a historical grounding. In other words, it is not by chance that we witness a proliferation of exception and exceptional measures in the wake of the October revolution and the end of the Great War. This can and should probably be read within the context of another Agambenian core concept – that of *stasis* and civil war[127] – but it does not necessarily warrant such a conflation between revolution and exception as the paradigm developed by the Italian philosopher would.

While indeed the exception unveils a structural tension within – of legality, that is – and it was historically theorised, it also operates as a particular mechanism within the sphere of politics by doing away with constitutional protections. The sovereign power, unfettered in the exception, does more often than not seem tainted by a specific ideological colour and does have a specific historical and memorial weight. While indeed the exception unveils a limit of the law – and is structurally nested within the operation of modern legality – it is hardly ahistorical. By taking for granted the very premise of the possibility of articulation of law as normativity – a necessary step needed for the functioning of the exception – the Agambenian paradigm projects law's inability to ground itself at the level of human history. Such a step, on the path opened by Schmitt, rightly points to the law's limits, but it does so only by keeping alive the necessarily formal dimension of law as a pure potency. Accordingly, it displaces the Schmittian criticism of the neo-Kantian presuppositions that gave Kelsen's theory its standing, but it expands them to the level of all Western legal history. To be sure, this is a necessary step – even from within a post-Kantian position – but it needs to be supplanted by a deeper historical analysis that goes beyond the construction of a paradigm. Accordingly, the *state of exception* in Agamben's rendition has the function of recalling, if not restating the obvious. As Georg Lukács noted in his criticism of Schmitt, any legal problem 'depends whether the competent legal authority decided it thus or otherwise; but the character, composition, etc., of that authority are pre-determined by politico-social and ultimately economic factors'.[128] Such a critique is not to be dismissed as a mere restatement of crude econocentrism, but ultimately raises the question of the outside-of-the-law that finds a place and is rendered visible within the structure of the exception.

126 Agamben, *Homo Sacer*, 14.

127 Giorgio Agamben, *Stasis: Civil War as a Political Pradigm*, Nicholas Heron transl. (Edinburgh: Edinburgh University Press, 2015), 1–18.

128 Georg Lukács, *The Destruction of Reason*, Peter Palmer transl. (Atlantic Heights: Humanities Press, 1981 [1962]), 654.

In his analysis of Hobbes' *Leviathan*, Giorgio Agamben focuses on the peculiarities of the iconography presented on the frontispiece of this book. His careful analysis of an otherwise over-read and mostly misinterpreted representation brings Hobbes' argument under a new light as a profanation, a work able to reveal the secret of political power by a détournement of theological topoi.[129] Irrespective of the substance of the argument, Agamben offers a number of important insights into his reading strategy that are useful for our own purpose of grasping the nature of the exception. Accordingly, the frontispiece is 'a door or a threshold that would lead, even in a veiled manner, into the problematic nucleus of the book'.[130] Such a strategy of disclosing through concealing, specific to the esoteric tradition, appeals to a reader – 'as any reader worthy of the name should be – capable of not allowing the particular details and modalities of exposition to escape them'.[131] Yet, the esoteric knowledge and its mode of dissemination are somewhat akin to riddles, mysticism and philosophy, and this is perhaps the heuristic status of Agamben's paradigm of exception. As he writes,

> every esoteric intention inevitably contains a contradiction, which marks a point of distinction with respect to mysticism and philosophy: if the concealment is something serious and is not a joke, then it must be experienced as such and the subject cannot profess to know what he or she can only oblivious to; if, conversely, it is a joke, in this case the esotericism is less justified.[132]

Read through such lenses, the state of exception is perhaps the esoteric veil that covers the status of legality within modernity. As such, it is not only able to capture the specific tension between validity and efficacy of the legal norm but also opens the path for a whole series of intellectual attempts at grounding the law within the unfolding of a time in which 'all that is solid melts into air'.[133] Through the frontispiece of the exception, as painted by Agamben in his genealogy of the concept, we are able to grasp as if through a glass, darkly, the operation of the exception as well as its intellectual *archè*.

However, as is the case with any frontispiece, it is followed by a work that is yet to be written. This is a work that would take the history of law's self-erasure seriously on several levels. First, at a jurisprudential level, by placing at its core the formal status of legality, that of a structure that is always at wrest with itself and which, as any symbolic structure, is haunted by a foundational erasure and thus is never complete. From this point of view, Jacques Lacan's concept of the

129 Agamben, *Stasis*, 48–49.
130 Ibid., 21.
131 Ibid., 22.
132 Ibid.
133 Karl Marx and Friedrich Engels, *Manifesto of the Communist Party* (New York: International Publishers, 2007 [1847–1848]), 12.

Real in its relation to the Symbolic offers an edifying insight into this operation: in its initial construction, the Symbolic, as an order of signification that produces meaning and reality, is carved out through a constant negation of the primeval matter of the *psyche* which is the Real.[134] This process is not dissimilar to the ways in which law is historically separating itself from politics, sovereign power and religion. Yet, in *Seminar XI*, Lacan veers from a description of the Real as a primeval traumatic encounter that is not mediated by the Symbolic towards a notion of the Real as by-product of the very institution of the Symbolic order.[135]

The analogy with the state of exception is striking: from within the standpoint of the law, the exception stands for the remainder of the unarticulated Real, of an outside-of-the-law that cannot be otherwise captured than by law's self-erasure. Positing the exception at the core of law's formal understanding is crucial in order to grasp is never-completed, always ungrounded status. First, then, this jurisprudential stand necessarily calls for an understanding of the law as a historical category, insofar as what stays outside of the articulation of the law is the remainder of historical struggles in which social forces collide in giving shape of the sphere of legality.

Second, as a matter of historiography, the state of exception forces us to inscribe legality in a broader timeframe and to refine our uses of concepts that historians and political theorists borrow from the arsenal of jurisprudence. Questions such as legitimacy and legality thus become particularly complex and demand a due analysis with a view to clarify both the agency and the limits of historical subjects. For instance, if one is to take the paradigm of the exception seriously, important questions related to the *lawless* character of authoritarian regimes do indeed need to be evaluated, just as the very symbolic line between liberal legality and its authoritarian other needs to be revisited.

But this refinement does not regard only our legal past. On the contrary, such important questions related to law's structural inability of grounding itself as a system of signification does call for a need to revisit our present as a part of a historical becoming. In simple words, the present effective erasure of legality – from the proliferation of emergency measures to the minute rewriting of legality and constitutional practices – should be understood as what it is: a moment in a historical unfolding of the exception. It is not an attack on liberal legality as such, but rather an unearthing of its inner limits and of the authoritarian potential nested at its core. Documenting the history of this process through which the law positively undermines itself is the work that stays beyond the esoteric veil of the exception.

134 Bruce Fink, *The Lacanian Subject: Between Language and Jouissance* (Princeton, NJ: Princeton University Press, 1995), 24.

135 Charles Shepherdson, *Lacan and the Limits of Language* (New York: Fordham University Press, 2008), 27.

Chapter 3

The other side of the exception

Sovereignty, modernity and international law

Przemysław Tacik

Introduction

Few philosophical books are remembered by the date of their first publication; even fewer jurisprudential works earn this honour. Giorgio Agamben's *Homo Sacer* – the founding volume of the project published in 1995[1] – triumphed in both categories. It belongs to a highly exclusive group of texts which do not provide a philosophical reformulation of legal studies, but rather take both philosophy and jurisprudence to a new common field in which the legal and the philosophical become indistinguishable. The revolution inaugurated by Agamben's work – although in many respects aptly disguised by references to Carl Schmitt, Walter Benjamin and Hannah Arendt – develops in a philosophical rather than jurisprudential pace. Its real impact will have become assessable after decades, not years. In this sense Agamben's stunning popularity among legal scholars – sometimes, admittedly, leading to banal application of his concepts – is not yet representative for the historical meaning of his thinking. The Agambenian breakthrough requires further development: the philosopher himself recognises it in his attempts to complete the still open-ended *Homo sacer* project.[2] Sometimes, however, the conceptual blow is too powerful to be exhaustively contained in one series and

1 Giorgio Agamben, *Homo sacer*, Daniel Heller-Roazen transl. (Stanford, CA: Stanford University Press, 1998) [original edition: *Homo Sacer. Il potere sovrano e la vita nuda (Homo sacer, I)* (Segrate: Einaudi, 1995)].

2 Agamben, *Homo sacer; Stato di Eccezione. Homo sacer II, 1* (Torino: Bollati Boringhieri, 2003); *Il regno e la gloria. Per una genealogia teologica dell'economia e del governo. Homo sacer II, 2* (Torino: Bollati Boringhieri, 2009); S*tasis. La guerra civile come paradigma politico. Homo sacer II, 2* (Torino: Bollati Boringhieri, 2015); *Il sacramento del linguaggio. Archeologia del giuramento. Homo sacer II, 3*, (Roma-Bari: Laterza, 2008); *Opus Dei. Archeologia dell'ufficio. Homo sacer II, 5* (Torino: Bollati Boringhieri, 2012); *Quel che resta di Auschwitz. L'archivio e il testimone. Homo sacer. III* (Torino: Bollati Boringhieri, 1998); *Altissima povertà. Regole monastiche e forma di vita. Homo sacer IV, 1* (Vicenza: Neri Pozza, 2011); *L'uso dei corpi. Homo sacer IV, 2* (Vicenza: Neri Pozza, 2014).

demands long-term efforts to realise all its implications. In order to do justice to the historical significance of *Homo sacer* it thus seems indispensable to continue the path it traced with loyalty to its vocation, even if occasionally against the grain of Agamben's own remarks.

One of the areas in which Agamben's project remains glaringly underdeveloped is international law. There seem to be a few reasons for this. First, Agamben openly concentrated on state power as well as its emanations or theological/philosophical models. International law is stunningly absent in this approach, as though all the paradoxes and tensions inherent in the law were limited to the realm under sovereign power, not the one which extends over it. However, this does not have to be the case, given that the position of exception is linked to the essence of language in which all law – including international law – is expressed. Second, Agamben's approach is used rather sparingly in the doctrine of international law. The adaptation of state-centred reflection on the law, sovereignty and exception to this domain demands deeper reformulation of the *Homo sacer* perspective and, as such, attracts few theorists. Third and most important, the manifest lack of theoretisation of international law in Agamben's work is not just a result of the philosopher's own preferences. As I will attempt to argue, this lack might be read as a symptom which, once revealed as such, exposes underdevelopments and questionable assumptions in apparently unrelated areas of his *œuvre*. Posing questions about international law touches upon Agamben's views on historical continuity and modern specificity. For these reasons, international law is not just another area of legality to which the theory of sovereignty and exception might be 'applied', but a field that challenges the theory itself and demands its reconsideration. As soon as we leave the boundaries of state-centred jurisprudence, not only will Agamben's theory appear in a different light, it might also contribute to better understanding of international law itself.

This chapter will be organised in the following manner. First, I will attempt to find a category deeper than exception – conflation – that accounts for the structural paradoxes of Agamben's thought, such as the tension between apparent temporal universality of his theory and its effective confinement to modernity. Then I will use it in order to ask whether the Agambenian account of historical continuity of sovereignty is justified. As it will appear, the emergence of international law in early modernity constitutes a stumbling block for this assumption. Taking into account the international law perspective on sovereignty, I will investigate the nature of modern sovereignty with the aim of extrapolating Agamben's thought. Finally, I will reinterpret his understanding of camps in order to find a more in-depth outlook on international law so that it might be confronted with the impact of Agamben's innovativeness.

Underneath the exception: conflation

In order to confront the thought-provoking absence of international law in Agamben's work, we need first to scrutinise the foundations of his intellectual edifice in order to understand why it is so firmly riveted to the state-centred and sub-sovereign vision of the law. Contrary to what might appear at first sight, the answer is to be found not in one of his hallmark concepts, the exception, but in its underlying philosophical category: conflation. Ubiquitous as it is in Agamben's writings, it remains almost untouched by his own reflection even though it gives the rhythm and provides a denouement of this thinking.

For obvious reasons it is Agamben's theory of exception – and its particular application to the state of exception as a legal device – that attracts most attention in jurisprudence. Focus on the state of exception allows legal scholars to omit the philosophically explosive potential of Agamben's work and concentrate on his contribution to understanding one of the well-established notions of constitutional law. Nonetheless, the concept of exception is much broader and philosophically charged:

> The exception is a kind of exclusion. What is excluded from the general rule is an individual case. But the most proper characteristic of the exception is that what is excluded in it is not, on account of being excluded, absolutely without relation to the rule. On the contrary, what is excluded in the exception maintains itself in relation to the rule in the form of the rule's suspension. The rule applies to the exception in no longer applying, in withdrawing from it. The state of exception is thus not the chaos that precedes order but rather the situation that results from its suspension. In this sense, the exception is truly, according to its etymological root, taken outside (*ex-capere*), and not simply excluded.[3]

The exception is therefore a crossing between generality and individuality, built not upon the model of proportionality and commensurability between the two,[4] but on their inherent discrepancy, which emerges in *suspension* of the rule. In a sense, Agamben reasserts Wittgenstein's rule paradox as interpreted by Saul Kripke[5]: there is, in fact, no simple determinative relation between the rule and an individual case. The nature of this creation-through-withdrawal and, in particular, the degree to which the 'determinative agency' is to be ascribed to the rule rather than to the other pole of this relation

3 Ibid., 17–18.

4 In this respect Agamben finds Kant to be 'on a false track'. Agamben, *State of Exception* (*Homo sacer II, 1*), Kevin Attell transl. (Chicago and London: University of Chicago Press, 2005), 39.

5 Saul A. Kripke, *Wittgenstein on Rules and Private Language: An Elementary Exposition* (Cambridge, MA: Harvard University Press, 1982).

remains unclear. Moreover, it seems to change over the course of Agamben's writings. The above-cited fragment puts stress on the rule creating the exception. However, quite quickly this imbalance is corrected and both the rule and the case are given a secondary position to the exception itself, which simultaneously links and creates them:

> The situation created in the exception has the peculiar characteristic that it cannot be defined either as a situation of fact or as a situation of right, but instead *institutes a paradoxical threshold of indistinction between the two* [emphasis added]. It is not a fact, since it is only created through the suspension of the rule. [...] In this sense, the sovereign exception is the fundamental localization (*Ortung*), which does not limit itself to distinguishing what is inside from what is outside but instead *traces a threshold (the state of exception) between the two, on the basis of which outside and inside, the normal situation and chaos, enter into those complex topological relations that make the validity of the juridical order possible* [emphasis added].[6]

The tension between the rule and the fact finds its resolution in a typical Agambenian manoeuvre: no primacy is given to either poles of the opposition; but a third, more powerful category is introduced to defuse them. It is not produced, but it has always been already there. Not accidentally, Agamben theorises it as a kind of space that 'precedes' the elements which enter it. Its boundaries are comparable to the event horizon in astrophysics. Whatever two elements overstep them ('crosses the threshold of indistinction' in Agambenian parlance), they lose the very possibility of being differentiated. Musing on what they truly are in this area is senseless – ontology coincides here with epistemology and whatever cannot be attested, does not exist. In the zone of indistinction the elements *conflate*. To add one last twist to the paradox, the conflation functions like a contagious zone that expands to suspend our knowledge: no question on the primacy between the elements and the conflation itself might be asked because the conflation consumes it as well.

I suggest that we understand Agamben's conflation as a *process* in which the difference between two terms or concepts is suspended. The difference does not disappear; it rather continues itself as a trace that becomes overwritten with its own insignificance. William Watkin brilliantly identified the area emerging after conflation, listing synonyms that Agamben uses for it:

> Agamben habitually places the reader in what he calls a zone or threshold of indistinction, inoperativity, indiscernibility, suspension or indifference. He

6 Ibid., 18–19.

> uses various terms to name the zone and various other terms to designate its specific quality, but the structure is always the same.[7]

Conflation differs therefore from the zone or threshold of indistinction insofar as it refers to the transition of an opposition from the world of acting differences to the area where they are suspended. Nonetheless, conflation retroactively overwrites itself, suspending the difference between the world of differences and the zone of indistinction. The latter seems to await the opposition as an event horizon of a black hole engulfs matter.

The spatial imagery that Agamben resorts to is unsurprising if we take into account Derrida's struggles for articulating the neutral category 'underneath' binary oppositions. Categories like 'supplement', 'pharmakon' or 'hymen', meant to capture the neither-nor beyond metaphysics,[8] eventually lead to a spatial category: *khôra*. It is the ultimately neutral non-concept because it does not take part in the play of oppositions but merely gives them space as the all-encompassing receptacle.[9] Agamben's 'zone of indistinction', or 'zone of indifference', functions analogically: it receives binary terms and suspends the question about their mutual relation or primacy.

The notion of 'conflation', which produces exception in the heart of the law, is much more widespread in Agamben's thinking than the exception itself, even if implicitly. If his philosophy is viewed from the structural, not material, point of view, conflation is a basic figure of this thought. It does not seem preposterous to claim that it is his primary contribution to philosophy at its fundamental level. The (state of) exception would be then just one of many instances that conflation accounts for. Given that a thorough exemplification of its usage would demand a separate paper, let us settle for just some telling applications.

Conflation appears in Agamben's writings as a process of entering a space in which multiple categories become indistinguishable.[10] In *Homo sacer* this space is referred to as a zone of indistinction for 'the categories whose opposition founded modern politics (right/left, private/public, absolutism/democracy, etc.)'.[11] In the legal context, conflation engulfs 'exclusion and inclusion, outside and inside, *bios* and *zoē*, right and fact',[12] as well as 'nature and fact',[13] 'law and fact',[14] 'law and violence',[15] or constituting power and

7 William Watkin, *Agamben and Indifference: A Critical Overview* (London: Rowman & Littlefield, 2014), xi.
8 See Rodolphe Gasché, *The Tain of the Mirror. Derrida and the Philosophy of Reflection* (Cambridge, MA: Harvard University Press, 1986), 148–151.
9 Cf. Jacques Derrida, *Khôra* (Paris: Galilée, 1993), 20–29.
10 See also Watkin, *Agamben and Indifference.*
11 Agamben, *Homo sacer*, 4. See also 122.
12 Ibid., 9.
13 Ibid., 21.
14 Agamben, *State of Exception*, 26.
15 Agamben, *Homo sacer*, 31, 33.

constituted power.[16] As to bare life, conflation encompasses the sacrifice and homicide of *Homo sacer*[17] as well as the life of the sovereign and of *Homo sacer*,[18] 'animal and man',[19] public and private life.[20] Indistinction might also absorb reign and government in contemporary democracies ravaged by the Debordian society of spectacle.[21]

Yet beyond these familiar conceptualisations that revolve around the idea of exception, Agamben uses the category of conflation in all areas of his thinking, including postmetaphysics, aesthetics, theory of language and theology. Conflation concerns as various oppositions as: mystery and history (becoming indistinguishable in the end times),[22] subject and object (in adventure),[23] justice and salvation (coinciding in Pilate's judgement on Jesus),[24] the dead and the living (in God's eternity),[25] creation and destruction (in modern capitalism),[26] words and things (in the very construction of the oath),[27] words and effects (in liturgy)[28] or *pars destruens* and *pars constituens* in philosophical research.[29]

This brief overview demonstrates that conflation possesses a few key features. First, it is a universal mechanism: both a figure of thinking and a real process. In this respect it resembles Hegel's logic, but with suspension instead of *Aufhebung*. Second, it does not seem to be time-irrelevant, but rather associated with a particular moment of time. Agamben either hints that it emerges with the onset of modernity or stresses that it becomes particularly conspicuous in contemporaneity. Whenever Agamben applies it to the pre-modern era, it seems that the re-interpretation of pre-modern phenomena has been made possible only with the use of the concept of conflation, in itself originating in modernity. Yet indistinction, once applied to pre-modern categories, dislocates them temporarily: their original, pre-modern placement conflates with the modern position from which they are grasped. As a result, they are no longer either pre-modern or modern.

16 Ibid., 41.
17 Ibid., 83.
18 Ibid., 96.
19 Ibid., 105.
20 Agamben, *State of Exception*, 83.
21 Agamben, *Il Regno e la Gloria*, 10.
22 Giorgio Agamben, *Il mistero del male. Benedetto XVI e la fine dei tempi* (Roma e Bari: Laterza, 2013), 32.
23 Giorgio Agamben, *L'avventura* (Roma: Nottetempo, 2015), 59–60.
24 Giorgio Agamben, *Pilato e Gesù* (Roma: Nottetempo, 2013), 63.
25 Giorgio Agamben, *Autoritratto nello studio* (Milano: Nottetempo, 2017), 166.
26 Giorgio Agamben, *Creazione e anarchia. L'opera nell'età della religione capitalista* (Vicenza: Neri Pozza, 2017), 132.
27 Agamben, *The Sacrament*, 46.
28 Agamben, *Opus Dei*, 96–97.
29 Agamben, *L'uso dei corpi*, 9.

Third, in one of his latest books, *Karman*, Agamben invents another synonym for conflation. Investigating once again the murky zone between rules and practice,[30] this time embodied in the tension between act and imputability, Agamben suggests a neutral term for what lies between them: 'a pure gesture' (*un puro gesto*).[31] It eludes the opposition between means and ends, becoming 'unjudgeable' (*ingiudicabile*).[32] This saving category is an obvious counterpart to the earlier theorisation of conflation between trial and punishment,[33] so well fathomed by Kafka. This juxtaposition demonstrates that conflation is a universal and ambivalent category. It might be both recognised in its many incarnations as a dangerous process (for instance in blurring the line between law and violence) and a saving notion. Symptomatically, Agamben seeks the antidote to the evil in the very same conflation, which responds for it.[34] In this line of thinking, he is clearly indebted to the Heideggerian legacy. The chain of concepts which embody Agambenian liberation: 'the suspension of the suspension',[35] the Sabbath, the messianic era, letting-be (manifestly borrowed from Heidegger) is conflation transformed into a redeeming device. Paradoxically, conflation engulfs itself in its both variations, bringing ultimate demise and salvation into the zone of indistinction.

If so, the concept of conflation – contrary to its limited application in the notion of exception – would be strictly modern. It either describes modern phenomena or, when applied to pre-modern mechanisms, reconstructs them within the modern field of knowledge. With this recognition the conspicuous absence of international law in Agamben's work might be recognised as part and parcel of his misrepresentation of modernity by the misleading assumption of historical continuity.

Sovereignty and historical continuity

Agamben's misrecognition of the role of international law is strictly correlated to his universalising conceptualisation of sovereignty. As long as sovereignty is conceived as a trans-historical property of power in its relation to the law,

30 This tension, viewed through the lens of the opposition (and conflation) between form and life, was extensively explored in: Giorgio Agamben, *The Highest Poverty. Monastic Rules and Form-of-Life*, Adam Kotsko transl. (Stanford CA: Stanford University Press, 2013), xi-xiii, 26, 62, 84–86, 115, 143–145.

31 Giorgio Agamben, *Karman. Breve trattato sull'azione, la colpa e il gesto* (Torino: Bollati Boringhieri, 2017), 136.

32 Ibid.

33 Giorgio Agamben, *Il fuoco e il raconto* (Roma: Nottetempo, 2014), 18.

34 In this respect, Agamben's concept of inoperativeness (*inoperosità*) is a 'positive' incarnation of conflation. Building politics and poetics on it (see Agamben, *Creazione e anarchia*, 47) are equivalent to Lévinas' gesture of ethical reversal of Heideggerianism.

35 Giorgio Agamben, *The Open: Man and Animal*, Kevin Attell transl. (Stanford, CA: Stanford University Press, 2004), 92.

understanding international law as born from the emptiness that emerged in early modernity in the over-sovereign space is barred.

Although Agamben's thinking seems to be deeply indebted to Heidegger's, his consideration of historicity is less self-reflective than his master's – who, beginning with *Sein und Zeit*, struggled to relativise his own thought to a particular moment in the historical development of Being.[36] As I demonstrated earlier, the concept of conflation – the philosophical foundation of Agamben's work – is highly paradoxical if analysed from the point of view of temporality. It oscillates dialectically between its modern features and the apparent trans-historical applicability. The philosopher not only does not take into account this paradox but also seems to surrender to it. His work is ravaged by the tension between finding historically universal explanations and acknowledging the ground-breaking cut of modernity. Nonetheless, Agamben does not explore it in a reflective manner, but disguises it under a falsely comforting image of historical continuity, understood as both (1) unproblematic applicability of concepts born in one epoch to another and (2) long-lasting influence of conceptual frameworks, notwithstanding epochal shifts.

This tension is equally recognisable in the conceptualisation of exception. In the second volume of *Homo sacer* Agamben clearly recognises the modern origin of the state of exception as a legal institution, identifying its beginnings with the French Revolution and focusing on its application in the aftermath of the First World War.[37] Then he re-interprets Schmitt's conception of sovereignty, in itself deeply rooted in the discussions and legal reality of the Weimar Republic and referring to the modern era.[38] Finally, he stresses that the proliferation of exception is a particular *signum temporis* of our age, tormented by the global civil war.[39] All these clues suggest that the state of exception is a properly modern phenomenon, linked to the construction of modern sovereignty.

However, Agamben immediately resorts to two strategies that obfuscate the radicalism of the modern cut. First, he juxtaposes modern concepts and legal institutions with Roman and medieval ones. The unreflexivity of this step is discernible in the following fragment of *State of Exception*:

36 Whether this was successful is another matter. See William D. Blatner, *Heidegger's Temporal Idealism* (Cambridge: Cambridge University Press, 1999) and Marlène Zarader, *The Unthought Debt. Heidegger and the Hebraic Heritage*, Bettina Bergo transl. (Stanford, CA: Stanford University Press, 2006).

37 Agamben, *State of Exception*, 11–22.

38 Cf. Carl Schmitt, *Political Theology. Four Chapters on the Concept of Sovereignty*, George Schwab transl. (Cambridge, MA and London: MIT Press, 1985), 16–35.

39 Cf. Giorgio Agamben, *Stasis. Civil War as a Political Paradigm*, Nicholas Heron transl. (Edinburgh: Edinburgh University Press, 2015), vi, 1–2.

> There is an institution of Roman law that can in some ways be considered the archetype of the modern *Ausnahmezustand*, and yet – indeed, perhaps precisely for this reason – does not seem to have been given sufficient attention by legal historians and theorists of public law: the *iustitium*. Because it allows us to observe the state of exception in its paradigmatic form, we will use the *iustitium* here as a miniature model as we attempt to untangle the aporias that the modern theory of the state of exception cannot resolve.[40]

At no point is this assumed continuity, based on a selective affinity between *Ausnahmezustand* and *iustitium*, confronted with the essentially modern character of the former, which was previously implicitly acknowledged. The Heideggerian legacy in Agamben's thinking is manifestly at work in the attempt to always posit a certain historical institution or concept in the lieu of origin, which is meant to properly explain the contemporary confusion around its late incarnations. Heidegger's preference for ancient, especially pre-Socratic Greece is here replaced by a particular fondness for ancient Rome and the medieval Christian legacy. Apart from Heidegger, Agamben inherits from a group of German Weimar or post-Weimar thinkers – Carl Schmitt, Karl Löwith and Jakob Taubes – who all explored and propounded the 'theological continuity' theorem. According to them, Western thinking and political institutions are still determined by the legacy of theological patterns and concepts of Christianity.[41] Notably, Agamben does not confront this premise[42] with the breakthrough of modernity that he himself assumed.[43] Nonetheless, the paradoxical nature of the concept of conflation should attract his attention. If properly reconsidered, it concerns history as well as conceptual oppositions; thus, it undermines the somewhat ramshackle underpinning of Agamben's historical constructions.

40 Agamben, *State of Exception*, 41.

41 Schmitt, *Political Theology*, 36; Jacob Taubes, *Occidental Eschatology*, David Ratmoko transl. (Stanford, CA: Stanford University Press, 2009), 13; Karl Löwith, *Meaning in History: The Theological Implications of the Philosophy of History* (Chicago: University of Chicago Press, 1949). See also the critique of Löwith in: Hans Blumenberg, *The Legitimacy of the Modern Age*, Robert M. Wallace transl. (Cambridge, MA and London: MIT Press, 1985), 27–121.

42 Agamben's profound affinity with this paradigm reaches its peak when the philosopher claims that probably all philosophy of history is constitutively Christian. See Agamben, *Il mistero del male*, 15.

43 It is most astonishing in the paradigmatically modern phenomenon of the camp. Tawia Ansah perspicaciously noted that '[f]or Agamben, to effect the transhistoricity of the camp, the historical camp must be sedimented and immanentized: one singular event can be traced back to the beginnings of the philosophical and theological tradition, to Athens or to Eden, depending upon one's point of origin.' Tawia Ansah, 'Auschwitz as *Nomos* of Modern Legal Thought' (2010) 22 (1) *Law and Literature* 145.

Second, Agamben displays a propensity for conceptual universalism. Properly modern phenomena, such as the state of exception, are explained with reference to features of language or humanity, which are posited as trans-epochal. The most eminent examples concern the anthropological machine theorised in *The Open*[44] or the features of the human being as a speaking creature, which are responsible for the trap of normativity, exception and suspension, as well as for the Western politics.[45]

The relation between the modern specificity of Agambenian concepts and his both historical and universal explanations remains almost untouched in the philosopher's own reflection. It is all the more intriguing given that some of the constructed links sound particularly questionable. For example, Agamben explicitly deduces modern biopolitics[46] and capitalism[47] from Christian theology, which sounds like an echolalic variation on Heidegger. 'Prehistory is more true than history',[48] he claims, arguing for an intellectual archaeology[49] which will demonstrate the *arche* – both the origin and the determining principle[50] – of our current conceptuality. Nevertheless, by smoothly passing over the question of historical continuity and universalism Agamben misreads his own account of the outbreak of modernity and its role for international law. The concept of conflation, although itself of seemingly modern origin, engulfs the very possibility of proper historical differentiation.

The outbreak of modernity and the rise of international law

Agamben's sovereign, modelled after the well-known Schmitt's definition, is not only monolithic[51] but also analysed from the point of view of its relation with the order that it tops. Such a sovereign – as the sole decision-maker of the state of exception – remains a paradoxical point of the legal order, both founding and destabilising it. What is absent in this vision, however, is the paradigmatically modern politico-legal area above the sovereigns.

44 Agamben, *The Open*, 27–30, 80.
45 Giorgio Agamben, *Che cos'è la filosofia?* (Macerata: Quodlibet, 2016), 25–29, 40; *The Sacrament of Language*, 10–11; *L'uso dei corpi*, 334.
46 Agamben, *Il Regno e la Gloria*, 13–16.
47 Agamben, *Creazione e anarchia*, 130.
48 '*La preistoria è più vera della historia*' [Agamben, *Autoritratto nello studio*, 154].
49 Agamben, *Creazione e anarchia*, 9.
50 Ibid., 91–94.
51 There has been considerable criticism of the unidimensionality of Agamben's vision of the sovereign which, among others, pointed to the fact that the sovereign state is not a sole decision-maker, but an intricate web of institutions whose power is always more or less balanced. See Adam Ramadan, 'Spatialising the refugee camp', (2013) 38 *Transactions of the Institute of British Geographers* 65; Elspeth Guild, 'Agamben face aux juges. Souveraineté, exception et antiterrorisme', (2003) 51 *Cultures et Conflits* 130.

International law in its proper sense was born in early modern Europe. In the Middle Ages the theologico-political structure of the continent was based on the imagined Christian community which had two pivotal positions at the top of it. God was imagined as the absolute ruler and keystone of the symbolic order. Between God and the level of state rulers, there was a mezzanine position, a ruler *pro tempore* of Europe: this position was an object of competition between the pope and the emperor. Despite its many incoherences and internal tensions, the Christian community of Europe was imaginable in terms of totality.

The onset of modernity, however, led to structural displacement in this order. First, state rulers gradually began to arrogate themselves the role of absolute sovereigns, which is best epitomised in Jean Bodin's canonical theory of early modern sovereignty. In Bodin's view, the sovereign does not recognise any power over his position except for God's; he decrees laws, but is not subjugated to them.[52] In other words, the level of state rulers becomes the epicentre of politico-legal power and a critical knot between violence and power.

Second, modern sovereign's demand for power is localised: it is limited to the territory of their states. The two traditional aspects of sovereignty (parenthetically, criticised by Schmitt in his introduction of the exception-based definition of the sovereign[53]) – internal (absolute power over the social life of the state) and external (independence from external sources of power) – revolve around the idea of a determined territory. Repelling external claims to power over the territory and affairs of a modern state founds sovereignty on the negative power that allows this state to found its legal system on its own unfounded decision. For the same reason total jurisdiction over state population must be exclusive. This negative power guarantees independence of sovereigns. Modern sovereignty is therefore based on the concept of recognising other sovereigns' rights and mutual co-existence. As Schmitt noted, international law constructs the border not in order to exclude, but to recognise the sovereign neighbour.[54] This negative aspect of sovereignty is not just a by-product of the creation of modern states. On the contrary, it is a key factor in their emergence, indissolubly linked to the positive aspect.

Third, mutual recognition between sovereigns is based on a set of paradoxes. Each arrogates to himself/herself the total and supreme power, but at the same time recognises other sovereigns' equal right, if only spatially separated. Recognition emerges in the emptiness that is produced in the space above the sovereigns. Whereas the Christian community assumed it to be part

52 Jean Bodin, *Les six livres de la république* (Paris: Fayard, 1985), 191–228, 297–299.
53 Schmitt, *Political Theology*, 16–35.
54 Carl Schmitt, *Der Nomos der Erde im Völkerrecht des Ius Publicum Europaeum* (Köln: Greven, 1950), 22.

and parcel of a positively constructed politico-legal order, early modernity identifies it with a state of nature between equal sovereign individuals. Jean Bethke Elshtain perspicaciously noted that modern sovereignty is built up via a negative reference to the supreme position of power, which ceased to exist with the demise of the medieval symbolic totality of Europe.[55] In this sense, being sovereign means actively rejecting any claim of power over oneself. *Pars in parem non habet imperium* is a maxim that founds international law as an order built primarily upon the concordant will of sovereigns, custom and general principles of law.

Hegel, a notorious eulogist of the sovereign logic, expressed the basic framework of international law in a short fragment from *The Philosophy of Right*:

> International law arises out of the relation to one another of independent states. Whatever is absolute in this relation receives the form of a command, because its reality depends upon a distinct sovereign will. … There is no judge over states, at most only a referee or mediator, and even the mediatorial function is only an accidental thing, being due to particular wills.[56]

A state is not a private person, but in itself a completely independent totality. Hence, the relation of states to one another is not merely that of morality and private right. It is often desired that states should be regarded from the standpoint of private right and morality. However, the position of private persons is such that they have over them a law court, which realises what is intrinsically right. A relation between states ought also to be intrinsically right, and in mundane affairs that which is intrinsically right ought to have power. But as against the state there is no power to decide what is intrinsically right and to realise this decision. Hence, we must here remain by the absolute command. States in their relation to one another are independent and look upon the stipulations that they make one with another as provisional.[57]

Despite profound transformations of international law after the Second World War – which led to the creation of a new international order in which war is generally illegal[58] – this branch of law is still ravaged by ineffectiveness and self-doubt which has no counterpart in other branches. As Hegel noticed, international law is born in the inter-sovereign void. It has no arch-sovereign, no court of highest instance whose jurisdiction would not stem from states'

55 Jean Bethke Elshtain, *Sovereignty. God, State, and Self* (New York: Basic Books, 2008), 77–158.
56 Georg Wilhelm Friedrich Hegel, *The Philosophy of Right*, S. W. Dyde transl. (Kitchener: Batoche Books, 2001), 262, 264.
57 Ibid., 262–263.
58 Ian Brownlie, *Principles of Public International Law* (Oxford: Oxford University Press, 2008), 729–747.

consent, and no universal system of sanctions. As such, it is a total and permanent zone of indifferentiability between law and fact. If norms of international law stem generally from the will of sovereigns, their consent might be withdrawn with the effect of deactivating the norm. Even though contemporary international law often prohibits renunciation of treaties,[59] the very construction of sovereignty is aimed at providing the ultimate possibility to repeal one's own decision. In such cases, notorious ineffectiveness of international law blurs the division between rule and application, making the former often just an argument in a dispute settled by factual confrontations of power. Among all branches of law Nietzsche's remark on Heraclitus is perhaps most pertinent to international law: 'the judges themselves seemed to be striving in the contest and the contestants seemed to be judging them'.[60]

Consequently, international law is a notorious field of paradoxes which still give rise to numerous volumes attesting to its problematic character or even, as in the famous case of Hans Kelsen, identifying it with 'primitive law'.[61] Nevertheless, from the point of view of Agamben's approach to jurisprudence it is more than problematic: it constitutes the other side of exception without which the theory of sovereignty is wanting. The inherent void of international law matches the zone of exception that the sovereign creates internally. In this light, the sovereign is nothing but an empty place of naked self-grounding and self-justifying power which exerts its influence both internally (over the legal order that it both founds and suspends) and externally (in the empty space of inter-sovereign relations).

Modern sovereignty: displacing Agamben

It seems therefore that Agamben's approach to the relation between sovereignty and exception requires further development, which would relate it to the question of modernity's uniqueness. Modern sovereignty is perhaps not just yet another incarnation of the same concept, but a distinct category that should be interpreted within its own politico-legal order rather than

59 See ibid., 620–626.

60 Friedrich Nietzsche, *Philosophy in the Tragic Age of the Greeks*, Marianne Cowan transl. (Washington: Regnery, 1962), 57.

61 'International law, as coercive order, shows the same character as national law, *i. e.*, the law of a state, but differs from it and shows a certain similarity with the law of primitive, *i.e.*, stateless society in that international law (as a general law that binds all states) does not establish special organs for the creation and application of its norms. It is still in a state of far-reaching decentralization. It is only at the beginning of a development which national law has already completed.' Hans Kelsen, *Pure Theory of Law*, Max Knight transl. (Clark, NJ: The Lawbook Exchange, 2005), 323. See also Hans Kelsen, *Principles of International Law*, R. W. Tucker transl. (New York: Holt, Rinehart & Winston, 1967). On Kelsen's evolution of views on international law see: François Rigaux, 'Hans Kelsen on International Law', (1998) 9 *European Journal of International Law* 325.

compared, somewhat artificially, to its previous models. Agamben's theory captures the specificity of modern sovereignty – primarily due to its roots in Schmitt's definition and the use of the category of conflation, but then extrapolates and mystifies its historical continuity.

Seen from this perspective, modern sovereignty presents a more complex phenomenon than the monolithic locus of decision on the exception. It is always displaced, imagined as being somewhere else but practised here and now – always in the name, on behalf, officially temporarily and exceptionally, but in truth permanently and without true justification. In this sense, Agamben's assumption about modernity (or, more often, late modernity) as an expanding space of exception should be viewed more broadly: modernity is an epoch structurally reigned by a displaced power which always seems provisional but in fact remains unassailable. Exception is only one of its manifestations.

The perspective of international law – as a specifically modern phenomenon – demonstrates that Agamben's view is limited. The assumption of continuity does not let him notice the truly modern shift in the functioning of sovereignty. Just as the state transforms itself from early modern absolute monarchy, in which the monarch embodies sovereignty, to the proper modern state in which the so-called 'nation' becomes the sovereign, so does international law pass from the concentration on state power to highlighting the role of the population. The modern state seems to be fully under the command of its nation, which is claimed to be sovereign – internally and in external relations. But this nation cannot exist in international relations without a state that simultaneously determines its character, boundaries (through the institution of citizenship), language and biological features.[62] Even though modern sovereignty belongs to the nation, it is exerted – on its behalf – by the state, which in theory is nothing and in practice everything. It seems to be nothing but a small displacement between population and state,[63] yet in truth it concentrates exceptional power and tends to spiral into a furious attempt to finally make nation and state overlap, as exemplified in the practice of the Nazi state. Naturally, this practice seems to be in stark contrast with contemporary functioning of states that are committed to protect their population and respect human rights. But in truth it is perhaps only now – after the Second World War and the subsequent evolution of states – that we might understand modern sovereignty.

What seems pivotal in its functioning is the fact that it presents itself as a vanishing mediating point between the nation as the reigning sovereign and the governed population. In *Il Regno e la Gloria* Agamben explores the rift between reign and government consisting of displacement between the

62 See Eric J. Hobsbawm, *Nations and Nationalism since 1780: Programme, Myth, Reality* (Cambridge: Cambridge University Press, 1990).
63 Cf. Agamben, *Stasis*, 36–40.

nominal locus of power and its executive centre. But this rift is in fact the basic paradox of the modern state in which the population is the nominal sovereign, whereas everyday government is performed in its name, but with full effectiveness.[64] Claude Lefort convincingly demonstrated that modern democracy is built upon the emptiness of the locus of power, which is always occupied temporarily.[65] Extrapolating Agamben allows us to conclude that the paradox of sovereignty – and its split into nominal reign and factual government – is built upon the negativity which rules the inter-sovereign space, making it a domain of permanent conflation between law and fact.

The exceptional internationality of camps

In the final part of this chapter, I am going to reconsider the phenomenon of Nazi camps, trying to extrapolate Agamben's thought[66] into new areas, in which the international dimension would be as important as the internal one.

As Foucault noted in his *Collège de France* lectures,[67] early modern states were concerned primarily with territory, whose inhabitants more or less shared the fate of their land. At the end of 18th century, however, the paradigm changed and states began to concentrate on population, viewed as a biological matter, which needed training and correction.[68] In international law, this trend started to be noticeable much later. But when it finally appeared, it did not replace previous international law with a completely new one, just as – on the national level – sovereignty did not disappear but was handed by the monarch to the nation. Contemporary international law is a compound of early modern international grid of sovereigns and a new dimension of population. Just as modern sovereignty is an empty place both dividing and uniting state and nation, so the international law must coincide two contradictory dimensions: of sovereign states and of populations.

This contradiction is visible in multiple paradoxes. Once we grant to population the right to self-determination, it collides with state sovereignty and the inviolability of its territory – and makes this right (outside the context of decolonisation) notoriously ineffective and often just declaratory.[69] Another example concerns human rights: international law forbids genocide and crimes against humanity but relies on the power of the main perpetrators

64 Cf. Agamben, *Il Regno e la Gloria*, 303–313.
65 Claude Lefort, *On Modern Democracy* in: *Democracy and Political Theory*, David Macey transl. (Minneapolis, MN: University of Minnesota Press, 1988), 17–20.
66 See Giorgio Agamben, *Remnants of Auschwitz. The Witness and the Archive*, Daniel Heller-Roazen transl. (Cambridge, MA: MIT Press, 2002).
67 Michel Foucault, *'Society Must Be Defended'. Lectures at the Collège de France, 1975–1976*, François Ewald transl. (New York: Picador, 2003), 35.
68 Ibid., 239–265.
69 See Jörg Fisch, *The Right of Self-Determination of Peoples: The Domestication of an Illusion*, Anita Mage transl. (Cambridge: Cambridge University Press, 2015).

of these crimes – states – whose cooperation with international bodies is the primary condition of human rights protection. Thus, contemporary international law is in constant tension between sovereign rights of a state and rights of the population. These two contradictory principles are held together, at great expense, by the whole system of international law based on sovereignty. This dualism should not be perceived as a transitional stage from full state sovereignty to future government of humankind. On the contrary, a Hegelian conclusion seems more pertinent: if they coexist in tension, but still function, they must be parts of the same politico-legal device, which carries out its power – also biopolitical power – despite having no ground.

In this context, the phenomenon of Nazi camps provides an example of extrapolated logic of purely modern sovereignty.[70] The camps were the definitive places in which the German state carried out the envisaged purification of the German population. Fencing off the special territory concentrated those who were to be excluded from the *Volk* and in this sense produced an extra-national space, populated by the de facto nationless. The outbreak of the Second World War prompted the Nazis to disregard citizenship altogether and apply universal race politics that generally took no account of individuals' legal bond with their states.

In this sense, camps constituted a zone of the state of exception in not only domestic but also international law. Within their territory, not only were international conventions suspended, but the mere recognition of other states as entities that might claim the right to protect their citizens. Nazi Germany happened to desist from detaining foreign citizens or to release them if it feared retaliation. However, within the territory of the camp such considerations were already of no account. In this regard, the German state acted as if any rights of other states to their population were suspended. It was clearly manifested by a conflict between the Vichy government and the Third Reich over the deportation of French Jews. Initially, the Vichy government collaborated in deporting Jews without French citizenship and opposed the Nazis when it came to French citizens.[71] Then, however, the Third Reich disregarded any autonomy left to the Vichy and moved to the deportation of all people whom the Nuremberg laws defined as Jewish. Therefore, in forcing its direct rule over bare life, the Third Reich exceeded the usual rights of a sovereign to its population. Its power seemed to overtake the power of any other state, regardless of the territory. In this light we can understand Hannah Arendt's thesis that the Nazis regarded external relations in internal, police terms.[72] The Third Reich put itself in the

70 Cf. Bülent Diken and Carsten Bagge Laustsen, 'The Camp', (2006) 88 (4) *Geografiska Annaler. Series B, Human Geography* 446.

71 Raul Hilberg, *The Destruction of European Jews* (New York and London: Holmes & Meier, 1985), vol. II, 609–659.

72 'For it is evident that those who regard the whole earth as their future territory will stress the organ of domestic violence and will rule conquered territory with

position of a universal police power, for which there were no borders. By suspending recognition, Nazi Germany actually put itself in the position of a pan-sovereign, which maintains relations not with any intermediary political power, but with bare life itself.[73]

From the point of view of international law, it would be easy to understand the Third Reich as a persistent negator of international norms that arrogated to itself absolute sovereignty. Nonetheless, it did not undermine the triad: exception-based international law–sovereign state–population. It rather reconfigured and thus made visible the complex and unobvious relation between the two zones of exception, under and above sovereign power: international law and bare life. The sovereign withdrawal of consent to international obligations, later pushed to the extreme forms of practical suspension of international law, was a strict corollary to extending absolute biopower of human beings under Nazi control. In a thought-provoking manner the suspension of recognition on the international plane corresponded to creation of a practically a-national zone within the camps, populated by people of numerous ethnicities and languages.[74] By usurping universal biopower, Nazi Germany suspended to a certain extent the premise of international law: the correspondence between states and populations. In this sense, camps were proto-national spaces of bare life, which escaped the primal division of the modern world into nationalities.[75] Interestingly, the post-war system of human rights protection based on international law – established after the return of this division – is based on establishing a specific

police methods and personnel rather than with the army. Thus, the Nazis used their SS troops, essentially a police force, for the rule and even the conquest of foreign territories, with the ultimate aim of an amalgamation of the army and the police under the leadership of the SS.' Hannah Arendt, *The Origins of Totalitarianism* (San Diego: A Harvest Book, 1979), xxxvi.

73 See also Agamben, *The Open*, 76.

74 Primo Levi noted the effect it produced: 'The confusion of languages is a fundamental component of the manner of living here: one is surrounded by a perpetual Babel, in which everyone shouts orders and threats in languages never heard before, and woe betide whoever fails to grasp the meaning.' Primo Levi, *If This Is a Man…*, Stuart Woolf transl. (New York: Orion Press, 1959), 36.

75 To a certain degree, the Third Reich succeeded to export this model to other countries, thereby undermining the basic principles of international law. As Hannah Arendt noted, 'the increasing groups of stateless in the nontotalitarian countries led to a form of lawlessness, organized by the police, which practically resulted in a co-ordination of the free world with the legislation of the totalitarian countries. That concentration camps were ultimately provided for the same groups in all countries, even though there were considerable differences in the treatment of their inmates, was all the more characteristic as the selection of the groups was left exclusively to the initiative of the totalitarian regimes: if the Nazis put a person in a concentration camp and if he made a successful escape, say, to Holland, the Dutch would put him in an internment camp.' Arendt, *The Origins of Totalitarianism*, 288.

alliance between the two zones of exception, international and sub-sovereign. Based on mutual commitments of states, some post-war human rights instruments (especially the European Convention on Human Rights) built an edifice of objective obligations of states which are meant to safeguard rights of individuals.[76] Yet this objective system is based on obliteration of the possibility of states to withdraw their consent. Internationally guaranteed human rights are therefore built upon the same disguise of exception.

Consequently, Agamben's theory needs to be developed in order to encompass two sides of the sovereign. Both are based on exceptions: national law on the possibility of being suspended through a sovereign decision and international law on unilateral withdrawal. As human rights constitute a critical knot between the two, their legal status is feeble and conditional. Perhaps then their universalism should be treated as a mediating counterpart of the sovereign exception.

Conclusion

The conspicuous absence of international law in Agamben's work seems strictly correlated with his misrecognition of the specificity of modernity. Consequently, the Agambenian approach to jurisprudence combines profound perspicacity with surprising blind spots. It is only with understanding the paradoxical nature of international law that two zones of exception might be discerned in their mutual entanglement.

Contemporary human rights law conceals a mystified biopolitical device, which might easily dispel the universalism of protection and give way to reuniting the two zones of exception in one territory of the camp. The nation state, based on a paradoxical difference between the nation and the state, which will never overlap, will always be tempted to spiral into the definitive attempt to identify them. In the post-war era nation states not only still exist but the world population has been trapped in their cooperative exertion of power. They carry out universal police, but neatly distributed into national instances. Parallel coexistence of two principles of international law – of sovereign states and of populations – constitutes a permanent biopolitical device. A device which, pushed to the extreme in the camps, leaves as a remainder and a reminder humanity itself. If an ideal nation state governs over the nation in the name of the nation, the phenomenon of Nazi camps reveals its hidden zone of exception. In the camp the sovereign governs not over a nation, but over a remainder of humanity; and not on behalf of the

76 As famously stated by the ECtHR in the *Ireland v. the UK* case (judgment from 18 January 1978, app. no. 5310/71), 'Unlike international treaties of the classic kind, the Convention comprises more than mere reciprocal engagements between contracting States. It creates, over and above a network of mutual, bilateral undertakings, objective obligations, which, in the words of the Preamble, benefit from a 'collective enforcement' (§ 239).

nation, but on no one's behalf. This is the zone of exception, in which the suspension of international law conflates with the suspension of domestic legal norms.

Agamben's seduction with the Heideggerian paradigm in which danger and salvation conflate profoundly mystifies this complex relation.[77] The remedy for the modern zone of indistinction cannot reside in its reinterpretation as the messianic era, in which law is suspended: this is nothing but extrapolation of the paradigmatically modern device imprinted in the construction of the nation state. If any remedy can be sought, it must be located outside modernity. Therefore, Agamben's propensity to universalise and de-historicise only perpetuates what it denounces. The messianic era of suspension is nothing that awaits the entire history, but a disastrous temptation at the crossroads between international and domestic law. What can await us, however, is the true end of modernity: an event whose scope and sense must elude every modern eye.

77 Agamben shares with Heidegger many fundamental determinations of thinking. One which seems particularly pernicious is the mystifying cult of passivity, parenthetically privately professed also by Carl Schmitt. See Klaus Figge, Dieter Groch, *'Solange das Imperium da ist': Carl Schmitt im Gespräch 1971* (Berlin: Duncker & Humblot, 2010), 54.

Chapter 4

Minor law

Notes towards a revolutionary jurisprudence

Tormod Otter Johansen

Introduction

A characteristic specific to contemporary Western society is its autonomous sphere of legal rules and the order set up to deal with those rules, which includes legislators, courts, and the police. However, this social sphere of law is no longer just a part of society. Instead it now seems to encroach upon and act as the hegemonic structure for all parts of society. Juridical argumentation, legislation, and rights discourse is the dominant mode of political thinking and acting today, from economic processes to the family, from religion to solidarity.

This chapter interrogates two of the most radical attempts at thinking about law beyond the horizon of this hegemony. The first attempt is made by Evgeny Pashukanis, who argues that law as such will be extinguished in a future society. The second is that of Giorgio Agamben, who argues that law will continue, but that it will take on a radically different role, emptied of force and no longer married to sovereign power. Informed by their arguments, I attempt to sketch out a third path: that law could shift from its hegemonic position and become what could be called *minor law*. This minor law would not be non-violent, nor would it be without coercive force, but it would exist in a qualitatively different position than law does today.

If law is moved into a minor position it will also be put in an exceptional position. The trajectory of modern society is one where law has increasingly become the dominant form of social organisation. It has embedded itself in social life as the normal structure conflict resolution and governing. Agamben's claim is that law and the exception to law, in declarations of state of exception, camps, etc., have reached an apex where the norm and the exception are indistinguishable.[1] Whether or not one agrees that law and its exception are no longer possible to distinguish, it is

1 Giorgio Agamben, *State of Exception* (Chicago: University of Chicago Press, 2005), 87.

significant that even deviations from legal normality are stated in legal language. When torture, camps, drone strikes, invasions and other acts with specious legal basis are legitimised today, it is done through legal argument.[2] Nothing, even the violent actions of the most powerful actors in the world, escapes legal language.

The wager in this chapter is that beyond the hegemony of the legal, and beyond the permanent state of exception that Agamben has argued we live in, lies the possibility of a world where law and legal processes again become true exceptions. True exceptions in the sense that legal rules and procedures become actually rare and, even more importantly, that most social interaction will be conducted without laws and legal rules being relevant. When laws, courts and jurists are engaged it will when absolutely necessary, similar to how the state of exception in its original form was a rare and truly exceptional phenomena.

I claim that there exists a third alternative between the ontological overcoming of law in the Benjaminian-Agambenian notion of a coming world where law is no longer in force, or married with violence, but only studied; and the irrelevance of law in communism that Pashukanis sees as the end goal of revolution. The third alternative is that law might not be overcome or left by the wayside of history, but that it can take on a new minor position next to other social forms and cease to be the major form of organising social relations it is today. This third way is not the reformist socialist approach of gaining state power to use the state and its legal order to effect a more just and egalitarian order.[3] It is presupposed here that the major shift a communist revolution entails, if possible and actually realised, would be an overall reduction in coercion. This is at the core of communist thought and the promise that the Marxist tradition continuously reaffirms.[4]

Pashukanis's main claim is that law and legal relations will disappear and be replaced by technical regulations to coordinate human action and moral rules that will be voluntarily followed, instead of criminal and other forms of law.

In Agamben's philosophy of a coming community, a world beyond the present is sketched where law will still continue to exist,[5] but it will be released from all power and force and therefore, with the Judaic law of Halacha as a template, only studied. For Agamben, following Benjamin,

2 Note the infamous 'Torture memos' by John Yoo, prepared in absolute secret to give legal legitimation to CIA torture.
3 Whether such a path is open at all is debatable, but that is not the path I investigate in the following.
4 Cf. Michael Head, *Marxism, Revolution and Law: The Lively Debates of Early Soviet Russia* (Saarbrücken, Germany: VDM Verlag Dr. Müller, 2010), 19.
5 Giorgio Agamben, *The Coming Community* (Minneapolis, MN: University of Minnesota Press, 1993).

law will still exist, yet it will not be entwined with violence and coercion, and it will likely be followed voluntarily. While any straightforward comparison and critique of these two thinkers necessarily does violence to their work and legacies, the reason for this study is not to disprove the validity or value in their respective philosophical positions. Rather, it is focused on sketching out the possibility of a third way between *the disappearance of law* and *the continuation of law without force.* This is possible due to the value of Pashukanis's and Agamben's contributions. Even if law and the juridical, both in theory and in praxis, have been amply studied and critiqued in the Marxist tradition, these studies have mostly focused on inquiring into, and critiquing the role of, legal norms and institutions in the present social order, and the role of law in creating and maintaining capitalism.[6]

This study's purpose is to connect Agamben with Pashukanis, partly through the idiosyncratic but still openly Marxist thinker, Benjamin. Agamben might not be a Marxist, but he is a thinker working and writing in relation to this tradition. Not least his important positioning early in *Homo Sacer*, where he criticizes keeping the state as the 'fundamental horizon' when the 'weakness of anarchist and Marxian critiques of the State' was to not have investigated the State as its originating structure as such. Agamben is clearly situated in an antagonistic position vis-à-vis the state, and therefore on the side of the anarchist and Marxian tradition:

> But one ends up identifying with an enemy whose structure one does not understand, and the theory of the State (and in particular of the state of exception, which is to say, of the dictatorship of the proletariat as the transitional phase leading to the stateless society) is the reef on which the revolutions of our century have been shipwrecked.[7]

There is a general lack of studies on law and the juridical in relation to the future aspect and goal of Marxist thought: revolution and suspension of the current capitalist order. Here the singular contribution from Pashukanis stands out, even though it is embedded in his specific Soviet context, and was

6 And here I place Agamben in this tradition as well. (See especially Daniel McLoughlin, 'Introduction: Agamben and Radical Politics', in McLoughlin (ed.), *Agamben and Radical Politics* (Edinburgh: Edinburgh University Press, 2016), 5, and the edited volume it introduces as a whole. McLoughlin points out that the shift in Agamben's work towards economy and government partly makes up for the critique he has received in not adequately regarding the issues that are the main focus of the Marxist tradition, Daniel McLoughlin, 'Rethinking Agamben: Ontology and the Coming Politics', (2014) 25(3) *Law and Critique* 323.

7 Giorgio Agamben, *Homo Sacer: Sovereign Power and Bare Life* (Stanford, CA: Stanford University Press, 1998), 11.

later swept away in the catastrophe of the Stalinist era.[8] Pashukanis is unique in that he specifically addresses the question of law and revolution in relation to communism from a juridical perspective. This gives this theme more depth than it receives in the peripheral comments from Marx and Engels, as well as compared to the sweeping fragments in Lenin's work. The greatest lack is still that this approach and Pashukanis's theory was not picked up and developed afterwards. Unfortunately, the questions of law in revolution, and after revolution, fell silent for decades.

While this central theme of law and revolution from a legal theoretical perspective is central to jurisprudential thought in a Marxist tradition, it is still in its infancy.[9] The notion that this is appropriate, since we shouldn't worry about questions regarding the organisation of social life beyond the boundary of revolution, is here rejected. It might be that any attempt to contribute to a field we may call *revolutionary jurisprudence*, with the aim of studying the role of law in and beyond revolution, also necessarily consists of speculation. But speculation is different from programmatism that attempts to prescribe future action. The possible futility and harmfulness of theories of future actions should not scare us away from proper speculation. Speculation is an act of thinking beyond the present by way of looking at what is already here.

On the path of minor law, many, perhaps even most, laws will wither away because they will be unnecessary and able to be replaced with other forms of social coordination that do not involve violence and coercion. This is a result of the overall reduction in coercion necessary in a world without wage labour, markets and private property. Some laws might still exist, concerning violence against persons or for the protection of children. These can possibly, but not necessarily, be coupled with coercive force, with violence. This would still entail a radical shift from the contemporary situation where legal regulation is a hegemonic type of social organisation and continues to expand to encompass attempts to solve all problems in human life. To turn this trend around would mean that law would not disappear, but would be subordinate and put in a minority position vis-à-vis voluntary and non-coercive forms of social organisation.

8 See Head, *Marxism, Revolution and Law: The Lively Debates of Early Soviet Russia*, chapter 8. The rising interest in Pashukanis's thought, not least in international law, during the latter decades should be noted: see China Miéville, *Between Equal Rights: A Marxist Theory of International Law* (Leiden: Brill, 2005).

9 Cosmin Cercel, *Towards a Jurisprudence of State Communism: Law and the Failure of Revolution* (Abingdon: Routledge, 2018), 50.

Law without coercion

Daniel Loick suggests that it is possible in theory, and perhaps in practice, to think that law can continue to exist in the future without being conjoined with sovereign power and violence. Law would then be compatible with a "radically democratic society" where law is not enforced through coercion and instead "takes on the character of a voluntary and therefore an-archic association". Law would take the form of a communal agreement and still "coordinate collective action and the cooperation of the whole society".[10]

Loick's critical project is, among other things, a damning critique of the moral legitimacy of law as such.[11] However, it still constitutes a careful attempt to reconstruct a meaningful role for law beyond the horizon of state power, the latter being a reality and assumption we seem almost incapable of reaching past today.

One question is whether or not the law that would subsist in a post-sovereign world would be law at all. The main example of a non-sovereign body of law in Loick's text is the Judaic law of Halacha, which is upheld in the sense that it is voluntarily transferred, studied, interpreted and followed by Jewish people.[12] A critique of this empirical example could be made, vulgarly, by referring to both the violent historical effects of Jewish law inside communities and families and the partial application of its laws in the contemporary state of Israel.[13] But Loick's theoretical point concerns the actual realisation of law without coercion, where the Jewish tradition surely provides many such examples. Judaic law in this mode is not connected to a sovereign state power, which enforces the law through violence or the threat of violence.

In other words, Halacha has functioned in a recognisably legal fashion, concerning rules of conduct and adjudicating different matters of life and action inside participating communities. In that sense, it is juridical, just like common, civil or international law. But it has also not always been conjoined with sovereign power, with a state that enforces it. Rather, it once functioned as an integrated, if not immanent, aspect of Jewish communal life.

The example of Halacha is therefore apt for the purposes of Loick's project since it amounts to a sort of rehabilitation of law as a legitimate force in social life, after it has suffered through a strong critique of its violent illegitimacy. His wager seems to be that law with violence is not good, but perhaps law without violence could be. The attempt by Loick is centred on a saving or

10 Daniel Loick, *A Critique of Sovereignty*, Amanda DeMarco transl. (London: Rowman & Littlefield, 2019), 216.

11 Loick points to the irony of the attempts to legitimate violence, Loick, 71ff.

12 Loick, 194f. This is a central example to Agamben as well, not least inspired by the work of Benjamin.

13 Loick also defends against such critiques in Daniel Loick, 'Law without Violence', in Christoph Menke (ed.) *Law and Violence: Christoph Menke in Dialogue* (Manchester: Manchester University Press, 2018), 104.

redemption of law, so that it can still prevail as an important, though not coercive nor violent, form of social organisation. I am sceptical of Loick's solution. My suggestion in the final section of this chapter will be that law might need to be retained, and that it will then still be violent and coercive, but that it will nevertheless exist in a different position and state compared to our present situation.

This chapter will not discuss Loick's attempt further, but will look at two more radical approaches to the future of law. For, if one alternative is to save law from violence (and Loick is not the first to attempt this), another alternative is to say that law, if it is to function as a means of social organisation, can only do so as a violent force. In other words, if we want to leave violent sovereign law behind we need to leave law behind as a social force as such. This wager is even more radical than Loick's. Whether it is more naive or realistic than Loick remains to be seen.

Both Pashukanis and Agamben, from their differing theoretical and historical perspectives, have formulated theories on the overcoming of the violent reality of law in our present societies. But these hypothetical overcomings of law have been formulated as requiring not just a new role for law in social organisation as with Loick, but rather the end of law as a social instrument.[14] Let us now turn to Pashukanis's intervention in the Marxist tradition.

The apex of bourgeois law and its end

This analysis will not amount to a comprehensive discussion of Pashukanis's theory of law, but will instead focus on the question of law in communism.[15] To be able to discuss this aspect of his theory, what we could call the speculative moment, we need to concisely describe his theory of law and then explain how it lends itself to the idea that law will be extinguished in a future society.

The basic premise of Pashukanis's theory is that law as such is based on economic relations. But he was critical of the Marxist attempts up until his time to regard law as a simple instrument of class rule. Instead of focusing only on this aspect of state-mediated coercion, Pashukanis offered a theory that took as its starting point what he considered the simplest legal relation, that of a contract regulating the exchange of commodities. This gave rise to the designation "commodity theory of law", a phrase Pashukanis approved of.[16] In the case of a

14 Loick refers extensively to Agamben as an important interlocutor in his work. Pashukanis does not figure in the text, although other thinkers in the Marxist tradition do.

15 For a more thorough account see Michael Head, *Evgeny Pashukanis: A Critical Reappraisal* (Abingdon: Routledge, 2007). Also the use of Pashukanis by Miéville, *Between Equal Rights: A Marxist Theory of International Law.*

16 It was Andrey Vyshinsky's invention. See Head, *Evgeny Pashukanis: A Critical Reappraisal*, 179.

worker and employer, the exchange is that of work against salary. This is the true content of the legal relation according to Pashukanis:

> Law in its general definitions, law as a form, does not exist in the heads and the theories of learned jurists. It has a parallel, real history which unfolds not as a set of ideas, but as a specific set of relations which men enter into not by conscious choice, but because the relations of production compel them to do so. Man becomes a legal subject by virtue of the same necessity which transforms the product of nature into a commodity complete with the enigmatic property of value.[17]

Pashukanis's notion of law centres on what he perceives to be the peculiar characteristic that distinguishes it "from every other social order in that it comprises isolated, private subjects."[18] Persons have claims to rights and assert them against others. This is different from other forms of "regulatory rules" of moral, aesthetic or utilitarian nature. "For Pashukanis, private law was the 'fundamental, primary level of law'."[19] It was the ultimate basis for all other forms of law, including family law, criminal law and constitutional law.

This also leads him to regarding everything other than private law in its pure form as either a twisted form of private law thinking or as something other than law. He disregarded public law as a secondary and derivative phenomena. "The system of civil law is therefore characterised by simplicity, clarity and completeness, while the theories of public law are replete with constructs that are rigid, artificial and grotesquely one-sided."[20] The distinction of legal relations, as different from other social relations, is therefore a result of the development of the capitalist economical order. The legal relation of private interests has at its core, and it reaches its apex in, bourgeois-capitalist society.[21]

But while the intricacies of Pashukanis's general theory of law are interesting in themselves, we here need to turn to what it implied for law in a future communist society. He does not offer any elaborate theory of law in communism, since his main conclusion is that it will be extinguished:

17 Evgeny Pashukanis, *The General Theory of Law and Marxism*, 1980, available at www.marxists.org/archive/pashukanis/1924/law/.

18 Ibid., chap. 3.

19 Head, *Evgeny Pashukanis: A Critical Reappraisal*, 179.

20 Pashukanis, *The General Theory of Law and Marxism*, 1980, chap. 3.

21 'Far from being a natural or eternal institution of human society, law was a peculiar form that arose from definite commodity exchange relations that had arisen historically at a certain stage of economic and social development and would die away once that stage had passed.' Head, *Evgeny Pashukanis: A Critical Reappraisal*, 173.

> Marx therefore envisioned the transition to developed communism, not as a transition to new forms of law, but as the withering away of the legal form in general, as the liberation from this inheritance of the bourgeois age which the bourgeoisie was itself condemned to endure.

While this formed the end goal of revolution, the intervening period of socialism might still need law because it would retain exchange in the sphere of distribution— the buying and selling of goods would still prevail. These are at the same time bourgeois and capitalist aspects of the socialist transition state, under the dictatorship of the proletariat. Were class relations to be finally abolished, laws and legal relations would no longer be needed or, perhaps, even possible because private exchange would no longer take place.

Pashukanis imagines the end of law as a necessary outcome of the end of bourgeois class society. Law as a form of social organisation has reached its peak in capitalist society, where it has acquired its purest form. The demise of bourgeoisie society also means the "withering away of law in general, i.e. the gradual disappearance of the juridic element in human relationships".[22] The Pashukanian path is therefore a promise of the realisation of communism as an end of all law. This leaves law no role, not even as a nonviolent, noncoercive form of organisation. In its place, there will still exist "regulation", but Pashukanis sharply distinguishes these technical rules from law.

Concerning other forms of social organisation, he simply rejects them as being legal at all. Military units are subordinated to the will of the commander; the Jesuit order is comprised of members fulfiling the will of the leader. These forms of hierarchical social organisation therefore have "nothing in common with the legal form". Similarly, fully realised communism would be a state of things where no private interests needed to assert their claims against others. Therefore, the legal form would no longer be of any use. The social organisation would then not be legal in nature. Instead of the government of persons there would be the administration of things, as Engels formulated it.[23] In Pashukanis, this even amounts to a destruction of ethics, since moral obligation only makes sense in a class society where the right of one implies the obligation of another.[24]

It is an important discussion whether Pashukanis's concept of law, or rather the legal form, is too narrow. His dismissal of public law and state power as

22 Pashukanis, *The General Theory of Law and Marxism*, 1980, chap. 3.

23 Karl Marx and Friedrich Engels, *Collected Works. Vol. 25, Anti-Dühring; Dialectics of Nature* (London: Lawrence & Wishart, 1987). See also Cercel, *Towards a Jurisprudence of State Communism*, 92.

24 'Pure utilitarianism, striving to disperse the metaphysical haze which surrounds ethical doctrines, leads to conceptualizing good and evil from the perspective of harm and benefit. Thereby, of course, it simply destroys ethics, or rather tries to destroy and transcend them.' Pashukanis, *The General Theory of Law and Marxism*, 1980, chap. 6.

more or less irrelevant for law as such, especially given the transitional Soviet state, are problematic. An integral part of his law-transcending theory is a conceptualization of the use that the proletariat must make of the legal form in a transitional socialist phase. Law together with other aspects of bourgeois society, such as morality and the state, will play a role before communism can be realised.[25] The question of whether his conception of law or the legal form as restricted to only those relations that are founded in exchange – and equally, whether every form of law can be derived from such a concept of private law – can definitely be discussed and critiqued.[26] Further, whether the distinction between the "law" of bourgeois society and the "regulation" of socialist society holds water is key to interpreting the value of his theory. But for the purposes of this text, it is not necessary to develop these aspects further. Pashukanis's work stands as a singular contribution in Marxist theory and in legal theory in general in that it tries to account jurisprudentially for the argument that law could be extinguished. It might be argued that the possibility, or in Pashukanis's case the promise, of the extinction of law is not more than a postulate in the theory. That might be too harsh since there is a somewhat developed argument for why that can and must be the case, at least inside the framework of Marxist thought. But even if it mainly functions as a postulate of the theory, this still amounts to quite a step compared to most theories of law that cannot even consider the end of law as a possibility.[27] We will now turn to a similarly radical theory, but one which surprisingly combines a retained role for law in a coming society at the same time as this role is completely transformed on an ontological level.

Destituent power and inoperativity

Law and its future is one of the many recurring and fragmentarily addressed themes in Agamben's oeuvre. The nexus of law and violent sovereign power that is at the core of the modern state is a central question not only in the whole *Homo Sacer* series but also in Agamben's previous and ancillary texts.

25 Pashukanis, chap. 6.

26 'Pashukanis' derivation of the legal form from the commodity form barred the possibility of grappling with pre-capitalist and even post-capitalist varieties of law and right.' Igor Shoikhedbrod, 'Estranged Bedfellows: Why Pashukanis Still Charms Legal Formalists', *Legal Form*, 15 June 2018, available at https://legalform.blog/2018/06/15/estranged-bedfellows-why-pashukanis-still-charms-legal-formalists-igor-shoikhedbrod/.

27 In another study, I aim to pick up the threads of the notion that law could end and develop them in a philosophical enquiry into what such an idea might actually mean. I would hesitate to mention a work in progress in print on the chance it doesn't materialise. And is it worth the reader's attention to mention it? Inside the discipline of law, the Scandinavian legal realism of the Uppsala School, certain radical neoliberals and anarchists on both the right and the left seem to be where thought connected to this idea might be found. The other great well of thought on the end of law is of course the theology of the Abrahamic religions.

In 2013, Agamben had reason to comment on his own attempts in a lecture titled "What is a destituent power?"[28]

He describes the intention of the *Homo Sacer* project and its archeology of politics as the attempt to shift "the very site of politics itself" and thereby move it from the place where Aristotle, Hobbes and Marx had it situated. In section six of the text, Agamben focuses on the concept of inoperativity, "an operation that deactivates and renders works (of economy, of religion, of language, etc.) inoperative". Inoperativity means the possibility to think of the human "as a being of pure potentiality (*potenza*), that no identity and no work could exhaust".[29] This is in stark contrast to the modern epoch, which is unable to think of inoperativity except as the negation of work, of operativity. Inoperativity has still been contained in different forms of exceptional activities such as the feast, which suspends the productivity of the everyday.

> But the feast is defined not only by what in it is not done, but primarily by the fact that what is done—which in itself is not unlike what one does every day—becomes undone, is rendered inoperative, liberated and suspended from its 'economy', from the reasons and purposes that define it during the weekdays (and not doing, in this sense, is only an extreme case of this suspension). If one eats, it is not done for the sake of being fed; if one gets dressed, it is not done for the sake of being covered up or taking shelter from the cold; if one wakes up, it is not done for the sake of working; if one walks, it is not done for the sake of going someplace; if one speaks, it is not done for the sake of communicating information; if one exchanges objects, it is not done for the sake of selling or buying.[30]

Inoperativity, then, stands for the possibility of doing what we always do, rather than something else, but released from the economy in which it is usually caught. Agamben describes this potential for making things inoperative as a *destitution*. And furthermore, that this destitution could "furnish a paradigm for thinking inoperativity as a model of politics". The feast also contains other examples of inoperative activities that Agamben mentions here and in other places: dance as the inoperative use of the body, masks as the neutralisation of the face, and, not least, the poem as the deactivation of the communicative function of language in order to put it to a new use. "What the poem accomplishes for the potentiality of speaking, politics and philosophy must accomplish for the power of acting."

Here we are closing in on the future for law and the juridical. In contrast to the constituent power that tries to establish a new order, "a violence that

28 It might be noted that this concise text has the potential to function as a prolegomena to the *Homo Sacer* project and Agamben's thought as a whole.

29 Giorgio Agamben, 'What Is a Destituent Power?', transl. Stephanie Wakefield, (2014) 32(1) *Environment and Planning D: Society and Space* 69.

30 Giorgio Agamben, *Nudities* (Stanford, CA: Stanford University Press, 2010), 69.

establishes and constitutes the new law", Agamben suggests that we should aim to think of a *destituent power* whose definition is the task of the coming politics. Here Agamben chooses to develop the question of what destitution could mean by grappling with the seminal text for the question of the future of law, Benjamin's "Critique of violence".[31] Benjamin interrogates what a breaking of the sovereign law and its violence could mean, which is a new historical epoch based "on the destitution (*Entsetzung*) of law with all the powers on which it depends, and as they depend on it, therefore ultimately on the destitution of state violence".[32] Benjamin finds an example of such a destitution of law in the proletarian general strike. This strike does not use the violence available in the legal categories of the present relation between labourers and capitalists, but rather inaugurates a new reality where law is completely transformed. This destitution therefore would mean something close to the extinction of law that Pashukanis suggests. Benjamin calls for a divine violence to end the mythical violence of the sovereign power of the state and the current order.

But Agamben is even more aligned in his next example. Paul, in Corinthians 15:24, argues that the relation between the messiah and the law is not only that he will make law, together with all authority and power, inoperative. The messiah will also conserve the law through this inoperative action. This *Aufhebung* then preserves the law as much as it makes it inoperative by 'deactivating its action with regard to sin'.[33]

In the remainder of his text Agamben connects this to his notion of a form-of-life, "a life that can never be separated from its form, a life in which it is never possible to isolate something like a bare life", in other words, a life that is not caught in the violent grip of law bound up in sovereign power.[34] What might this mean specifically for law and the juridical?[35]

31 This is also the central text for Loick, *A Critique of Sovereignty*. See also Loick, 'Law without Violence'.

32 Agamben, 'What Is a Destituent Power?', 70. Translated as 'suspension' or 'abolition' in other versions, see Walter Benjamin, 'Critique of Violence', in Peter Demetz (ed.), *Reflections: Essays, Aphorisms, Autobiographical Writings* (New York: Harcourt Brace Jovanovich, 1978), 300. Also Walter Benjamin, 'Critique of Violence', in Marcus Bullock and Michael W. Jennings (eds), *Walter Benjamin: Selected Writings. Vol. 1, 1913–1926* (Cambridge: Harvard University Press, 2004), 251.

33 Agamben, 'What Is a Destituent Power?', 71.

34 This also forms the explicit and central theme of the final volume in the *Homo Sacer* series, Giorgio Agamben, *The Use of Bodies* (Stanford, CA: Stanford University Press, 2015).

35 Even though these questions are by necessity intertwined, and concern a common core. A clear example of this is the quote Steven DeCaroli has rescued from an impromptu discussion in Greece, where Agamben connects the need of the form-of-life with the need to avoid the constitution of a new law: 'We have to stop thinking of any revolutionary action as directed toward the constitution of a new juridical order. Benjamin calls this pure violence, which is a violence that will never constitute a new juridical order. You depose without restoring another. If you are really, strongly and clearly able

To expand on that we need to turn to another text, the second instalment in the *Homo Sacer* series, *State of Exception*. Here Agamben attempts to investigate the question Benjamin raises, which Agamben points out both primitive Christianity and the Marxist tradition have also formulated: "What becomes of the law after its messianic fulfillment?" Agamben refers directly – although without any actual explication – to Pashukanis and the Soviet debate as another formulation of the same question: "And what becomes of the law in a society without classes? (This is precisely the debate between Vyshinsky and Pashukanis.)"[36] In his attempt to answer this, Agamben turns to another, perhaps even more general, example of inoperative use, namely play:

> One day humanity will play with law just as children play with disused objects, not in order to restore them to their canonical use but to free them from it for good. What is found after the law is not a more proper and original use value that precedes the law but a new use that is born only after it. And use, which has been contaminated by law, must also be freed from its own value. This liberation is the task of study, or of play. And this studious play is the passage that allows us to arrive at that justice that one of Benjamin's posthumous fragments defines as a state of the world in which the world appears as a good that absolutely cannot be appropriated or made juridical.[37]

The law is thereby rescued from extinction; it is retained and even bears the promise of justice. Agamben points out in his reading of Benjamin that it is not this activity that gives justice, rather it opens the possibility that we might arrive at justice through the opening of a gate, as Benjamin writes. "The law—no longer practiced but studied—is not justice, but only the gate that leads to it. What opens a passage toward justice is not the erasure of law, but its deactivation and inactivity—that is, another use of law."[38] Catherine Mills argues that the specific choice of play is a way for Agamben to choose a middle path between endless deferral, as in deconstruction, and eschatology, which purports the end of time as such.[39] The other alternative, that of letting law become extinct, as Pashukanis suggests, would for Agamben threaten the rise of a new violent and sovereign law.

Agamben's project has a much grander objective than the specific aspect of the future of juridical structures and law I focus on. His main theme

to demonstrate the illegitimacy of the political order, in a way you are deposing it.' Agamben, quoted in Steven DeCaroli, 'What Is a Form-of-Life?: Giorgio Agamben and the Practice of Poverty', in McGloughlin (ed.), *Agamben and Radical Politics*, 226.

36 Agamben, *State of Exception*, 63.

37 Ibid., 64.

38 Ibid.

39 Catherine Mills, 'Playing with Law: Agamben and Derrida on Postjuridical Justice', (2008) 107(1) *South Atlantic Quarterly* 30.

concerns the consequences of our ontological status and the way we comport ourselves to existence as such, towards Being in the wake of Heidegger. But the fact that both legal concepts, institutions and the often enigmatic "law" itself plays such a recurring role in Agamben's texts also points towards the question of the future or end of law as fundamental in his philosophical and ontological work.

I interpret Agamben's account as a possible description of or argument for the possibility of a change of the juridical through and beyond a revolution, even if it would be of a different kind than the Marxist and anarchist revolutionary programs and attempts from which he distances himself.[40] The question of whether Agamben himself is a representative or adheres to the possibility of a communist revolution is here in a way suspended. In that sense, this text does not try to interpret his often enigmatic stance on issues of political change in general and communism in particular. Instead, it tries to use his post-juridical thought for the purposes of revolutionary jurisprudence.

Agamben is, among other things, inspired by Benjamin's formulations on the "study of law" as a future use of law, the same template as Halacha, the Judaic law that is the object of tradition and study. This activity of studying is not described as primarily a practical tool for the communicative need of the community to choose and legitimate collective action. Instead, law will still exist in a sense similar to the Jewish example, in that it is studied, but without any coercive power of other humans. As we have seen, Agamben even describes this activity as playing, where the law is left as a discarded object from a previous era, suitable for use as a toy. He likens law to many other artifacts and activities from history that have been "profaned" – in other words, put to a new use beyond their previous roles in religion, warfare or law. This implies an even more extreme future for law than it being just non-violent. It no longer fulfills any practical or utilitarian function, but is instead released from any function beyond its use as an object of study, or play.

We now play with religious symbols, with left-over things and with profaned rituals. Even these rituals in themselves contain elements of play at their core.[41] But what would it even mean to play with law as a disused object? Aren't law and the juridical anathema to playfulness or play? Perhaps, this is conceivable because of the very possibility that law could be freed from the apparatus of teleological action and become the object of study and play. Even though the ontological shift that the coming community, the new forms-

40 He does that explicitly, see footnote 3 above.

41 In *Karman* Agamben attempts to locate the activity or the means without end. His main example, established in a typical eclectic reading and Indo-European etymology is that of dance, the acting that has no end that therefore 'never settles into a *crimen*, into a culpable and imputable act'. Giorgio Agamben, *Karman: A Brief Treatise on Action, Guilt, and Gesture*, Adam Kotsko transl. (Stanford, CA: Stanford University Press, 2018), 82.

of-life, or the inoperative destituent power must act on every apparatus that our present world contains and is structured around, law is the most extreme case. The catastrophe is, in Jessica Whyte's terms, most acute in law and therefore it harbours the greatest potential for redemption.[42] If we can play with law, or study it without it being applied, we can destitute anything and everything.

The problem with Agamben's suggestion that law could subsist after its connection with sovereign violence is severed is perhaps simply that it seems too hopeful, too messianic. This is not a strong argument against it, since the structure of a messianic argument implies that not only major change but also the most radical change thinkable is possible.

In any case, to develop the theme of law beyond revolution that I have presented with the help of Pashukanis and Agamben, I will now sketch another configuration of law in a post-revolutionary situation.

Minor law: beyond the hegemony of law

For Pashukanis's central examples, private law transactions such as payments or contract fulfilment, it is at least plausible that they would be exhausted in a world without private property. Similarly, the coming community outlined by Agamben is a world where legal contestation of rights loses its meaning, in the sense that legal relations would not organise the relations between the humans living in such a community.

While Pashukanis theorises inside the framework of a radical transformation of society, he still operates on an ontic level. Agamben suggests that a transition freeing humans from sovereign power would be an ontological shift, and at the same time it might not take the form of an all-encompassing social event, but rather exist as a promise in every situation.

In the framework of this chapter it can be posited that we might find ourselves, or that we might be able to realise, a world where sovereign, violent legal power does not hold the hegemonic position as the main form or enforcer of social organisation. In other words, where the guarantor of the social forms of property, individual rights, wage labour, criminal law, market relations and public administration is no longer the judicial system coupled with the police. It seems obvious that most of these institutions would either disappear, as might be the case with the private ownership of means of production, wage labour and markets, or be radically transformed, as in the case of the heterogeneous activities of education, care and other functions that public administration now fulfills. Michael Stolleis has succinctly formulated this crucial aspect of state theory, whether thinking inside a framework of reforms of the current social order or from a revolutionary perspective:

42 Jessica Whyte, *Catastrophe and Redemption: The Political Thought of Giorgio Agamben* (Albany, NY: State University of New York Press, 2013).

> What our ancestors thought about [the state] and how they shaped it is something we must understand at least in outline in order to decide what it is we ourselves want to do in the state and with the state. If we decide that we want to have as little as possible to do with the state and refuse to become engaged on its behalf, we must answer the questions of who is to protect us against violence; who is to be responsible for the services necessary for living and for the conveniences we take for granted; who will maintain transportation and communication systems; who will finance universities, libraries, museums, and much else.[43]

The case of criminal law, but even more so the role of social law in the protection of children and other vulnerable persons, can function as a specific focal point, since it seems to be one of the most problematic aspects of thinking law beyond sovereign power. The case against all law has to face the case of a child being severely mistreated. Even though this one case cannot be a general argument for the legitimacy of juridical structures, it is challenging to not see the need for societal responsibility of some sort. If the care of a child needs to be taken on by the community through coercive force, it necessarily implies the protection of rights, fair procedure and, in the end, institutional violence as a necessary means. Leaving the same matter to a simply moral organ, with no qualified recourse to force, does not seem more appetising to most modern senses. This is Lenin's position on the protection of people in a nutshell:

> We are not utopians, and do not in the least deny the possibility and inevitability of excesses on the part of *individual persons*, or the need to stop such excesses. In the first place, however, no special machine, no special apparatus of suppression, is needed for this: this will be done by the armed people themselves, as simply and as readily as any crowd of civilized people, even in modern society, interferes to put a stop to a scuffle or to prevent a woman from being assaulted.[44]

I do not find this attitude reassuring.

The general organisation of social life could probably survive on technical rules or regulations and voluntary acts of following these structures. This is in an important sense the implicit promise of communism, that the production in the economy and social interaction would not need to rely on wage labour, with its inherently coercive nature, or forced labour in any other form. Some crimes will implicitly disappear, such as private property crimes, although

43 Michael Stolleis, *Public Law in Germany: A Historical Introduction from the 16th to the 21st Century*, Thomas Dunlap transl. (Oxford: Oxford University Press, 2017), 9.
44 Vladimir Lenin, *The State and Revolution*, 1999 [1918], Lenin Internet Archive, available at https://www.marxists.org/archive/lenin/works/1917/staterev/, chap. 1.

probably not crimes committed towards individual property, acts of sabotage or the theft of common resources.

What should also be considered is the contingent nature of social structures and the potential for a multitude of different forms of social, juridical and quasi-juridical forms of organisation. The width of possible ways of human ordering, social organisation and dispute resolution cannot be evaluated in any depth here. It can however be claimed without exaggeration that many actual and possible forms of such social order exist, and have existed, where no law or legal order is present in the sense it is in contemporary Western society.

Simon Roberts suggests in his book *Order and Dispute* that the possible forms of, and variation in, types of ordering structures for human social conduct is great indeed. The anthropological literature contains a wide variety of social structures for ordering social life and resolving disputes.[45] That such a plethora of non-legal forms of coordination and dispute resolution exist, and have existed, makes it seems unnecessary and even naive to posit legal orders and law as necessary components of human society. Whether large and even global societal orders require law is another question, but it does not seem a priori necessary that it is the case. This opens up the possibility to go beyond a binary choice between society with law, with a legal order and juridical structures, and societies without. Rather, a multitude of different combinations of legal, quasi-legal and non-legal forms for ordering and dispute resolution are possible.

Pashukanis suggests a complete extinction of the juridical. Agamben in turn suggests that law can survive without power, as an object of study or play. And as we saw in the introduction, Loick suggests that it can exist as a voluntary form of social organisation. I suggest that another possible configuration of the legal and non-legal is that the former could be *extinguished* in part, *profaned* in part (made the object of study, play or voluntary commitment) and *developed or transformed* in part. This tripartite structure will perhaps on the outset look similar to contemporary societies, in that we live with all three aspects of ordering and dispute resolution norms already. We resort to the legal order and its violent guarantees, we act inside voluntary or non-legal normative orders – etiquette and decency are the classical examples – and we all know that legal rules and forms are sometimes extinguished, such as formal inequality between the sexes or legal slavery. These extinguished laws also form an important background for the legitimacy of the present legal order, as both its precursor and its other, so to speak.

45 'Despite the wide range of organizational forms which may be found in small-scale societies, the mechanisms for maintaining continuity and handling disputes tend almost universally to be directly embedded in everyday life, unsupported by a differentiated legal system.' Simon Roberts, *Order and Dispute: An Introduction to Legal Anthropology*, 2nd ed. (New Orleans, LA: Quid Pro Books, 2013), 15.

But the difference I have alluded to is that a post-revolutionary situation where the state no longer forms the sovereign nexus of power would amount to a situation where both proportions and the hegemony of these normative orders is radically shifted. A shift from the present hegemony of law would still amount to a radical shift. To go from a hegemonic and ever growing judicialisation and its swelling body of law to a situation where law only survives in a minority position would be qualitatively different. Would law, in a minor position, hold the promise of an emergence of new and more manifold forms of social organisation?

It might not only mean the pragmatic and utilitarian decision to keep the, by then, archaic form of legal violence, as a last resort against certain crimes. It could be that the new relative position of criminal law, social law for the protection of children, etcetera, might be kept, and would also qualitatively change these spheres of legal violence and rationality. In our present situation the choice of a non-legal or nonviolent form of dispute resolution or problem solution is seen as an exception to the normal course of things.[46] If emissions need to be reduced, children protected or the consumer business expanded, the first call is for legislation. Or if not immediate legislation, the threat that if other measures are not sufficient, legislation will surely follow. Even in personal life and in civil society the legal hegemony prevails, where every political or social goal is communicated through the language of rights or the legal responsibilities of the state. Conflicts with neighbours are not always brought to court, but the threat of legal action is implicitly or explicitly in the background.[47]

But it is possible to imagine the profanation of now violently guaranteed rules of administrative activity into mere technical rules, followed voluntarily by the participants in a joint venture. These rules now give the director general or local bureau chief the mandate to decide what someone in the workplace should do. These decisions are backed up by the threat of disciplinary action or termination of employment, and in the extreme, by the general laws of criminal liability. While the coercive aspects are relatively specific, they could perhaps be severed from the more technical and practical "rules" that organise the common endeavour.

This is different from criminal laws that directly have only a coercive or violent element. If these elements were severed from the criminal justice system, it is hard to see what would remain. Perhaps one could instead imagine alternative or more transformed forms of activities, such as reconciliation procedures. These share some of the same aims as criminal justice – revealing truths about past events, morally condemning certain actions, providing some sort of resolution for the parties involved – but

46 A historical reversal of the situation.

47 David Graeber, *The Utopia of Rules: On Technology, Stupidity, and the Secret Joys of Bureaucracy* (New York: Melville House Publishing, 2015), 32.

without the main outcome of a criminal procedure, namely retribution in form of a punishment. Reconciliation procedures look more different than criminal justice when compared to other legally bound activities, such as the heterogeneous forms of public or private administration or enterprises, after purging the coercive element. On the other hand, it is hard to know what schools, workshops, factories, hospitals, theatres or public transport would look like after the abolition of wage labour and coercive disciplinary systems. Maybe the descendants of our courts will be materially and aesthetically more similar to their forerunners than the universities and dental clinics.

It is possible to imagine juridical reasoning, and a process that in most regards is similar to the adjudication of a judge, without it being coupled with violent enforcing. This is not least the modus operandi of the academic jurist when in a dogmatic mode, or when an advocate general presents her suggested judgment to the court.

I therefore argue that law might still be needed, though not in the non-violent form Loick imagines, but rather in its specifically violent and coercive form.

This might still leave some areas where violent law is deemed socially necessary. But even when these minor, although important, areas are left inside a legal order with courts, police and perhaps even prisons as enforcers, we are still in a qualitatively different situation. Law might be contained, at least in a political situation where law as violent coercion is no longer deemed necessary or seen as the only option to enforce the political will of the community. Law will then be a true exception.

The profanation of law will therefore follow a broadly similar pattern to the profanation of the religious. Many social patterns, rites and different types of liturgical action from pre-modern times are now either secularised into political forms within the state or left as minority and private forms of activity within religious communities. But this does not mean that religion as such is over. Even though Agamben's profanation thesis is correct, it does not mean, and he doesn't seem to mean, that an era of religion is over. Rather it is a shift of emphasis or primacy. Instead of being both primary and suffused into every form of moral, scientific or legal argumentation, religious belief and practices are either transformed into profaned alternatives, like the religious rite becoming a children's game or Christian ethics becoming human rights, or they simply take a minority position alongside the now hegemonic secular forms of state ideology and practice.[48] This does not form a sequential order of distinct eras, of course, but rather overlapping structures, shifting throughout history. Whether religion as an explicit political signifier is on the rise is an empirical question, and the "re-

48 Consider the a priori commitment to deism in natural science up until modern times. This is a similar dynamic in the fields of ethics or law.

sacralisation" of politics could then be a reversal of the profanation of earlier religious forms of political and social order.

The path I sketch suggests neither sudden nor gradual shifts. It does require that radical changes happen, but the question of transformative periods, or rather immediate communisation, is not given. However, it seems that considering the Soviet example in the light of the theoretical works of Pashukanis, there is at least a question of the danger of using law and state violence in a transformative period as a tool for effecting the social change that is the end goal. To put it in juridical terms: could a court develop into a nonviolent institution gradually, or could a police force gradually become noncoercive?[49] Perhaps, but in institutions that both use violence as a means at their core and constitute the bedrock of state power through their wielding of the monopoly on violence, it seems hard to imagine. The transformation of a school that now has the legal right to demand pupils to attend, as just one aspect of the violence infused in that particular institution, into a voluntary enterprise where attendance is not forced, does not seem out of reach.[50]

The profanation of law does then mean that law would start to decline in importance, and that successively fewer and fewer spheres of human activity would be ordered through law backed by coercion and violence. This might seem in the abstract to be a minor shift, just another choice of coordinating structure or organisation. But considering the trajectory contemporary society is on it would actually amount to a significant change. If any contemporary examples of social activities that have become less juridified can be put forward, I dare to say that they are the exceptions that prove the rule. We live in the epoch of law and whether we are at its peak or its penultimate moment we still do not know.

49 I have learned anecdotally that the Kurdish Rojavan government police force Asayish has the aim that all citizens should be provided with police training, with the ultimate goal of dissolving the police force and replacing it with self-managed security by the citizens themselves. Dissolving the police by making everyone a potential police officer.

50 The interconnected aspect of schooling to the reproduction of the work force and the indoctrination of work ethic and societal ideology are still problematic and critical factors. Compare to Ivan Illich, *Deschooling Society* (London: Marion Boyars, 2002).

Chapter 5

The exception of the norm in the Third Reich

(Re)reading the Nazi constitutional state of exception

Simon Lavis

Introduction: permanent (Nazi) state of exception?

In historiography and jurisprudence, Nazi Germany is the place where the exception remains the exception and the extreme situation of the Holocaust, precisely because of its emblematic status within the Third Reich, is the very thing that alienates Nazi Germany from the *Rechtsstaat* and the rule of law. However, focusing deliberations about the state of exception on the aporia of the Holocaust risks reinforcing the perception that the Holocaust, and therefore Nazism as a whole, exists outside of the 'normal' legal system as a manifestation of lawlessness – a site of 'non-law'. This, in turn, asserts a point of rupture between Nazi 'law' and 'normal' law, which is philosophically problematic and does not fully capture the historical nature of the Nazi state.[1] Instead, to understand the move from law in the 'ordinary' Nazi state to 'law' as genocide it is necessary to interrogate the juxtaposition of the abyss and the legal normal.

The boundary between law and non-law, the norm and exception, is represented in a number of ways in the Nazi state and surrounding literature. It is a temporal boundary between pre-Nazi law in the *Rechtsstaat*, under the Weimar Constitution, and Nazi rule following the takeover of power, which is commonly characterised as lawless, particularly in influential studies.[2] It is a spatial boundary between sites and institutions where the normative, legal state continued to operate, and those, such as the camp system, used to implement the Holocaust, where arbitrary, prerogative power is considered to have dominated.[3] It is also a theoretical boundary

1 Simon Lavis, 'The Distorted Jurisprudential Discourse of Nazi Law: Uncovering the "Rupture Thesis" in the Anglo-American Legal Academy', (2018) 31(4) *International Journal for the Semiotics of Law* 745.

2 See, for example, Franz Neumann, *Behemoth: The Structure and Practice of National Socialism 1933–1944*, 2nd ed. (London: Frank Cass & Co., 1967).

3 See Ernst Fraenkel, *The Dual State: A Contribution to the Theory of Dictatorship* (New York: Octagon Books, 1969 [1942]), although Fraenkel did characterise the prerogative state as part of the broader legal system.

between what constitutes valid law and what does not.[4] The state of exception, as the juridical response to a state of emergency, involves crossing the threshold between normal and exceptional legal situations, lawfulness and lawlessness, and so its examination has potential to illuminate this problematic zone in the history of Nazi legality. This chapter, therefore, is concerned with how contemporary theories of the state of exception may be used to interrogate and understand the boundary between the two sides of law in the Third Reich. In particular, it seeks to revisit Giorgio Agamben's work on the state of exception to establish what of value it can offer historians and theorists of law in Nazi Germany; how it can help us to read the juridical aporia of the Third Reich.

The Third Reich is intimately connected to Agamben's *Homo sacer* project and specifically his study of the state of exception.[5] Agamben relies heavily on the Nazi use of the state of exception to support his claims of a 'zone of indistinction' between fact and law. He locates this zone spatially in the 'camp', and specifically the Nazi concentration camp, reading Auschwitz as the paradigmatic example: 'precisely the place in which the state of exception coincides perfectly with the rule and the extreme situation becomes the very paradigm of everyday life',[6] and 'the hidden paradigm of the political space of modernity'.[7] Agamben is also heavily influenced by Carl Schmitt's writing on the state of exception, where Schmitt notoriously became a supporter of and implicated in the Nazi regime from its takeover of power in 1933.[8]

These connections invite a re-examination of the role of the exception in the Nazi legal system because of the history-theory nexus at play in both historical and jurisprudential narratives of Nazi law and Agamben's own theory. First, prevailing narratives of rupture and exceptionalism within scholarship about Nazi law, including the portrayal of the Third Reich as a fundamentally lawless state,[9] and difficulties with properly framing Nazi law

4 See the Hart-Fuller debate: H. L. A. Hart, 'Positivism and the Separation of Law and Morals' (1958) 71(4) *Harvard Law Review* 593; and Lon Fuller, 'Positivism and Fidelity to Law: A Reply to Professor Hart', (1958) 71(4) *Harvard Law Review* 630.

5 See especially the initial trilogy: Giorgio Agamben, *Homo Sacer: Sovereign Power and Bare Life*, Daniel Heller-Roazan transl. (Stanford: Stanford University Press, 1998); *Remnants of Auschwitz: The Witness and the Archive*, Daniel Heller-Roazan transl. (New York: Zone Books, 1999); and *State of Exception*, Kevin Attell transl. (Chicago, IL: University of Chicago Press, 2005).

6 Agamben, *Remnants of Auschwitz*, 113.

7 Richard Ek, 'Giorgio Agamben and the Spatialities of the Camp: An Introduction', (2006) 88 *Geografiska Annaler: Series B, Human Geography* 363, 368.

8 See, for example, Carl Schmitt, 'The Führer Protects the Law: On Adolf Hitler's Reichstag Address of 13 July 1934' in Anson Rabinach, Sander Gilman (eds), *The Third Reich Sourcebook* (Berkeley, CA: University of California Press, 2013).

9 See David Fraser, *Law after Auschwitz: Towards a Jurisprudence of the Holocaust* (Durham, NC: Carolina Academic Press, 2005); Simon Lavis, 'Nazi Law as Non-law in Academic Discourse' in Stephen Skinner (ed.), *Ideology and*

as a legal-theoretical enterprise, raise questions about whether Agamben's notion of a 'zone of indistinction' is an aid or a hindrance to a better understanding of Nazi legality. Does the positing of a theoretical, juridical space-between help to clarify the effective interpretation of the Nazi use of law or only douse it further in confusion? Second, Agamben's treatment of the historiography of the Third Reich (and of history in general) has been heavily criticised, raising questions concerning how helpful the Nazi example is for supporting Agemben's theory, and (again) how useful this model of the state of exception is for interpreting Nazi law.

This chapter evaluates how, notwithstanding criticisms, Agamben's state of exception helps us to interpret the empirical realities of exceptionality in the Nazi context that animates his concept. In light of this line of inquiry, it will make the argument that, while many of the criticisms of Agamben's treatment of Nazi history and instrumentalisation of the 'Auschwitz' paradigm are valid, his state of exception theory does help in two specific ways to further our understanding of the Nazi legal system. First, the collapse of the oppositions between law and fact into a zone of indistinction draws attention to the point where the two elements of Ernst Fraenkel's dual state collide, enabling us to develop our understanding of how the normative and prerogative states co-existed and were entwined in the Third Reich. The moment of political decision-making that is inherent in every legal decision, addressing which and how normative legal rules apply to a given set of facts, crucially is a moment of exception simultaneously within and without the law, which collapses the distinction between the exception and the (legal) rule. This moment was exploited in the Third Reich as increasing discretion was carved out by the decision-maker in each instance, to the point where the legal norm pursuant to which prerogative decisions were taken was itself determined by its discretionary form. Discretion, it might be argued, was the defining feature of the prerogative state, but this was enabled in law by the fundamental norm of the *Führerprinzip* (leader principle), and Agamben's theory assists us in elucidating the connection between prerogative power and its normative, juridical underpinnings.

Second, the state of exception helps to give legal-theoretical form to Ian Kershaw's influential explanatory historical concept 'working towards the Führer'.[10] The historical reality of the *Führerprinzip* as the controlling norm of Nazi rule, and dynamic policy radicalisation based on a dualistic relationship between the leadership and the lower ranks of the Nazi movement, which is effectively encapsulated by Kershaw's concept, can be understood juridically as the dispersed exercise of sovereign power. While Agamben's

Criminal Law: Fascist, National Socialist and Authoritarian Regimes (London: Hart, 2019).

10 Ian Kershaw, '"Working Towards the Führer." Reflections on the Nature of the Hitler Dictatorship', (1993) 2(2) *Contemporary European History* 103.

state of exception, adapted from Schmitt, problematically envisages a unified sovereign, this focus on sovereign power may be modified with reference to the exception-from-below[11]: the idea that sovereign decision-making can be understood as dispersed among a wide range of lower-level actors within the system. In Nazi Germany, despite the symbolic and concrete significance of Hitler as *Führer,* it is now well established that in many spheres the dynamic momentum of the system was enabled by a willingness and structural capacity for 'working towards the Führer'. This is illustrated by the example of the development over time and space of the concentration camp system, which was as reliant on local initiative and energy from below as it was on direct instruction from above.[12] This both exposes the problem with focusing attention in relation to the exception on a single sovereign decision-maker and further blurs the lines between the exception and the norm, such that in the Third Reich it becomes very difficult to tell the difference between the two. Through this, it is possible to obtain a clearer idea of how decisions, which may otherwise appear to persist outside of the legal system, could be seen to take juridical form in the Third Reich.

In order to advance its arguments, the next section of this chapter will briefly examine the juridical aspects of the Nazi takeover and consolidation of power to reveal the historical construction of the Nazi exception and explore how the theory of the state of exception has been used to interpret this. Following that, it will set out some of the criticisms of Agamben's theory of the state of exception, particularly in terms of its use of Nazi history, with a view to evaluating the validity of these criticisms and isolating those features of his theory it may be fruitful to explore further. It will then consider in more detail two ways the state of exception may be applied to the Third Reich in a way that is theoretically useful and takes into account the historical nature of the Nazi state. First Agamben's zone of indistinction will be used to interrogate Fraenkel's dual state model of the Third Reich. Then the usefulness of the notion of sovereignty as dispersed rather than singular and unified, with reference to Kershaw's idea of 'working towards the Führer', will be considered. Finally, it will conclude by returning to the theory of the state of exception to determine what may be salvaged from it in light of the foregoing discussions.

The idea of this research is certainly not to *legitimise* the Nazi regime, nor give any credence to the often outrageous norms, principles and outcomes that came to characterise its legal system and extra-legal conduct, but to

11 Roxanne Doty, 'States of Exception on the Mexico–U.S. Border: Security, "Decisions," and Civilian Border Patrols', (2007) 1 *International Political Sociology* 113.

12 See Jane Caplan, Nikolaus Wachsmann (eds), *Concentration Camps in Nazi Germany: The New Histories* (London: Routledge, 2010).

achieve two things. First, to understand better how and why Nazi law achieved contemporary legitimacy inside and outside of the Third Reich taking into account the necessary degree of consensus now accepted by historians to have been essential for the survival of the regime, alongside the undeniable terror and coercion.[13] Second, to explore further how to theorise the relationship between Fraenkel's observed normative and prerogative states in the Third Reich within a legal schema – to try to understand the nature of Nazi authority *as law*. This is not, as has been said, to lend Nazism any value that might be associated with the law, or at least the rule of law (which the Nazis certainly rejected), but to try to understand how law operates in the transformation of regimes such as Nazi Germany.

Constructing the Nazi exception

The history of the Nazi invocation of the exception is, initially at least, a straightforward one to tell. The constitutional story of the Nazi takeover and consolidation of power in Germany from 1933, pursuant to the provisions of the Weimar Constitution, has been narrated many times by historians and is fairly well understood, so what follows is only a very brief account of how the exception initially took legal form in the historical circumstances of the Nazi consolidation of power.

Article 48 of the persisting Weimar Constitution gave the Reich president broad powers to 'take such measures as are necessary to restore public safety and order', including temporarily suspending fundamental civil rights, 'if the public safety and order in the German Reich are considerably disturbed or endangered'.[14] By the time Hitler ascended to the role of Reich chancellor on 30 January 1933 (appointed by the president pursuant to Article 53 of the Constitution), Article 48 had already been increasingly used by President Paul von Hindenburg between 1930 and 1932 to rule by legislative decree in the face of majority opposition in the Reichstag parliament to successive, short-lived governments (also propagated by the president's Article 25 power to dissolve the Reichstag for new elections). Once Hitler had persuaded Hindenburg to grant a further dissolution of the Reichstag for new elections in order to secure majority support for his new government, emergency powers were used to issue the Decree for the Protection of the German People on 4 February 1933. This law was used to constrain the press and ban opposition meetings ahead of the forthcoming election,[15] which took place on 5 March 1933. Subsequently, the more notorious Reichstag Fire Decree (Decree for the

13 See Nathan Stoltzfus, *Hitler's Compromises: Coercion and Consensus in Nazi Germany* (New Haven, CT: Yale University Press, 2016).

14 Article 48, Weimar Constitution. The Constitution of the German Reich / August 11, 1919 / Translation of Document 2050-PS / Office of U.S. Chief of Counsel.

15 Ian Kershaw, *Hitler 1889–1936: Hubris* (London: Allen Lane, 1998), 439.

Protection of the People and State of 28 February 1933) utilised the Article 48 emergency provisions to suspend indefinitely key basic rights enshrined in the constitution. It also enabled the Reich government to override the powers of the German states (*Länder*). This decree is considered foundational to the constitution of the Third Reich. Michael Bazyler notes that it 'was never abolished during Nazi rule. In effect, Hitler ruled for the next twelve years under what amounted to *martial law*'.[16] In Ian Kershaw's view, this 'hastily constructed emergency decree amounted to the charter of the Third Reich'.[17]

Subsequently, however, on 24 March 1933, the passage of the Law to Remove the Distress of the People and the State (the Enabling Act) amended the Weimar Constitution to allow laws to be passed by the executive government without engaging the legislature, including laws that deviated from the constitution itself (within certain limits), thereby dissolving the distinction between administrative measures and ordinary law.[18] This was not passed using the Article 48 emergency powers or previously enacted emergency legislation, but pursuant to the otherwise ordinary Article 76 constitutional amendment powers, requiring a two-thirds majority of the Reichstag to assent to amend the constitution. It was, therefore, not strictly a formal part of the state of exception, but was made possible by the factual consequences of previous emergency legislation; for example, the impact of the 4 and 28 February decrees on the composition of the Reichstag following the March 1933 election.

The Enabling Act explicitly left the powers of the Reich president untouched (Article 2), but this obstacle to total power was removed on the event of Hindenburg's death on 2 August 1934, with the passage of the Law Concerning the Head of State of the German Reich, dated 1 August 1934. This combined the offices of chancellor and president and made Hitler the *Führer* and Reich chancellor, including supreme commander of the armed forces. This law, of formally questionable constitutional status, was affirmed by plebiscite on 19 August 1934.[19] It was an exception within the exception to the extent that it fell outside of the provisions of both Article 48 and the Enabling Act. It was

16 Michael Bazyler, *Holocaust, Genocide, and the Law: A Quest for Justice in a Post-Holocaust World* (Oxford: OUP, 2016), 6. [Emphasis added]. Martial law generally refers to the control of the state by military – as opposed to civilian – forces in an emergency; the suspension of the law to ensure a return to the law. In English law, 'neither more nor less than the will of the general who commands the army. In fact, martial law meant no law at all'; Duke of Wellington, 1851, quoted in Leon Radzinowicz, *A History of English Criminal Law and its Administration from 1750. Volume 4: Grappling for Control* (London: Stevens & Sons, 1968), 143–144.

17 Kershaw, *Hubris*, 459.

18 Peter Caldwell, 'National Socialism and Constitutional Law: Carl Schmitt, Otto Koellreutter, and the Debate over the Nature of the Nazi State, 1933–1937', (1994) 16 *Cardozo L. Rev.* 399, 413.

19 Kershaw, *Hubris*, 524–525.

arguably, therefore, in Schmittian terms a moment of constituent power.[20] At this point Hitler was 'institutionally unchallengeable, backed by the "big battalions" adored by much of the population. He had secured total power.'[21]

From this brief account we see that both legally constructed normative and emergency executive powers were utilised by President Hindenburg under Hitler's influence, and subsequently by Hitler himself, in a way that led to the undermining of the Weimar Constitution and the Nazi consolidation of power. In terms of the theory of the exception, there are different ways of understanding the significance of the use of emergency powers in this period, depending on whether one adopts a conventional, Schmittian or Agambenian view of the relationship between law and fact.

A conventional approach, which upholds the distinction between the law and the exception and emphasises the former as the normal situation, and represents the orthodox interpretation of the Nazi state, sees the initiation of the exception as the undermining of the legal and constitutional order. According to this, the Nazis exploited the Article 48 emergency powers to consolidate their grip on power, constructing a permanent state of exception through the use of increasingly quasi-legal and extra-legal measures. While shadows of the pre-existing legal system remained, much of Nazi rule in areas that mattered most to the leadership (e.g. racial policy) took place within an essentially lawless prerogative state. It was situation of fact unrelated to the law; Bazyler's twelve years of martial law.[22] The state of emergency, initially constituted by legal provisions was abused to enable the regime to act on the basis of an enduring suspension of the legal order. On this interpretation, the Reichstag Fire Decree was Kershaw's 'charter for the Third Reich' precisely because it *suspended* key aspects of the constitution, but was not a constitution as the constitution itself was now in abeyance.

A Schmittian approach, by contrast, holds that norm and exception maintain a relationship to one another. It places more emphases on the primacy and juridical significance of the exception in making possible the normal constitution, and the importance of the sovereign who is not subject to but stands in relation to the normative legal order because of its power to decide on the existence, scope and nature of the exception.[23] In this way, 'Schmitt's understanding of the state of exception is not quite a legal black hole, a juridically produced void. Rather, it is a space beyond law, a space which is revealed when law recedes, leaving the state, represented by the sovereign, to act'.[24] In Schmitt's writing the constitutional exception can take two forms:

20 Carl Schmitt, *Political Theology: Four Chapters on the Concept of Sovereignty*, George Schwab transl. (Chicago, IL: University of Chicago Press, 2005 [1922]).
21 Kershaw, *Hubris*, 524–526.
22 See fn 16 above.
23 See Schmitt, *Political Theology*.
24 David Dyzenhaus, 'Schmitt v. Dicey: Are States of Emergency Inside or Outside the Legal Order?', (2006) 27(5) *Cardozo Law Review* 2005, 2015.

commissarial dictatorship and sovereign dictatorship, and in both instantiations 'the juridical order is preserved even when the law itself is suspended'.[25] In a commissarial dictatorship,

> although the commissarial dictator acts outside the law, their actions retain a connection to the legal order in two ways: the existing constitution is not abolished but temporarily suspended; and the terms of its suspension are regulated by 'norms of the realisation of law'.[26]

Here the constitution is suspended in order to preserve the constitution; the law 'remains in force and is regulated by "techno-practical rules" that derive from that legal order'.[27]

In a sovereign dictatorship, 'the state of exception signifies the exercise of "constituent power": in effect, it is a moment where no constitution or law applies other than the sovereign decision itself'.[28] It is

> a revolutionary organization that aims to overthrow the existing legal order and produce the conditions in which a new constitution can be created. A sovereign dictatorship thus acts 'outside' the norms of the law because, by definition, it cannot be regulated by an existing constitution.[29]

In this form a connection to the juridical order persists because 'the law exists in the "minimal form" of an actually existent constituent power, which has not yet achieved a formal existence as a constituted legal system'.[30]

The Article 48 provisions in the Weimar Constitution naturally make no mention of using the emergency measures to reshape the constitution itself, referring instead to the *restoration* of public safety and order and the *temporary* suspension of selected fundamental rights. However, whatever the intentions of President Hindenburg in invoking Article 48 in February 1933 (and on prior occasions), Hitler made it clear that the Nazis intended to use constitutional methods to obtain power, not to restore the constitution, but rather to achieve the aim of entirely re-constituting the state to conform to the Nazi vision.[31]

25 Stephen Humphreys, 'Legalizing Lawlessness: On Giorgio Agamben's State of Exception', (2006) 17(3) *EJIL* 677, 680.
26 McLoughlin, 'The Fiction of Sovereignty and the Real State of Exception: Giorgio Agamben's Critique of Carl Schmitt', (2016) 12(3) *Law, Culture and the Humanities* 509, 514–515.
27 Ibid., 515.
28 Humphreys, 'Legalizing Lawlessness', 680.
29 McLoughlin, 'The Fiction of Sovereignty', 515.
30 Ibid.
31 See Hitler, September 1930, quoted in Jeremy Noakes, Geoffrey Pridham, *Nazism 1919–1945, Volume 1: The Rise to Power 1919–1934* (Exeter: University of Exeter Press, 1998), 90. See also Peter Caldwell, 'National Socialism and Constitutional Law', 399.

Schmitt's distinction between the commissarial and sovereign forms of exceptional dictatorship is not straightforward to apply to the facts of the Nazi takeover as, while constitutional emergency measures were used to create the exception, a largely ordinary law was used to begin to construct a new, Nazi constitution. The Reichstag Fire Decree appears, on the face of it, to be a commissarial instrument; a temporary delegation of extraordinary power to defend the state against acts of violence and restore public safety and order, using the extant constitutional state of emergency powers. The Nazis' explicit intentions in relation to the state and constitution, and their apparent manufacturing of the attack on the Reichstag building that immediately brought about the decree, however, suggest it was used by Hitler as a step towards sovereign dictatorship, allowing the conditions to be created in which a new constitution could be forged. Nevertheless, this decree was the instrument that suspended much of the constitution, but not, legally at least, the instrument pursuant to which the state was shaped according to the Nazi vision.

The March 1933 Enabling Act represents a clearer manifestation of sovereign dictatorship, even though it was passed using the ordinary constitutional amendment powers and with the consent of the legislature, albeit somewhat neutered in its opposition by violence, intimidation and the impact of preceding, exceptional legal measures. This instrument changed the way ordinary positive laws could be made and largely exempted them from pre-existing constitutional limitations, thereby underpinning a new Nazi constitutional framework for the state. Once subsequent laws are taken into account, including the Law Against the Founding of New Parties of 14 July 1933 (passed using the cabinet's Enabling Act powers), which made Germany a single-party state, and the aforementioned Law Concerning the Head of State of the German Reich, the Nazi exception may be more clearly viewed as a sovereign dictatorship, as total power under a new constitutional order was achieved. It is not, however, a simple case of the sovereign exploiting the powers bestowed by a commissarial exception to establish a sovereign dictatorship, both because the emergency powers were not directly used to fashion a new constitutional order and, if there was one locus of sovereign power, until August 1934 it was President Hindenburg rather than Chancellor Hitler.

The temptation, which also leads to the description of the Reichstag Fire Decree as a charter of the Third Reich, is to view the twelve years of Nazi rule as an extended and exploited form of commissarial exception; an exception initially constituted by the law, which goes rogue. According to this model, because the Nazis ruled largely by individual decrees and no new codified constitution was promulgated, the legal basis of the Nazi state was the suspension of the existing constitutional order: the removal of rights and liberties and the undermining of the independent authority of the *Länder*. It was the instrumental, ad hoc and decisionistic rule of the sovereign *Führer*, lacking any coherent constitutional basis or underlying legal principles.[32] This rule, for some, becomes so arbitrary and far removed from legal justification that it was essentially lawless. However, this view is problematized not only by the Nazis' own constitutional and ideological logic and attempts by Schmitt and others to rationalise the nature of the Nazi constitution, but also the normative content of Nazi laws and their continuing use up to and including in the Holocaust.[33]

A preferred Schmittian jurisprudential interpretation is to see the constitutive legal measures from the Enabling Act to the August 1934 law as an effective charter for the Third Reich. On this reading, the Nazis tore down the constituted power represented in the Weimar Constitution, and exercised the (allegedly but questionably supported) constituent power of the polity in a moment in which only the sovereign decision of the *Führer* existed, which then took shape in the form of a new *Führer* order. Nevertheless, this interpretation presents a number of challenges. First, it requires us to take Nazi (legal) ideology seriously, to assert that the Nazi leadership had in mind more than the instrumental wielding of absolute political power under the cover of a pseudo-legal cloak; that there was some form of coherence between ideology and legal principle. Second, even accepting this, the Nazi legal ideology, in the form of the *Führerprinzip,* rendered supreme the actions of the *Führer* as the direct manifestation of the *völkisch* will of the people, so it is a challenge to differentiate meaningfully in the Nazi context between arbitrary decisionism and a newly constituted state. This also makes it difficult to conceptualise Nazi rule theoretically with respect to the state of exception. In either case, however, Schmitt's approach emphasises the juridical nature of the exercise of sovereign power in the realm of the exception, which always persists in relation to a normal constitutional order, countering the view that it is a legal black hole, an essentially lawless space.

Agamben's approach to the exception addresses directly the challenge presented by the realisation that the Nazi exception is not entirely constituted by the suspension of the ordinary law, nor does it explicitly create a new constitutional order, and nor is it entirely lawless; so it does not conform neatly to either conventional or Schmittian models of the state of emergency. Agamben builds on Schmitt's insights into the role of the sovereign and the juridical nature of exceptional power, but interrogates more closely the border

32 See Neumann *Behemoth.* Cf. Simon Lavis, 'Nazi Law as Pure Instrument: Natural Law, (Extra-) Legal Terror, and the Neglect of Ideology' in Michał Gałędek and Anna Klimaszewska (eds), *Modernisation, National Identity, and Legal Instrumentalism: Studies in Comparative Legal History. Volume II: Public Law* (Leiden: Brill, 2019).

33 See David Fraser, 'Criminal Law in Auschwitz: Positivism, Natural Law and the Career of SS Lawyer Konrad Morgen' in Stephen Skinner (ed.), *Ideology and Criminal Law: Fascist, National Socialist and Authoritarian Regimes* (London: Hart, 2019).

between the norm and the exception and finds both the conventional and Schmittian interpretations ultimately unsatisfactory for illuminating this boundary. He questions how the legal order can contain a lacuna unrelated to law, but also how the suspension of the law can be contained within it. This leads to his determination that 'the state of exception is neither external nor internal to the juridical order, and the problem of defining it concerns precisely a threshold, or a zone of indifference, where inside and outside do not exclude one another but rather blur with each other'.[34]

For Agamben it is the very case of Nazi Germany that illuminates the zone of indifference between the inside and outside of the law and renders Schmitt's analysis of the exception inadequate because it confounds the categories of commissarial and sovereign dictatorship and the way Schmitt conceptualises the relationship between the rule and the exception. Agamben asserts that in 1933, 'Germany found itself technically in a situation of sovereign dictatorship, which should have led to the definitive abolition of the Weimar Constitution and the establishment of a new constitution',[35] but this did not occur. Instead, the Nazi regime 'allowed the existing constitution … to subsist and … placed beside the legal constitution a second structure, often not legally formalized, that could exist alongside the other *because* of the state of exception',[36] thereby conflating the rule and exception: 'this confusion between the exception and the rule was precisely what the Third Reich had concretely brought about, and the obstinacy with which Hitler pursued the organization of his "dual state" without promulgating a new constitution is proof of it'.[37]

According to Agamben, Schmitt's theory does not account for this situation; 'the machine can no longer function … the rule, which now coincides with what it lives by, devours itself'[38]. As McLoughlin states:

> By indefinitely suspending the law, the Nazi party produced a 'normal' constitutional structure characterized by the profound legal indeterminacy of the emergency situation … . Once emergency and normality, exception and law, are rendered absolutely undecidable, the sovereign is 'no longer capable of performing the task that *Political Theology* assigned to it': that of distinguishing between exception and law on the basis of a distinction between emergency and normality.[39]

In light of this, Agamben collapses the distinction between law and exception and eschews the relationship between the legal and extra-legal in the

34 Agamben, *State of Exception*, 23.
35 Ibid., 58.
36 Ibid., 48 [Emphasis added].
37 Ibid., 58.
38 Ibid.
39 McLoughlin, 'The Fiction of Sovereignty', 518.

exception, so '[e]very fiction of a nexus between violence and law disappears here; there is nothing but a zone of anomie, in which a violence without any juridical form acts'.[40] Agamben, with reference to Walter Benjamin, shifts the focus slightly away from the law, as 'while Schmitt harnesses the power of the exception back to the juridical order, Benjamin releases that power into a new politics beyond law and beyond the state',[41] but with purportedly much more radical implications for both law and politics than are propounded by the conventional approach.

Agamben's Nazi problem

There is ostensibly an opportunity with Agamben's focus on interrogating the border between norm and exception for enhancing our legal theoretical and legal historical understanding of the role of the exception in the Third Reich, and consequently of Nazi law and its implications for the modern state. However, Agamben is not without his detractors in this area. Indeed, significant disciplinary and methodological differences mean that major historians of Nazi Germany have not engaged with Agamben's philosophical writings or, where they have, it is often via a single intervention about *Remnants of Auschwitz*. Nevertheless, there are some scholars who have critiqued Agamben's work. This section will outline and address some key criticisms of Agamben's representation and treatment of the Third Reich in his writing.

We have seen that Agamben's chief concern with Schmitt's theory of the exception is that his efforts 'amount to a denial of the existence of an extralegal reality: the existing "juridical order" becomes total'.[42] Agamben uses the Third Reich to explain and illustrate the challenge Schmitt faces; the blurring of fact and law in Nazi Germany: 'Not only is the law issued by the Führer definable neither as rule nor as exception and neither as law nor as fact. There is more: in this law, the formation of a rule … and the execution of a rule … are no longer distinguishable moments'.[43] So, for Agamben, in this situation the fiction on which the relationship between the law and the exception is based becomes unsustainable, with catastrophic consequences. The state of exception

> is founded on the essential fiction according to which anomie … is still related to the juridical order and the power to suspend the norm has an immediate hold on life. As long as the two elements remain correlated yet conceptually, temporally, and subjectively distinct … their dialectic–though founded on a fiction–can nevertheless function in some way. But

40 Agamben, *State of Exception*, 59.
41 Catherine Mills, *The Philosophy of Agamben* (London: Routledge, 2014), 66.
42 Humphreys, 'Legalizing Lawlessness', 682.
43 Agamben, *Homo Sacer*, 98.

> when they tend to coincide in a single person, when the state of exception, in which they are bound and blurred together, becomes the rule, then the juridico-political system transforms itself into a killing machine.[44]

Agamben, famously, makes a leap from the operation of the exception in the mass killings in the camp system of the Holocaust to a claim that 'the voluntary creation of a permanent state of emergency … has become one of the essential practices of contemporary states, including so-called democratic ones'.[45] Historians and theorists, however, have questioned both Agamben's elucidation of the Nazi exception and his conceptualisation of modern state practice in this way. Often, for scholars of the Third Reich, Agamben's use of Auschwitz as paradigmatic of the camp system and the 'nomos of the modern' is the focus of criticism. He is accused, among other things, of using poetic, abstract and non-concrete writing, adopting an unhistorical or ahistorical methodology focused on etymology rather than evidence, fetishising law and sovereignty, and simultaneously exceptionalising and universalising the Holocaust. There is only scope here to recapitulate briefly the most relevant of these criticisms.

A key framing of many of his detractors include that Agamben's version of the Nazi state and Auschwitz is both un-historical and un-legal. For the former, in the two senses that it is meta-historical – it does not work in historical time – and it is not an accurate description of the relevant history. For the latter, in the two senses that it does not correctly capture how law works, and it is not an accurate description of the relevant law. For example, Heike Schotten argues that 'Agamben indulges in a kind of "Holocaust exceptionalism" wherein the Holocaust is both the center and the apex of politics, political events, and political history (if not also of political "evil," a term that proliferates in Holocaust exceptionalist discourses)',[46] thereby simultaneously exceptionalising and universalising the Holocaust in unhistorical ways. Alison Ross has highlighted the extent to which Agamben appears to focus on defending his ideas rather than explaining events: 'as political theory Agamben's work founders because his core fidelity is not to explain complex events but to defend concepts with dubious explanatory value'.[47] This indicates, for Ross, 'perhaps that his theory is too speculative, too ready to forgo the task of analyzing actual practices and institutions in its "philosophical" attachment to articulate the "ultimate" or the "fundamental"'.[48] Esther Marion goes further down the same path, to claim that 'Agamben's

44 Agamben, *State of Exception*, 86.
45 Ibid., 2.
46 C. Heike Schotten, 'Against Totalitarianism: Agamben, Foucault, and the Politics of Critique', (2015) 20 *Foucault Studies* 155, 178.
47 Alison Ross, 'Agamben's Political Paradigm of the Camp: Its Features and Reasons', (2012) 19(3) *Constellations* 422, 425.
48 Ibid., 431.

analysis … effaces the very historical constitution of this aporia, which he structurally appropriates for assimilation into his philosophical discourse'.[49]

Mark Mazower highlights a number of objections to Agamben's analysis in relation to the historical specificities of Nazism, while also questioning his selection of Auschwitz as a privileged historical paradigm.[50] For example,

> Agamben does not really talk about extermination. He invokes the emblematic power of Auschwitz—its 'uniqueness'—yet his accounts of camp life come back again and again to life in the concentration camps, not the death camps, and his remarks about 'indeterminate life' only make sense in the context of the former.[51]

Mazower also highlights Agamben's reductionist tendencies when using the history of the camp system, for example that 'the idea that the camps were designed to be a deliberate experiment in metaphysical domination can be regarded as nothing more than a gross simplification'.[52]

The historian (although not ordinarily of Nazi Germany) Ichiro Takayoshi has gone further than most, systematically critiquing the factual basis of Agamben's analysis, with reference to *Homo Sacer*. Takayoshi asserts that Agamben's use of three key Nazi examples – the euthanasia programme, camp system and Nazi law – is flawed on a historical level,[53] which undermines his more profound philosophical claims. With regard to the state of exception, Takayoshi invokes Fraenkel's dual state to argue that the

> vapor of indistinguishability [between exception and norm] is dispelled once one reformulates this assertion as follows: during the Nazi rule, the state of exception … was prolonged, and in this very limited, literal sense, routinized (but never normalized). Vital components of the Weimar constitution were gradually dismantled and Nazi legal theoreticians employed juridical casuistry to construct a new theory of state. Nevertheless, the fact remains that the *Rechtsstaat* was never abrogated.[54]

This was because 'Hitler had an instinctive aversion to any legal constraints on his freedom of action and thus showed no desire for "normalizing" the

49 Esther Marion, 'The Nazi Genocide and the Writing of the Holocaust Aporia: Ethics and *Remnants of Auschwitz*', (2006) 121(4) *MLN* 1009, 1009.
50 Mark Mazower, 'Foucault, Agamben: Theory and the Nazis', (2008) 35(1) *Boundary* 2, 23, 31.
51 Ibid., 29.
52 Ibid., 31
53 Ichiro Takayoshi, 'Can Philosophy Explain Nazi Violence? Giorgio Agamben and the Problem of the "Historico-Philosophical" Method', (2011) 13(1–2) *Journal of Genocide Research* 47, 50–59.
54 Ibid., 56.

exception ... preferring instead to disregard the old legal system wherever expedient'.[55] In this system, the norm continued to exist alongside the 'sphere of lawlessness' that constituted the prerogative state, while Hitler as sovereign 'exercised the jurisdiction over jurisdictions and decided on the eligibility of its subjects for membership in the völkisch community'.[56] Ultimately, then, law and exception did not become indistinguishable but 'became even more sharply partitioned from each other. For the German state had every reason to be invested in policing the border between the two, in the manipulation of which lay one main source of Nazi violence'.[57]

This insistence on the clear distinction between law and lawlessness in the Third Reich is a fundamental feature of Takayoshi's critique of Agamben's merger of the two into a hybrid of fact and law. He contends that when Agamben takes his analysis of Nazi law into the camps, he 'is ascribing his far-fetched characterization ... which barely does full justice to the Führer law, to the camp, which was not merely distinct from legalized terror but found itself often in a complex mode of rivalry with the legal system'.[58] This general criticism is perhaps most tellingly employed in relation to the concrete example of the euthanasia programme, where Takayoshi asserts that

> the Third Reich, in the state of exception, did not strip the incurably ill of legal protection and kill them lawfully. A group of individuals possessing no legal authority broke the domestic law and murdered at least five thousand chronically ill children and over one hundred thousand adult psychiatry patients ... . Hitler could have issued a law, prescribing that the mentally and physically disabled be put to death because they posed a dead burden on the state (*Ballastexistenzen*). Instead of turning the incurably ill into 'homo sacer', however, Hitler chose to launch a clandestine operation. Drawing on the work of Lothar Gruchmann, Ian Kershaw notes that 'Even according to the legal theories of the time, Hitler's mandate could not be regarded as a formal Führer decree and did not, therefore, possess the character of law'. In this regard, there is an illuminating contrast between the 'euthanasia action' and the forced sterilization: the latter was a 'public procedure based on expert tribunals' and the former was a covert, illegal operation.[59]

In the case of the euthanasia programme, then, 'Hitler took great care to sidestep the normal administrative and legislative branches of the Reich government', to commit a crime that 'violated the domestic law of the Third Reich, however

55 Ibid.
56 Ibid.
57 Ibid., 56.
58 Ibid., 59. Cf. Fraser, 'Criminal Law in Auschwitz' in terms of the legal continuities between 'legalised' terror and the Holocaust.
59 Takayoshi, 'Can philosophy explain Nazi violence?', 52.

perverted it had already been'.[60] Takayoshi is also highly critical of Agamben's interpretation and application of Schmitt's writings, primarily because of Agamben's tendency to take Schmitt's claims at face value, thereby 'assume[ing] that their writings are accurate, reliable substitutes for the political and legal reality'.[61] So, if 'Schmitt wrote that fact and law became indistinguishable in the Third Reich, Agamben takes this statement to be the objective description of the historical situations, ruling out the possibility that Schmitt, like many other Nazi jurists, had vested interests in concealing the reality where law was, to their embarrassment, still distinguishable from fact'.[62]

The historical examples Takayoshi uses to question Agamben's arguments are convincing in so far as they are grounded in some sound historiographical evidence. Fraenkel's dual state, which implies the never complete destruction of the pre-existing, normative constitutional order of the state coupled with an always ad hoc, prerogative approach to new administrative orders and decrees, provides a good analytical account of the operation of the Nazi state. The description of a complex, sometimes conflictual relationship between the SS-run camp system and the regular legal system is a fair one, although the extent to which this can be used to support a clear differentiation between legal and extra-legal terror, normative and prerogative states is less certain. The example of the euthanasia programme does show that the Nazis sometimes chose not to propagate regular laws in certain areas, and indeed acted in breach of the existing legal framework, although this raises questions about what precisely constituted 'law' in the Nazi state. Finally, there is a good case for treating Schmitt's statements about Nazi law with extreme caution, given his association with the regime.[63]

However, the historical situation in the Third Reich does not provide as clear-cut a rebuttal of Agamben's argument as Takayoshi asserts. The endorsement of the conventional state of exception narrative is problematic in light of the ideological imperatives driving the new legal regime. This makes it possible to see some commonality across the alleged chasm between legal and extra-legal terror, the latter of which is seen to be the sole domain within which the camps operated. It calls into question whether deliberately hiding the euthanasia programme orders behind unusual instruments even for the Nazis, for fear of adverse public response, necessarily meant it fell outside of the broader legal norms of the system. In this context, Takayoshi's critique elides Agamben's claim about the undecidability of facts and norms, which meant that actions taken in the formalistically extra-legal sphere, but in the service of Nazi ideology, were unpunishable within the legal system and so not against the law in any meaningful sense.

60 Ibid., 53.
61 Ibid., 59.
62 Ibid.
63 See, for example, Benjamin A. Schupmann, *Carl Schmitt's State and Constitutional Theory: A Critical Analysis* (Oxford: OUP, 2017).

Re-reading the Nazi Constitutional State

The idea that the exception, particularly as exemplified in Nazi Germany, cannot have juridical form represents a paradigm of law, and more importantly lawlessness, which disrupts and obfuscates our understanding of Nazi legality.[64] While the criticisms discussed in the previous section expose significant problems with his use of Nazi Germany and 'Auschwitz' to support his project, by narrowing the scope of the inquiry considerably Agamben's evaluation of the state of exception can help to overcome the conundrum of a system of rule that appears to be at once both lawful (law-full) and lawless (law-less).[65] This section focuses on two ways in which, notwithstanding the weaknesses identified, Agamben's approach may be used to better understand the role of law in the Nazi regime, both of which are based to an extent on his willingness to take Nazi legal ideology seriously. Perhaps it should not be taken as literally as Agamben, who occasionally appears to accept too readily Schmitt's sometimes self-serving juridical justifications for the nature of Nazi rule after his conversion to the National Socialist cause, but seriously enough to interpret Nazi law as something more than a pure and cynical instrument of power and terror.[66]

The first is to use Agamben's idea of a 'zone of indistinction' to interrogate and advance Fraenkel's 'dual state' model of Nazi rule, which remains the pre-eminent and most enduring conceptualisation of Nazism as a legal regime,[67] but which arguably provides an incomplete legal-theoretical account of the Nazi state. The second is to use a refinement of the connection between sovereignty and the state of exception, which is advanced by Agamben based on Schmitt's writings, to try to make jurisprudential sense of key legal and functional concepts that were at the heart of the regime: the *Führerprinzip* and 'working towards the Führer'.

64 See fn 9 above.

65 Michael Stolleis, 'Law and Lawyers Preparing the Holocaust', (2007) 3 *Annual Review of Law and Social Science* 213. See also Simon Lavis, 'The Conundrum of Nazi Law: An Historiographical Challenge to the Anglo-American Jurisprudential Representation of the Nazi Past' (PhD, University of Nottingham, 2015 [unpublished]), available at http://eprints.nottingham.ac.uk/29061/1/Thesis_Final_April%202015_Hardbound%20Final_4118996.pdf

66 See Lavis, 'Nazi Law as Pure Instrument'.

67 Fraenkel, *The Dual State*. For a compelling recent attempt to revive Fraenkel's dual state theory for legal and political theory in relation to the Third Reich and beyond, see Jens Meierhenrich, *The Remnants of the Rechtsstaat: An Ethnography of Nazi Law* (Oxford: OUP, 2018).

Excepting the dual state

Agamben's willingness to interrogate the distinction between law and lawlessness in relation to the exception is helpful for problematising the influential 'criminal state' or 'rupture thesis' narrative around the Third Reich[68] and for understanding the relationship and delineation between legal and extra-legal measures in the Nazi regime. The question Agamben aims to address is how to understand a system where *form* and *force* of law become confused; where the formal requirements of law are hollowed out to the extent that formality has little meaning, but does not simply become the force of law absent its form because the validity of law in the system depends on something beyond or other than formal requirements. Applied to the Third Reich, this relates to the extent to which the pre-existing constitutional norms of the Weimar Republic continued to be in force (variously with and without application), while the new, Nazi law was, arguably, in places in application without always being normatively in force.[69]

The relevance and usefulness of this aspect of Agamben's work is best illustrated with reference to Fraenkel's dual state. This model recognised the parallel operation of both a residue of the pre-existing legal regime – the normative state – and the new, arbitrary regime – the prerogative state – representing 'a division between the existing constitutional structure and a system of extraordinary administrative and executive powers that operated outside or in contradiction to the established norms'.[70] Fraenkel rejected Franz Neumann's signification of the Nazi state as lawless[71] and instead incorporated both elements of the state within the conceptual realm of 'law'. However, notwithstanding his consideration of the doctrine of 'communal natural law',[72] which, he argued, 'is not in conflict with the arbitrary regime of the Prerogative State. Rather it presupposes its existence, for only the community and nothing but the community is of value',[73] Fraenkel does distinguish between the operation of legal norms and the assertion of prerogative political power, essentially placing the two states on separate juridical footings. There is some attempt to account for

68 Frederick DeCoste, 'Hitler's Conscience, Redemptive Political Emotions, and the Politics of Fear', (2012) 3 *Passions in Context* 1, 6–7; David Fraser, 'Evil Law, Evil Lawyers: From the *Justice Case* to the Torture Memos', (2012) 3.2 *Jurisprudence* 391; David Fraser, '(De)Constructing the Nazi State: Criminal Organizations and the Constitutional Theory of the International Military Tribunal', (2016–2017) 39 *Loy. L.A. Int'l & Comp. L. Rev.* 117. See also Lavis, 'The Distorted Jurisprudential Discourse of Nazi Law'.

69 Agamben, *State of Exception*, 36.

70 Richard Overy, *The Dictators: Hitler's Germany, Stalin's* Russia (London: Penguin, 2005), 62.

71 Neumann, *Behemoth.*

72 Fraenkel, *The Dual State*, ch 3 of Part II.

73 Ibid., 141.

both the role of elements of Nazi ideology in Nazi legality and its presence within the overall system of the prerogative state – a sphere of governance ostensibly outside the legal realm – but a distinction is drawn across the boundary separating the two states, between law and politics:

> since martial law has become permanent in Germany, exceptions to the normal law are continually made. It must be presumed that all spheres of life are subjected to regulation by law. Whether the decision in an individual case is made in accordance with the law or with 'expediency' is entirely in the hands of those in whom sovereign power is vested.[74]

However, too much of a difference is arguably constructed between the two systems, whereas they were not always functionally easily to differentiate, increasingly united by an ideology which permeated the legal system as a whole. As Michael Stolleis has made clear, 'it is a myth that some areas [of law] remained entirely untouched by the political claims of the system',[75] while it has been observed that 'the more closely we look at the mechanisms of the *Führerstaat*, the more categories such as "normative" and "prerogative state" … tend to lose their obvious meanings'.[76] Fraser's research into the role of law in the Holocaust, in the camp system, leads him to suggest an addition to the dual state that recognises the normativity underpinning the prerogative state as well as the mutual presence of both states with the structures engaged in the Holocaust.[77]

To return to Agamben, the focus on the borderland between legal and extra-legal provides the means to question such fine distinctions and may, in this case, encourage the drawing of the boundary between law and politics beyond the confines of the dual state, wherein both portions belong to a unified legal realm. The ideology of the regime was seen to inform a normativity underpinning the normative and prerogative states by the Nazis. For example:

> The law itself is nothing other than the expression of the communal order in which the people live and which derives from the Führer. The Führer law makes concrete the unwritten principles of the *völkisch* communal life. It is therefore impossible to measure the laws of the Führer against a

74 Ibid., 57.
75 Stolleis, 'Law and Lawyers Preparing the Holocaust', 216.
76 Thomas Schaarschmidt, 'Mobilizing German Society for War: The National Socialist *Gaue*' in Martina Steber and Bernhard Gotto (eds), *Visions of Community in Nazi Germany: Social Engineering and Private Lives* (Oxford: OUP, 2014), 102.
77 Fraser, 'Criminal Law in Auschwitz', 35.

> higher concept of the law because every Führer law is a direct expression of this *völkisch* concept of the law.[78]

While the Nazi's own legal justifications for the effectively absolute power of the *Führer* should be treated with care, incorporating the regime's ideology helps us to move past a key obstacle presented by the parallel existence of both old and new systems: did the Nazis found a new constitutional order or act entirely within an (increasingly expansive) suspension of the existing order? An argument for the latter is that the Nazis did not formally institute a new constitution or sets of legal codes in their ideological image. However, as Peter Caldwell has asserted, 'Nazism was not a movement of opportunism without coherent principles—rather, its very *principle* was a kind of constitutional opportunism',[79] and so 'Nazi anticonstitutionalism … was not merely an example of "pragmatism" or a "lack of principles," but rather an essential part of the National Socialist world view, manifested in real institutions as well as theory'.[80]

The result of this is perhaps better seen as a functionally hybrid – rather than a dual – system with an at times thin, but significant, connection to law across all of its façets. Decrees, orders, commands and other measures implemented by the regime, including those which infringed some of the basic principles of the rule of law such as non-retroactivity of criminal law, are not, it may be argued, ordinary legal rules. Nevertheless, those decrees, orders, commands and other measures were from early on the basic, ordinary norms of the Nazi legal system; i.e. they had full legal force, were posited correctly according to the (formally sparse) rules of the system, and persisted as commonplace rather than exceptional elements of the system. By recognising the conflation of law and non-law in the wake of the Nazi institution of the state of exception, and acknowledging it as a deliberate, ideological position capable of constituting a juridical order, Agamben's 'zone of indistinction' may paradoxically be treated as an invitation to study further the legal-historical constitution of the Nazi order, even while he attempts to escape from the jurisprudential hegemony over life that this implies, and in spite of the flaws in his representation of Nazi history.

The multi-levelled sovereignty of the Führerprinzip

Kershaw used the phrase 'working towards the Führer', borrowed from a 21 February 1934 speech by Werner Willikens, state secretary in the Prussian

78 Ernst Rudolf Huber, quoted in Jeremy Noakes, Geoffrey Pridham, *Nazism 1919–1945, Volume 2: State, Economy and Society 1933–1939* (Exeter: University of Exeter Press, 1998), 282.

79 Caldwell, 'National Socialism and Constitutional Law', fn 6, 400–401.

80 Ibid., 400.

Agriculture Ministry, to capture how the relationship between Hitler as *Führer* and the people of Nazi Germany operated. As such, it both explains the cumulative radicalisation that the regime engendered and encapsulates the functional nature of an administration that appears at once both extremely autocratic and polycratic.[81] As an explanatory concept for the Nazi state, it has proved hugely influential among historians, and has advanced academic understanding of the regime enormously.[82] The crux of the explanatory power of the concept is in describing the interplay between the different levels of hierarchy and engagement with the administration, in driving the regime forward and contributing to its radicalisation. Its achievement in doing so is in not diminishing the importance of the central focal point of Hitler's leadership while maintaining a prominent role for Nazi ideology. As Kershaw explains:

> Through 'working towards the Führer', initiatives were taken, pressures created, legislation instigated – all in ways which fell into line with what were taken to be Hitler's aims, and without the dictator necessarily having to dictate. The result was continuing radicalization of policy in a direction which brought Hitler's own ideological imperatives more plainly into view as practicable policy options.[83]

Therefore, 'working towards the Führer' brings to the fore an important aspect of the way the regime operated that raises doubts about the absolute, decisionistic sovereignty of Hitler. Yes, Hitler had the power and authority to take any decisions he wished, but this did not mean he took all decisions. Indeed, although it placed Hitler at the apex of the hierarchy, the leader principle – according to Peter Caldwell one of the two key tenets of Nazi rule[84] – empowered leaders at all levels to make independent decisions that were binding on those below them: 'each member of the hierarchy owed absolute obedience to those above and exercised authority over those below'.[85]

Consequently, the *Führerprinzip* does not exclusively refer to the absolute sovereignty of Hitler, and the idea of 'working towards the Führer' suggests a

81 Ian Kershaw '"Working Towards the Führer"' in Kershaw, *Hubris* (see page 529 for the origin of the phrase).

82 See, for example, Anthony McElligott and Tim Kirk (eds), *Working towards the Führer: Essays in Honour of Sir Ian Kershaw* (Manchester: Manchester University Press, 2004). See also Dan Stone, *Histories of the Holocaust* (Oxford: OUP, 2010), at page 55.

83 Kershaw, *Hubris*, 530.

84 The other being 'the principle of the essential unity of *Artgleichheit* (unity of species, type, or race) of the German *Volk*', Caldwell, 'National Socialism and Constitutional Law', 408.

85 Joseph W. Bendersky, *A Concise History of Nazi Germany*, 4th ed. (Maryland: Rowman & Littlefield, 2014), 39.

much more dispersed and devolved model of sovereignty than envisaged by Agamben. An example of this elsewhere is found in Roxanne Doty's application of Schmitt's theory of sovereignty to civilian border patrol groups on the southern border of the United States of America. Doty seeks, with reference to such groups, to explore and problematise Schmitt's concepts of sovereign and the decision, questioning 'where and who is "the sovereign" and what does it mean to "decide"?'[86]

Agamben's claim, taking a lead from Schmitt, is that 'the defining characteristic of sovereignty is that the sovereign determines when law is applicable and what it applies to, and, in doing so, must also create the conditions necessary for law to operate since the law presupposes normal order for its operation'.[87] Doty, however, asks whether the functions of the sovereign decision go beyond this, as this view of the decision suggests 'the moment of actual policy-making is the moment that brings into being the political when in actuality the political preexists any ultimate moment of decision on the part of political leaders or elites', because of the role of social forces in preempting and shaping official decision making.[88] Sovereignty is not therefore a single, unified entity, but 'is ethereal and hovers unsteadily around us, not firmly anchored, not solely public or private, legal or extra-legal',[89] and sovereign decisions are best understood in accordance with this more dispersed notion of sovereignty:

> Decisions disseminate across many landscapes and are held together by numerous fragile threads, which both presuppose and produce the enemy. These threads consist of beliefs, values, and unquestioned presuppositions found in the many facets of the movement as well as across the social field more generally.
>
> ... [W]idely dispersed utterances constitute a myriad of decisions and can come from what, on first glance, may seem irrelevant or peripheral, perhaps even fringe.[90]

One of the historiographical challenges for Agamben's adoption of both Schmitt's unified theory of sovereignty and his juridical justification of the *Führer* state is to overemphasise the totalitarian and monolithic nature of the Nazi regime, locating Hitler at the centre of all decision-making. Doty's version of sovereignty fits better with a Nazi administration in which those lower down, and sometimes outside of, the state hierarchy were empowered to take decisions that contributed to, and sometimes translated into, official legal and

86 Doty, 'States of Exception', 116.
87 Mills, *The Philosophy of Agamben*, 61–62.
88 Doty, 'States of Exception', 116.
89 Ibid., 132.
90 Ibid., 130.

policy measures, and which operated in a polycratic way with a dynamic relationship persisting between different levels in the hierarchy. Indeed, because of the totalising aims of the Nazis with respect to state and society and the content of the leadership principle, the role of civilians in the Third Reich in contributing to sovereign decision-making was, potentially, formally and practically more authoritative and officially sanctioned than Doty's civilian border patrol groups, especially when initiatives found favour with the Nazi leadership.

This application of sovereignty to the Third Reich builds on the fundamental tenets of Agamben's (and Schmitt's) analysis of sovereignty and the exception but in a way that better represents the historical and legal nature of the Nazi regime. In doing so it provides a way to disarm an important theoretical criticism of Agamben, that his notion of sovereignty is too monolithic, while showing how the notion of a sovereign power that exists within and across the norm-exception dichotomy may be grounded in a real historical situation. From a historical perspective, it demonstrates the legal relevance and significance of the *Führerprinzip* and 'working towards the Führer' as key concepts for understanding the operation of the Nazi state. Linking back to the dual state and the zone of indistinction, it also highlights the intrinsic juridical continuities across the two state spheres revealed by Fraenkel's analysis that again divert our attention to the point of amalgamation of norm and exception.

Conclusion: the exception of the norm

Despite the merits of some of the criticisms of Agamben's work, not least in its treatment of history, it is the thesis of this chapter that aspects of his state of exception do have something important to contribute to the legal and historical interpretation of law in Nazi Germany. The component that connects the two elements of Agamben's state of exception theory recovered in the preceding section, and which leads us inexorably to a focus on the point of convergence between the norm and the exception, is ideology. In terms of the limits of the dual state model when confronted with Agamben's zone of indistinction, the ethical norms of the regime applied across the supposed boundaries between normative and prerogative states; between what historians of the Third Reich refer to as legal terror and extra-legal terror. The Nazis, therefore, did not simply instrumentalise the law on the site of the suspension of the constitution but endorsed a grotesque philosophy that was not able, or intended, to be captured within the confines of a new, formal constitution. The laws – old laws, new laws, laws in force without application, laws applied without being in force – all operated in the service of the ideology, making it, from this perspective, difficult to draw a clear distinction between rule and exception.

In terms of the mutually enforcing ideas of dispersed sovereignty and 'working towards the Führer', it is the ideological tenets at the heart of the regime and its law, such as the *Führerprinzip*, which animated the basic method of operation that drove the regime's radicalisation. Equally, not being a juridical concept, when paired with Agamben's notion of sovereignty, the legal significance of 'working towards the Führer' is illuminated as it encompasses the implications of norms that operated inside both the conventionally normal and exceptional (legal and extra-legal) realms regardless of the formal, legal status of those norms. In doing so it highlights the zone of indistinction, the space between rule and exception, because on these terms there is again no way to distinguish between the two that is compatible with the fundamental tenets of the system. This is where Agamben's assertion about the undecidability of fact and norm resonates most.

The challenge with following Agamben down this path is twofold. First, how far can we, and should we, go along with Nazi ideology? Taking Nazi ideology seriously as a means of understanding the Third Reich, as so many historians are now willing to do, means also taking seriously its juridical manifestations as a means of understanding both the important role norms and normativity played in Nazi Germany[91] and the implications of this for legal theory beyond the Nazi past. However, it is equally important to be careful not to simply reflect Nazi propaganda, exemplified by some of Schmitt's own attempted justifications of Nazi rule.[92] Identifying the point where representing the actual significance of ideology to the functioning of the regime ends and over-emphasising the importance of aspects of Nazi rule that were a propaganda exercise begins is not straightforward.[93] Nevertheless, it is hoped that generally, and in this chapter, this problem can be overcome by making appropriate efforts to found jurisprudential claims in historical research.

Second, this approach confounds conventional historiography and legal theory. It is evident that the Nazi use of law does not fit neatly within the formal exception. However, Agamben goes further to argue that the exception is contained within any application of the law, in the moment of political discretion that initially separates and subsequently joins the legal norm to be applied to the facts subject to its application. This again draws our focus to the zone of indistinction between law and fact in a way that is pertinent to Nazi law. The gap that exists between factual situations and legal norms in the Third Reich was often much larger than we would usually expect in a legal system, and the legal norm often much less formally

91 Herlinde Pauer-Studer and J. David Velleman, 'Distortions of Normativity', (2011) 14 *Ethical Theory and Moral Practice* 329.
92 See, again, Schmitt, 'The Führer Protects the Law'.
93 See Ian Kershaw, 'Volksgemeinschaft: Potential and Limitations of the Concept' in Steber and Gotto, *Visions of Community*.

constituted, indeed sometimes reducible to the perceived will of the *Führer*. Consequently, in Nazi Germany, the zone of indistinction is particularly exposed and the very thing used to argue that the regime was lawless, particularly in the prerogative state where the Holocaust took place, is also the thing that may be used to argue that the regime was law-full – full of legal norms.[94] The combination of a stark distinction between the forms of Nazi laws and 'ordinary' laws and the extent of apparently arbitrary decision-making involved in bridging the gap needed to apply certain norms to particular facts is simultaneously indicative of a law/non-law divide and evidence for the convergence of the two. As such it exposes the root of the complex juridical relationship between exception and norm, which requires further interrogation in relation to both the Third Reich and other contexts.

94 Fraser, *Law after Auschwitz*.

Part 2

Histories of exception

Chapter 6

'Norm' and 'exception'

From the Weimar Republic to the Nazi state form

Dimitrios Kivotidis

Introduction

In this chapter, I aim to examine the unity between 'norm' and 'exception' as different forms of exercise of public power. I argue that both 'norm' and 'exception' are essential forms for the reproduction of bourgeois rule and that the change from one form to the other is contingent upon the intensification of socio-economic antagonisms (which manifest themselves in both class and intra-class conflicts). This argument is pursued based on an examination of the transition from the Weimar Republic to the Nazi state form, as reflected in the work of Carl Schmitt.

Schmitt's work will be assessed as a unified whole in its socio-economic and political context. This methodological choice will allow us to raise another theoretical point on the succession of different forms of state. During the interwar period in Germany, two major changes took place: one relating to the structure of the state and the other to the theory of the state. The bourgeois state underwent a process of deep crisis and transformation as it had to confront the antagonism of the first workers' state and the internal threat of the revolutionary working-class movement, as well as the socio-economic contradictions of capitalism that reached their peak at the economic crisis of 1929. These processes were bound to be reflected in the theory of the state, and the work of Carl Schmitt is a key example of this phenomenon.

The fundamental differences and nuances between the 'normal' and the 'exceptional' forms of exercise of public power is the point of departure of this analysis. The Weimar Republic is not the same as the Nazi state. This is precisely the point: they correspond to different levels of intensification of social antagonisms. The German Revolution of 1919 was defeated, but the German working-class struggle won vital concessions in the form of civil, political and social rights, which were enshrined in the Weimar Constitution. These concessions were embodied in the form of the welfare state and were abolished in the form of the Nazi state. However, in order to comprehend why these concessions were so easily abolished we have to figure out what is common to the two forms. What relations were reproduced by both the Weimar and the Nazi state? What social movements were prevented by both?

It is argued that Schmitt's theory of the state, reflecting a specific state form, responded to specific socio-economic conditions of intensified class and intra-class struggle that necessitated the change in the form of exercise of public power. To this end, the dualisms found in Schmitt's work (i.e. 'commissarial' and 'sovereign dictatorship', the 'quantitative' and the 'qualitative total state') will be examined alongside an analysis of the socio-economic reasons that necessitated the transition from the 'quantitative-Weimar' form to the 'qualitative-Nazi' form. These reasons include, but are not limited to, the need to reproduce the capitalist relations in the face of socio-economic and political crisis, as well as the need to facilitate the conditions for intensified exploitation, which would restore the profitability of German capital by crushing the labour movement and organisations.

In pursuing these arguments, the chapter is structured as follows: the analysis of Schmitt's theoretical framework begins with the conceptual pair of 'sovereign' and 'commissarial' dictatorship. Part I examines the commonalities and differences between the two. A discussion of the common origin of both normal and exceptional forms in the legitimating concept of the 'people' is followed by an examination of the difference between the two, i.e. the 'efficiency' in making the political decision against the 'enemy'. In Part II, the principle of 'efficiency' is examined in a move from the 'political' to the 'social' and the 'economic'. This is achieved by examining another one of Schmitt's dualisms, between the 'quantitative' and the 'qualitative total state'. A careful look at Schmitt's economic model reveals the reasons behind the transition from one form to the other: the reproduction of capitalist power, property and productive relations, as well as the facilitation of conditions for intensified exploitation of labour. The similarities and differences between the 'quantitative-Weimar' and 'qualitative-Nazi' forms are examined with reference to the class and intra-class antagonisms and contradictions of interwar Germany. Furthering this line of reasoning, Part III examines the prominent role of plebiscitary legitimacy in the 'qualitative-Nazi state', as well as the 'leadership principle' as it appeared not only in the field of public law but also in that of labour relations.

'Sovereign' and 'commissarial' dictatorship

I will begin the analysis with the first dualism, which is crucial for grasping the transition from one form (normal-Weimar) to the other (Nazi-exceptional): 'sovereign' and 'commissarial dictatorship'. These two kinds of dictatorship are both based on the concept of the 'people'. But, whereas in 'commissarial dictatorship' the deputies of the people, acting within the already constituted order, seek to preserve this order by suspending certain legal provisions, in 'sovereign dictatorship' the people's role as a legislator and as a dictator coincides in order to found a new constitution. The exercise of the people's constituent power is the distinguishing element of sovereign dictatorship. Here is how Schmitt describes the relationship between 'sovereign' and 'commissarial dictatorship':

> The legislator is nothing but right that is not yet constituted; the dictator is nothing but constituted power. When a relationship emerges that makes it possible to give the legislator the power of a dictator, to create a dictatorial legislator and constitutional dictator, then the commissary dictatorship has become a sovereign dictatorship. This relationship will come about through an idea that is, in its substance, a consequence of Rousseau's *contrat social*, although he does not name as a separate power: *le pouvoir constituant.*[1]

Two issues follow directly from the above. First, the relationship between dictatorship (i.e. exceptional use of power) and the law is always there and never questioned in both dictatorial forms. On the one hand, in 'commissarial dictatorship' it is the exercise of power unrestrained from law that safeguards the law itself. On the other, 'sovereign dictatorship' does not appeal to an existing constitution, but to one that is still to come. This is why the concept of 'constituent power of the people' is crucial here; because the 'people' as the carrier of this power relates it to the constitution-to-come as foundational to it.

This brings us to the second issue, i.e. the ideological function of the 'people'. Both forms of dictatorship are based on the idea of the 'sovereign people'. It is the 'people' that institutes the state with its constitution-making power on the basis of its 'political unity', we read in Schmitt's *Constitutional Theory.*[2] And it is in the interest of the 'people', i.e. it is in the 'general interest', that this constitutional order is suspended for exceptional power to safeguard it. However, the 'people', this classless and metaphysical subject, is a fiction. The concept of the 'people' is an illusory concept, albeit one with very actual effects in a social formation, precisely because it impedes the conceptualisation of society in its contradictory movement by obscuring the conflicting social interests behind the 'oneness' of 'popular sovereignty'. The 'people' as a whole cannot be sovereign because society is divided; the 'people' stands in for a whole, which consists of classes with conflicting interests, which cancel the possibility of a 'general interest', expressed in a 'general will'. 'Sovereign' and 'commissarial' dictatorship, normal and exceptional forms, are based on the idea of the 'people' (and the accompanying concepts of general will and general interest) as a legitimating fiction of class rule.

1 Carl Schmitt, *Dictatorship* (London: Polity Press, 2013), 111.
2 Carl Schmitt, *Constitutional Theory* (London: Duke University Press, 2008).

Where does this leave us concerning the nature of the Nazi state? Was it a 'permanent state of exception'? Was it a sovereign or a commissarial dictatorship? In order to answer this question we have to look at Schmitt's celebratory essay on the Nazi state, his 1933 *State, Movement, People.* There, Schmitt refutes the argument that

> the National-Socialist public law has only the value of a temporary, interim measure against the background of the earlier constitution, and that a simple bill passed by the Reichstag might again abolish the new constitutional legislation entirely and return to the Weimar Constitution.[3]

He argues instead that there are two issues to be taken into account with regard to the Enabling Act (or 'law of empowerment', i.e. the enabled amendment of the Weimar Constitution that gave the German executive the power to enact laws without the involvement of the Reichstag) of 24 March 1933. The first one consists of the fact that the elections of March 1933 'were in fact *a popular referendum, a plebiscite*, by which the German people has acknowledged Adolf Hitler, the leader of the National-Socialist Movement, as the political leader of the German people'.[4] According to Schmitt, the 'people' appears here to give ordinary elections the character of plebiscite. The 'pouvoir constituent' and the 'will of the people' are invoked here by Schmitt to found the Nazi state. And this invocation points towards the concept of sovereign dictatorship with regard to the emergence of the Nazi state. On the other hand, Schmitt emphasises the importance of the fact that this transition should take place legally.[5] The Enabling Act came into legal existence in conformity with Article 76 of the Weimar Constitution, which required a two-thirds majority for laws amending the Constitution, but that

> does not mean that one may still nowadays consider the Weimar Constitution as the foundation of the present-day State structure, but only that the law represents a bridge from the old to the new State, from the old base to the new base.[6]

Here, therefore, the change to the exceptional form is accommodated within the normal-parliamentary form. The Nazi state form combines the elements of norm and exception and is a perfect example of the unity of and continuity between these forms. This unity is captured by Ernst Fraenkel's concept of the 'dual state'. Fraenkel's central argument was that the Nazi

3 Carl Schmitt, *State, Movement, People: The Triadic Structure of the Political Unity* (Washington, DC: Plutarch Press, 2001), 5.
4 Ibid.
5 Ibid., 6.
6 Ibid.

state consists of two constituent and equally necessary elements, namely a state of exception and arbitrariness, which he calls 'prerogative state', and a state of legal normality, which he calls 'normative state'. He argues that the 'prerogative state' is the result of a process through which the National Socialists 'were able to transform the constitutional and temporary dictatorship (intended to restore public order) into an unconstitutional and permanent dictatorship and to provide the framework of the National Socialist state with unlimited power'.[7] However, the limits of this 'prerogative state' are set out by the reproduction of the 'normative state', whose existence as a 'normative state' was essential because it protected the institutions of private property, contract and private enterprise, which were still the basis of the German social formation.[8]

Norm and exception are united in the source of authority of the Nazi state form too. The fact that the Reichstag voted its own disempowerment with the Enabling Act of 1933 is proof of this. Legality becomes its own legitimation since the transfer of power is carried out in accordance to the laws in force at the time of the transfer, which provide it with the necessary legitimation and grant it legal validity. One could argue that the two legal instruments used to consolidate the rule of the Nazi party – i.e. the 'Decree for the Protection of the People and the State' of 28 February 1933, passed under the emergency provision of Article 48 of the Weimar Constitution (otherwise known as the 'Reichstag Fire Decree'), and the 'Enabling Act' of 24 March 1933 – correspond to the different types of dictatorship, the former being an instance of commissarial while the latter an instance of sovereign dictatorship. Both, however, facilitated the consolidation of Nazi rule in intricate relation with the notion of the 'people' – the former protecting the 'people', the latter being an expression of the 'people's' constituent power.

Consequently, 'commissarial dictatorship' and 'sovereign dictatorship' show their indissolubility at this point, something evident in Schmitt's famous definition of sovereignty. They are indissoluble because they refer to different processes of legitimating the exercise of public power. 'Sovereign dictatorship' refers primarily to the idea of the 'people', of a constituent power as the law-positing, establishing power of the legal rule. 'Commissarial dictatorship' refers primarily to the idea of 'general interest' which the dictator promotes. However, the dictator in this case acts according to a strict mandate on behalf of the people. Consequently, the ideological function of the people and its role in the reproduction of a regime of power, property and productive relations is central for both Schmittian types of dictatorship.

7 Ernst Fraenkel, *The Dual State: A Contribution to the Theory of Dictatorship* (Clark, NJ: The Lawbook Exchange, 2010), 5.
8 Ibid., 86.

We end up with a prima facie paradoxical conclusion that the source of legitimacy of the Nazi state was the law itself, but at the same time the source of the new constitution has to be the 'people'. The validity of the new constitutional order does not derive from the old Weimar Constitution, which is now superseded, but from the constituent power of the German 'people'. This paradox is resolved only if we take into account the common basis of both norm and exception, commissarial and sovereign dictatorship, on the same legitimating mechanism of 'peoplehood'. The conflict between the antithetical conceptualisations of law – as a normative and as a voluntaristic phenomenon – was resolved in the actual case of the transition from the Weimar to the Nazi state form by revealing law as being based on both norm and will. It was important for the so-called 'German revolution' to take place through legal means because this would provide it with the necessary legitimacy.[9] Nevertheless, it was for the same reasons equally important that the metaphysical concept of '*pouvoir constituant*' is there in its absence.

Having looked at the common legitimating basis of the two forms it is now necessary to examine what element of novelty the Nazi state form and Nazi legal ideology, as expressed in Schmitt's work, bring about. This new distinguishing element is the *efficiency* in making the political decision and in dealing with the 'enemy'. Based on the above, it is argued that the pamphlet *State, Movement, People* is the key to understanding Schmitt's theory of sovereignty and the exception. Until then Schmitt has not named the 'enemy'. His theory has already taken sides, but the 'enemy' remains unnamed so long as it is only the 'legal state' which is attacked.

The bourgeois *Rechtsstaat* and the neutral function of law is criticised precisely for not being able to make the political decision. In his *Legality and Legitimacy*, Schmitt attacks the neutrality and the functionalist nature of the legislative state. In particular he makes the case that the two-thirds majority required for the amendment of the constitution is problematic because it gives equal chance to all parties to ascend to the seat of government and take advantage of the 'political premium' this permits. In *State, Movement, People* it becomes obvious that the enemy of the state, the enemy of the 'people', the force that threatens the 'political unity', can be no other than the enemy of the bourgeoisie whose stated goal is overthrowing the capitalist relations of production/exploitation. As he writes:

9 The important ideological effect of Hitler being seen as coming to power by the most strictly constitutional means, notwithstanding the coercion against and immediate arrests of members of the Communist Party and trade-Unionists between the Reichstag Fire Decree and the voting of the Enabling Act, is reflected in statements such as the one by Kautsky, that 'the Dictatorship has the mass of the population behind it': see Rajani Palme Dutt, *Fascism and Social Revolution* (London: Martin Lawrence, 1934), 148–149.

> One could not wait for the empowerment of a system, which by its own weakness and neutrality was in no way capable of recognising even a mortal enemy of the German people, in order to abolish the Communist Party, the enemy of the State and of the people.[10]

It becomes clear that the political premium should not be exploited by the communists, but only by the Nazi Party in order to safeguard the bourgeois state with the passing of the Enabling Act. This provides us with the substantive content of the – not so formal any more – decisionist theory of Carl Schmitt. The new form of the Nazi state can make the political decision and crush the enemy which threatens the reproduction of bourgeois rule; and this is what the old form of the *Rechtsstaat* could not deal with efficiently.

The 'legal state' with its inherent contradictions and its functionalist neutrality cannot make the political decision and exclude the communists from the equal chance of rising to power. It is only for this reason that the 'legal state' is criticised by Schmitt; because it does not correspond as a form to the needs of the ruling class in a situation of intensified exploitation and class struggle. On the other hand, the Nazis made use of the two extra-ordinary law-makers – both the extraordinary law-maker *ratione materiae* (Art. 76 of the Weimar Constitution) and the extraordinary law-maker *ratione necessitatis* (Art. 48), as defined by Schmitt in his *Legality and Legitimacy* – so as to change the organisational structure of the bourgeois German state, get rid of its neutral functionalist character, and effectively crush the communist threat after recognising it as the enemy.[11]

Besides crushing the 'enemy', the Nazi state and its corresponding legal ideology performed the equally important function of unifying the ruling class and consolidating the bourgeois rule. Therefore, the notion of 'political unity', which in Schmitt's 1928 work *Constitutional Theory* serves as the basis of the constitution-making power of a unified 'people', gives its place to the principles of 'leadership' and 'ethnic identity', which can accommodate more efficiently the most aggressive form of reactionary policies of the capitalist state. However, the ideological function served by both notions is the same: the construction of an abstract people, of a unified whole which obscures the fundamental division between exploiting and exploited classes, with the added effect of ameliorating the intra-class contradictions within the exploiting class itself; a vital need of interwar German bourgeoisie. As Schmitt writes, 'The Reich Chancellor is the political leader of the German people, *politically united* in the German Reich. The primary importance of the political leadership is a fundamental principle of the present-day public law.'[12]

10 Schmitt, *State, Movement, People*, 3.
11 Carl Schmitt, *Legality and Legitimacy* (London: Duke University Press, 2004).
12 Schmitt, *State, Movement, People*, 8–9.

The 'leadership' principle as the cornerstone of political unity of the German people follows upon the plebiscitary legitimacy of the president. Consequently, in Schmitt's works of 1933 'political unity' turned into 'ethnic identity' and the 'constitution-making power' of the 'people' turned into the 'leadership' principle (*Führerprinzip*). This new notion of the people, identified with the *Führer*, is the new foundational and legitimating principle of the Nazi state. This plebiscitary form corresponds to the new levels of intensification of capitalist contradictions but performs the same mystifying and legitimating function, contributing to the reproduction of the same capitalist relations. It marks the passage from a 'quantitative total state' (a welfare state with a pluralist party system representing different class interests) to a 'qualitative total state' (a strong one-party state to represent the interests of the ruling class), to use Schmitt's definition.

Elections in the former, as was the case under the Weimar Constitution, had become an option that split the German people into many incompatible parties. On the contrary, elections in the 'qualitative total state' such as the German elections of 12 November 1933 were part of the 'great plebiscite' on which the German people assume a foremost position in the politics of the Reich government by responding to the appeal launched by the political leadership.[13] According to Schmitt, the one-party Nazi state is the form corresponding to the truly unified 'people', now substantively unified based on 'ethnic identity' and the *Führerprinzip.* Moreover, this form corresponds precisely to the ideology of class collaboration, which accompanied the new level of intensified exploitation, and to the need of consolidation of the bourgeois rule through the amelioration of intra-class conflicts and the elimination of centrifugal tendencies.

'Quantitative' and 'qualitative total state'

Let us further examine the conceptual pair of 'quantitative' and 'qualitative total state' in order to shed light on the reasons that led to the change from 'normal' to 'exceptional' forms of exercise of bourgeois rule. The move from the 'quantitative' to the 'qualitative total state' was necessary for reasons of efficiency in dealing with the socio-economic contradictions that posed a threat to the reproduction of capitalist relations in interwar Germany. It is important to note that the concept of 'socio-economic contradictions' used here is not limited to class struggle between two opposing classes, but extends to intra-class contradictions. These include the intra-class conflicts of the German ruling class that had to be overcome. Therefore, the demand for *efficiency* can be understood as the need for a strong state to make the political decision to oppose the enemy – i.e. a rising working-class movement – as well as the need for consolidating the bourgeois rule against centrifugal tendencies.

13 Ibid., 10–11.

Schmitt's theory of state, reflecting a specific state form, responds to specific socio-economic conditions (of intensified class and intra-class struggle), which gave rise to the most aggressive form of exercise of state power. This is particularly evident in Schmitt's preferred economic model, which aims to empower capital by freeing it from the regulatory burdens of the democratic welfare state. It has been argued that Schmitt provides a political theory of 'authoritarian capitalism', but one in which authoritarian political institutions are masked by an appearance of popular legitimacy.[14] In particular, Schmitt's qualitative total state provides for the 'legal and institutional preconditions for a system in which capitalist proprietors engage in conscious forms of joint supervision of the economy'.[15] According to this reading,

> Where economic decisions are likely to have a 'public' significance, state planners would not dominate the entrepreneur. Instead, entrepreneurs would engage in forms of planning. In Schmitt's own terms, the state planners should not dominate; rather, the (economically) dominant should plan. [...] [The] state must do all it can to encourage private capitalists to engage in relatively far-sighted, sensible forms of economic coordination.[16]

Schmitt's advocating for a qualitative total state which guarantees authentic state sovereignty while simultaneously managing to provide substantial autonomy to owners of private capital, appears in his 1933 essay 'A Strong State and Sound Economics'[17] and was foreshadowed in a 1930 lecture presented to a prominent organisation of German industrialists,[18] the

14 William Scheuerman, *Carl Schmitt: The End of Law* (London: Rowman & Littlefield, 1999), 101.
15 Ibid., 103–104.
16 Ibid.
17 Carl Schmitt, 'Starker Staat und gesunde Wirtschaft: Ein Vortrag vor Wirtschaftsführern', (1933) *Volk und Reich*, no. 2, 89–90; Carl Schmitt, 'Machtpositionen des modernen Staates' [1933], in Carl Schmitt, *Verfassungsrechtliche Aufsätze aus den Jahren 1924–1954*, 371. According to Franz Neumann, in his 1932 address, Schmitt invented a distinction between 'two kinds of totality, the Roman and the Germanic'. Roman totality was quantitative; the Germanic, qualitative. The former regimented all spheres of life, interfering with every human activity. In sharp contrast, the Germanic remained content with a strong and powerful state that demanded full political control but left economic activities unrestricted. Schmitt's doctrine is, of course, no more Germanic than its opposite is Roman. In fact, it had been formulated much more clearly and realistically by an Italian, Vilfredo Pareto, who espoused political authoritarianism and economic liberalism simultaneously and who influenced the early economic policies of Mussolini. See Franz Neumann, *Behemoth: The Structure and Practice of National Socialism* (Chicago: Ivan R. Dee, 2009).
18 See Schmitt's (untitled) lecture in Max Schlenker (ed.) *Mitteilungen des Vereins zur Wahrung der gemeinsamen wirtschaftlichen Interessen in Rheinland und*

Langnamverein, when he called for a 'rollback of the state [in the economy] to a natural and correct amount'.[19] The qualitative total state must replace its quantitative counterpart, a weak, social-democratic inspired interventionist state. The capitalist economy should be self-administered, meaning that the economic leaders, owners and managers need to be given substantial autonomy in their industries and factories, and they need to be freed from social-democratic forms of regulation.[20]

Schmitt's argument here is still one of 'efficiency'. Not only the 'efficiency' of the qualitative total state in making the political decision but also the 'efficiency' of the qualitative state with regards to economic planning: for Schmitt, the economically dominant should plan and the state should provide the legal and institutional preconditions, as opposed to a system in which a pluralist party and welfare state reflects the working-class struggle in the form of concessions and freedoms granted to the exploited class in order to avoid a radical overthrow of the property regime. Therefore, the exceptional form safeguards the bourgeois rule not only by eradicating the communist threat but also by promoting and consolidating the interests of monopoly capital.

In both its program and its fact, the so-called 'qualitative total state' bases itself on the fundamental condition for the reproduction of capitalist relations, i.e. private property. The exceptional form is thus essential for the reproduction of normality, or to use Fraenkel's terminology, the 'prerogative state' and the 'normative state' have a symbiotic relation: exceptional powers and arbitrariness are necessary in order to reproduce the conditions of capitalist production and as long as they do not threaten the reproduction of these conditions. In his first Reichstag speech on 25 March 1933, Adolf Hitler said: 'The government will on principle safeguard the interests of the German Nation not by roundabout ways of bureaucracy organised by the state but by encouraging private initiative and by recognising private property.'[21] This function the 'qualitative total state' shares with its predecessor,

Westfalen (Düsseldorf: Matthias Strucken, 1930), 458–59. A translation is found in Renato Cristi, *Carl Schmitt and Authoritarian Liberalism* (Cardiff: University of Wales Press, 1998), 212–233.

19 Scheuerman, *Carl Schmitt: The End of Law*, 288.

20 An example of this self-administration of capital, enabled by the qualitative total state, can be found in an order of the minister of economics of 12 November 1936, which transferred a great deal of responsibility for the supervision of the activities of the cartels from governmental authorities to bodies of the economic self-administration. The minister wrote: 'It is my intention to obtain the co-operation of private economic organisations in the execution of the supervisory activities of the cartels which my ministry has hitherto exercised alone. The administrative bodies of the private economic organisations should be responsible for seeing that the cartels are in harmony with the economic policy of the government in every respect.' See Fraenkel, *The Dual State*, 97.

21 Ibid., 60.

i.e. the 'quantitative total state', which according to Schmitt was 'a totality of weaknesses'.[22]

It should not be forgotten that after the end of the First World War and Germany's defeat, an intensified economic and socio-political crisis broke out in the country. In November 1918, many German cities were the locus of armed insurgencies, which led to the overtaking of governmental buildings and the declaration of soviet (workers' councils) rule, while a revolutionary government was formed, which ruled over a substantive part of the country. After a series of conflicts, in January 1919 the armed militia of the workers were defeated and Karl Liebknecht and Rosa Luxemburg, the leaders of the Spartacists, were murdered by the Freikorps.

The Weimar Constitution must be assessed in this context as the constitution of a bourgeois state in the need to reproduce itself in the face of multi-level threat.[23] The public legal form is assessed in its unity with the socio-economic and political context; and the Weimar form was assumed by a bourgeois state in need of reproducing itself. The Weimar Constitution, which crystallised a new form of bourgeois state, can be seen as the German ruling class's response to the proletarian revolution: a state not indifferent to the movement of economy, a state that does not recognise as its subject only the private citizen but also the members of the exploited classes, which it seeks to include in its provisions.

Originating in the context of highly intensified contradictions, the Weimar Constitution was an example of the move from an individualist to a more corporate[24] model of constitutionalism, performing two important and inter-related functions, i.e. the constitutionalisation of labour law and the introduction of measures of 'economic democracy'. However, despite the declared intentions of its authors to combat the imbalance between capital and labour, inherent in capitalist relations, the roots of the imbalance, located in the private ownership of the means of production, were reproduced. Therefore, in spite of its progressive nature, the Weimar Constitution ultimately served to reproduce the capitalist relations of production by performing (objectively, even though not consciously at all times) three very important functions: demobilising the labour movement; promoting policies of class collaboration; and promoting an ideology of non-radicalism.

22 Carl Schmitt, 'Sound Economy – Strong State', Appendix to Cristi, *Carl Schmitt and Authoritarian Liberalism*.

23 On this issue see Enzo Traverso, *Fire and Blood: The European Civil War, 1914–1945* (London: Verso, 2016) and Pierre Broué, *The German Revolution, 1917–1923* (Chicago: Haymarket Books, 2006).

24 For the purposes of the following analysis corporatism refers to the state model which is based on the one hand on the political principles of 'national sovereignty' and on the other on the socio-economic principles of collaboration of the various classes engaged in production; see Fausto Pitigliani, *The Italian Corporative State* (London: P. S. King, 1933).

Ultimately, it is argued that Weimar is an example of how the constitutional form (the *corporate-welfare* form of the Weimar constitution) could neither contain nor withstand the capitalist antagonisms and contradictions it overlaid. It sought to preserve the basis of the German capitalist social formation, i.e. private ownership, while recognising the existence of dominated classes and incorporating rights pertaining to the latter. It thus contributed to the reproduction of the regime of power, property and productive relations of capitalism, albeit in a form different from any other capitalist state encountered thus far. However, after the 1929 capitalist crisis, it became evident that the welfare state could no longer accommodate the interests of the ruling class and was eventually negated by the qualitative form of the Nazi state.

If the 'quantitative-Weimar' form was vital for the reproduction of capitalist relations in the face of the 1919 working-class revolt, the 'qualitative-Nazi' form was vital for the reproduction of the same in the face of intensified socio-economic contradictions following the Great Depression. The new form of exercise of public power was more effective in ensuring the reproduction and profitability of capitalism by negating the form of the quantitative total state that was unable to make the political decision and could no longer accommodate the contradictory interests of the ruling class.

It has to be noted that the German ruling class of the interwar period was not a metaphysical subject, which decided *en bloc* and had a single uniform voice. On the contrary, it was replete with conflicting interests that struggled against each other for the best way out of the crisis and for the state form to best accommodate this process.[25] However, it is argued here that these conflicting groups were unified in the process of dealing with the common enemy, i.e. the working-class movement, for facilitating conditions of intensified exploitation, based on the extraction of absolute surplus value. It was for this reason, ultimately, that the dictatorial form of the Nazi state came to being: to consolidate the bourgeois rule and facilitate the intensification of exploitation.

As far as the intra-class conflicts are concerned, it has been argued that during the interwar period the German businesses were divided into two main groups: those that demanded a policy of free trade, such as the textile and pharmaceutical industries, and those that tended towards protectionism, such as the industries of agriculture, iron and steel.[26] By the end of the 1920s, the leading role had fallen to the former, the so-called new industries, i.e. the large-scale finishing ones such as the big chemical firms, the heavy machine manufacturers and the electro-industry, while the iron and steel industries had slipped into a subordinate position. This was hardly to the liking of the latter,

25 Alfred Sohn-Rethel, *Economy and Class Structure of German Fascism* (London: Process Press, 1987).
26 Ibid., 16.

whose aims for realising the full productive potential of their plant could be served only by a determined policy of re-armament.[27]

The process of concentration of the decisive elements of German monopoly capital in a new grouping of interests is described by Alfred Sohn-Rethel. According to his analysis, on the one hand the establishment of fascism in Germany in January 1933 was a result of the political victory of the dysfunctional groups of big and small businesses over the financially sound parts of the German economy, since, by the end of 1932, the near entirety of German finance capital had coalesced on a policy bent on violent expansion and war.[28] Germany's production capacities were far too large for its own narrow market. Hence, the need for a larger internal market arose. This was expressed in the Nazi theory of the 'living space', but also in the expansion of the armament policies.

On the other hand, the victory of one group of businesses over the other, as expressed in the decision of the German investment industries to expand their monopoly market by means of their Central European policy, was underlined by and corresponded closely with the common interest in suppressing wages and increasing the number of working hours. If wages were not curtailed as soon as possible, capital would be. This is because the crisis had seen a large section of industry caught between the variable costs of wages and the fixed ones of capital. If losses were not compensated by wage cuts, many businesses would be pushed over the brink.[29] A reversion of the capitalist mode of production from relative to absolute surplus value extraction (i.e. intensification of exploitation through increase in the number of working hours and drop in real wages) was necessary for the German capital not to spiral downwards into inescapable crisis again, as it did in 1929.

Of course, the attack on workers' rights and the implementation of policies directed at the lowering of labour costs did not begin with Hitler's rise to power. Ever since September 1926, the German industrialists had showed that they could no longer afford the gains won by the working class between 1918 and 1923 by issuing a statement attacking the so-called 'too generous distribution of social benefits' and calling for a 'reduction of the burden of taxation' in order to 'restore the profitability of the economy'.[30] Just weeks after the Wall Street crash, the League of German Industry called for the welfare state to be 'adapted to the limits of economic sustainability' decrying 'unjustified and immoral abuse' of social security benefits because in their eyes the economic crisis had been caused by a bloated welfare state, high wages and short working hours.[31]

27 Ibid., 46.
28 Ibid., 89.
29 Ibid., 55.
30 Ibid., 8.
31 Marcel Bois, 'Hitler Wasn't Inevitable', *Jacobin*, 25 November 2015, available at www.jacobinmag.com/2015/11/nuremberg-trials-hitler-goebbels-himmler-german-communist-social-democrats/

What German finance capital needed above all was to break out of the falling rate of profit by the only means in existence that depended neither on other capitalist powers nor on the world market, i.e. a forced raising of the rate of surplus value by the slashing of the workers' wages.[32] This economic need was met by Hitler's policies that consisted of a systematic lowering of wages. The millions of unemployed were gradually re-employed at rates of pay no higher, or hardly so, than their unemployment benefit. This was vividly captured by the slogan 'Work for all, not wealth for all', as the Nazis expressed it after they had smashed the trade unions. The great mass of financially weak firms welcomed Hitler's economic 'revival' methods insofar as through them they could escape the more or less acute danger of bankruptcy.[33]

But the aggressive policies necessary to achieve this systematic lowering of wages involved a sustained attack on workers' rights that were safeguarded by the Weimar Constitution. The leaders of German industries were well aware that the policies they were compelled to pursue in the economic crisis, with the attacks on all sections of the workers, including those who had gained by the previous social legislation, would inevitably result in the weakening of the basis of Social Democracy. These policies could not be realised in conditions of intensified class struggle and growing militancy of the workers, unless the bourgeois elite was able to smash not only the proletarian political organisations but also the mass basis appropriate to the previous system of control through relative surplus value production, namely the trade unions and social democracy. The best analysis of the reasons that necessitated the change from the Weimar to the Nazi form was made before the Reichstag on 21 May 1935 by Adolf Hitler himself:

> In order to assure the functioning of the national economy it became *necessary to arrest the movement of wages and prices.* It was also *necessary to stop all interferences which are not in accord with the higher interests of our national economy,* i.e. it was *imperative to eliminate all class organisations which pursued their own policies with regard to wages and prices.* The destruction of the class-struggle organisations of employers as well as of employees required the analogous *elimination of those political parties* which were financed and supported by those interest groups. This process, in its turn, caused the introduction of a new constructive and effective 'living constitution' and the refoundation of Reich and State.[34]

32 Sohn-Rethel, *Economy and Class Structure of German Fascism*, 89.
33 Ibid., 39.
34 As quoted in Fraenkel, *The Dual State,* 187 [emphasis added].

As a former Nazi official, Albert Krebs described in his memoirs: '[n]ot all capitalists were particularly enthusiastic about the Nazis, but their scepticism was relative and ended as soon as it became clear that Hitler was the only person capable of destroying the labour movement'.[35] The Nazi state form and the Nazi economic model formed a unified yet contradictory whole, which is reflected in the concept of 'qualitative total state' in Schmitt's theoretical framework. These new economic and political forms corresponded to the intensified capitalist contradictions after the capitalist crisis and the objective need to restore the profitability of German enterprises by advancing a new political system that would crush the working-class movement.

The essence of National Socialist social policy consisted in the reproduction of the class character of the German social formation, in the attempted consolidation of its ruling class, in the atomization of the subordinate strata through the destruction of every autonomous group mediating between them and the state, and in the creation of a system of autocratic bureaucracies interfering in all human relations.[36] The maintenance of capitalist ownership, 'private enterprise', and the recovery of 'profits' and 'profitability' accompanied with moderate state intervention in a regulatory role were characteristics of the interwar corporatist state, and were reflected in Schmitt's economic model of the 'qualitative total state'.

We conclude that the Nazi form of government, as well as the Nazi economic model, was necessitated by the intensification of class and intra-class conflicts. The deadlock in the economy and the contradictions between protectionism and inflation were manifestations of capitalist contradictions. But the capitalists were unified against the main opponent, namely the working class organised in workers' unions and workers' parties. The measures against the workers had to be passed and for this the communist threat had to be extinguished. This urgency for action on the part of the industrial capitalists was reflected in the use of the extra-ordinary law-making provisions, of Article 48, in the Reichstag Fire Decree, and of Article 76 in the passing of the Enabling Act, which consolidated the Nazi rule.

State form and intensified exploitation

The Nazi state form reproduced the foundational condition of the capitalist relations of production (i.e. private property) in the face of rising class and intra-class contradictions. In order to achieve this goal it functioned so as to unify the competing ruling-class fractions, containing any centrifugal tendencies. Simultaneously, and equally significant, it enabled the conditions of intensified exploitation by violently suppressing the labour movement and

35 Albert Krebs, *The Infancy of Nazism: The Memoirs of Ex-Gauleiter Albert Krebs* (London: New Viewpoints, 1976).

36 Neumann, *Behemoth*, 365.

eliminating any resistance to aggressive capitalist policies. It can safely be argued that throughout its existence the Nazi form was vital for maintaining the legal foundations of the capitalistic economic order.[37]

Having looked at the main factors, which necessitated the change in the form of exercise of public power, it is time to reflect upon the specific function of plebiscitary legitimacy, as concretised in the principles of 'leadership' and 'political unity' which appear in Schmitt's work. What novelty does this form bring? How does the main legitimating mechanism, based on the concept of the 'people', adapt to the new socio-economic configuration? To begin answering this question it is important to go back to Schmitt's 'quantitative-qualitative' total state distinction and revisit his idea of the political. As mentioned above, the legal *Rechtsstaat* was considered inefficient and was criticised by Schmitt precisely because it failed to make the ultimate political decision, i.e. it failed to decide between 'friend and enemy'.[38]

This legal *Rechtsstaat* was also a 'quantitative total state' in the sense of providing many parties or interest groups with the chance 'to make their political decision' and decide on their 'friends and enemies'[39]. Against this total state, against the neutralised liberal democratic state, Schmitt advocates the total de-politicisation of civil society and the total concentration of political power in an authoritarian state. To repeat a point raised earlier, the 'political' decision (as well as the use of the 'political premium' to enact this decision) is not for everyone. It appears then that Schmitt is fundamentally against 'the political'. His concept of the political is a form of bourgeois ideology to the extent that the socio-political content of the decision on the friend and enemy is revealed and thus the decision itself is reserved for the representatives of the interests of the bourgeois class. Social groups, trade unions, must have no political voice of their own. They must not be allowed to express their own economic and political interests. A qualitative total state rises above the conflicts within society, and ensures its reproduction, while suppressing these contradictions. The question 'in whose interests' has already been answered above.

This deep de-politicisation of society had to take place in the form of its opposite, i.e. extreme politicisation. One aspect of this was the process of blurring, or rather a redrawing, of the dividing line between political and non-political acts.

The second law regarding the jurisdiction of the political police, i.e. the Gestapo (*Gesetz über die Geheime Staatspolizei* of 30 November 1933), provided for the abolition of judicial review of all acts of the Gestapo, but also of all acts of ordinary police pursuant upon special orders of the Gestapo, all

37 Fraenkel, *The Dual State: A Contribution to the Theory of Dictatorship*, 72.

38 Carl Schmitt, *The Concept of the Political*, George Schwab transl. (Chicago: University of Chicago Press, 1996 [1929]), 26.

39 Ibid., 27–28.

acts of the ordinary police pursuant upon general orders of the Gestapo and all acts of the ordinary police which fall within the jurisdiction of the Gestapo.[40] The classification of more and more actions as 'political', rather than private, so that they would fall within the jurisdiction of the Gestapo, whose actions were not subject to judicial review, was essential for the exceptional Nazi state form.

Furthermore, this process of politicisation appears in the form of the plebiscite and the identification of rulers and ruled. In his early analysis of the Weimar form, even before the Nazi form, the election of the *Reichspraesident* was interpreted by Schmitt as something different from a democratic election[41]; it was seen as a plebiscitarian acclamation. It is no wonder then that in the Nazi form of the plebiscite, popular sovereignty reaches an extreme point of hollowness. Only a decisionist president, a leader (*Führer*) could escape civil society's centrifugal pluralism, and 'unify the people' by holding its trust. It could thus provide the perfect legitimating mechanism for a class-collaborative form of state to reproduce the conditions of intensified exploitation necessary for the recovery and expansion of German capital.

The plebiscite, this new form of legitimation, was cohesive with (even though different from) parliamentary elections, which it superseded. They both share an abstract and class-less conception of the 'people'. The people appear on stage when they are asked to vote, and then recede in the background once they have 'blessed' and legitimised a new round of policies, which they have supposedly chosen in an expression of the 'general will'. But whereas in liberal democracy an election provides an opportunity for freewheeling debate about candidates and political parties, and the election is seen as culminating in some 'normativisation' (i.e. a piece of general law deriving its legitimacy from rational debate), the Schmittian plebiscite is simply a 'decision giving expression to an act of will', a means by which the popular masses can hope to approximate 'a pure decision not based on reason and discussion and not justifying itself'.[42] The plebiscite as a distinctive form has the advantage for the ruling class to present the voters with only an extremely limited choice, a polarising and reductionist distortion of the many-sided reality. Moreover, it deals in binaries and has the added advantage of the voters' utter dependence on the way the question is formulated (as Schmitt himself points out in his 'Legality and Legitimacy').

Therefore, plebiscitary legitimacy and the leadership principle served a double purpose: on the one hand they acted as a unifying force against centrifugal tendencies, a form accommodating the reconsolidation of German capital. On the other hand they provided the legitimating mechanism necessary for the conditions of intensified exploitation. For this reason, the effect of

40 Ibid., 27.
41 Schmitt, *Constitutional Theory*.
42 Scheuerman, *Carl Schmitt: The End of Law*, 102.

the leadership principle was not confined to constitutional law but is encountered in Nazi Germany's labour law too. The Nazi state was a 'qualitative total state' indeed, as it set up the German Labour Front comprising both employers and employees, no longer called by the old names but now termed 'leaders' and 'followers'. The Law for the Organization of National Labour was issued on 20 January 1934 and under it the German Labour Front was the inclusive organisation of German brain and hand workers.[43]

It is pertinent here to raise a comparative point on the relation between the German Labour Front and the Weimar system of labour law. First, with regards to Weimar, paragraph 1 of the Works Council Law of 4 February 1920 states as one of the two basic objectives of the Works Councils: 'to support the entrepreneur in fulfilling the works-objectives'[44]. Similarly, paragraph 1 of the 1934 Law for the Ordering of National Work provides: 'The entrepreneur, as leader of the works, and the employees and workers, as his following, work together in the works for the advancement of the works-objectives and for the common service of people and state.'[45] It is evident that both provisions share the notion of 'works-objectives', which obfuscates the contradictory interests of capital and labour in the production process. Moreover, the provisions share a depiction of the employer as the leader of this works-community, even though the leadership principle is much more obvious in the Nazi legislation.

Returning to the German Labour Front, this was a crucial element of the qualitative total state, as it was the main mechanism of class collaboration. The interests of workers, i.e. the 'followers', were identified with the interests of capitalists, i.e. the 'leaders'. We find here the leadership principle at work in the sphere of labour law. The 'leader' makes the real decisions and this fact became undeniable in 1935, when the Reich Chamber of Economics (a bureaucratic organisation, containing all the employers in Germany, controlled by the Ministry of Economics) joined the Labour Front.[46] The German Labour Front employed the *Führerprinzip* in the economy and, as the main form of class collaboration, provided the Nazi regime with the social power base necessary for its reproduction. Nazism as reconsolidation of the bourgeois regime would be unsuccessful unless it managed to bind to itself social strata which socially do not form part of the bourgeoisie but which would afford it the inestimable service of anchoring its rule in the people.[47] If the Labour Front was the mechanism used to make this in the economy, plebiscitary legitimacy and the leadership principle were the main legitimating mechanisms to achieve this in the sphere of constitutional law and ideological legitimation of power.

43 Norman Thomas, 'Labour Under the Nazis' (1936) 14(3) *Foreign Affairs* 424.
44 David Kettler, 'Works Community and Workers' Organization: A Central Problem in Weimar Labour Law', (1984) 13 *Economy and Society*, 278, 296.
45 Ibid.
46 Ibid.
47 Scheuerman, *Carl Schmitt: The End of Law*, 122.

It follows from the above that changes in German constitutional law and changes in German labour law were intertwined during the interwar period. The reason for this was shown to have been the intensification of social and economic contradictions. Abolishing the rights to strike and collective bargaining and crushing the working-class movement while creating a new social basis based on the principle of class collaboration could not have been achieved unless the form of exercise of public power had changed. The interwar model of the corporate state[48] was based on the one hand on the principles of 'national sovereignty' and 'national unity' and on the other hand on a concept implicit in the state system, which Fascism desires to build up – namely, the economic collaboration of the various categories engaged in production.[49] Schmitt's theoretical framework accommodates both these principles, as is evident in the above analysis.

We conclude that the normal and the exceptional forms of exercise of public power are different but not separated. They are rather united in their difference. A fundamental necessity underlies both norm and exception: the necessity of a regime of power, property and productive relations. The ordinary function of the rule of law, which safeguards this regime, is conditional upon the non-occurrence of the always existent and imminent danger, which Schmitt terms as the 'ever-present possibility of conflict'.[50] It has been argued that this 'ever-present possibility of conflict' stands for the intensification of social antagonisms. This concept includes a multiplicity of factors (intra-class conflicts and class struggle) that might necessitate a change in the form of exercise of public power.

48 Franz Neumann held that the Nazi state form was incompatible with the model of the corporate state because for National Socialism the primacy of politics is decisive. The reason he gives for this is that the Nazi Party never allowed itself to put the economic questions into the foreground and to announce comprehensive economic official party programs. It always insisted on the primacy of politics over economics and therefore consciously remained a political party without any basic economic orientation: see Neumann, *Behemoth*, 232. However, the structural role of a political party in a social formation is hardly restricted to its political intentions and announcements through party programmes. It is, on the contrary, assessed by the objective effect its policies have in the social formation. Neumann himself acknowledges that the role played by the German Labour Front was one of promoting ideas and practices of class collaboration, under the influence of corporative ideas: see Neumann, *Behemoth*, 414. In this respect the Front served five crucial functions: the indoctrination of labour with the National Socialist ideology, the taxation of the German working class; the securing of positions for reliable party members, the atomization of the German working classes, and the exercise of certain inner trade-union functions: see Neumann, *Behemoth*, 417.

49 Fausto Pitigliani, *The Italian Corporative State.*

50 Carl Schmitt, *The Concept of the Political.*

Conclusion

The above analysis showed the indissoluble union between 'norm' and 'exception', as well as between all the other dualisms employed by Schmitt to characterise the different forms of exercise of public power. Schmitt's dualisms were examined in their socio-political context to unearth the content that the different forms corresponded to. This move from political theology to political economy meant that we had to discuss not the state in the abstract, but the capitalist state, not sovereignty in the abstract, but the economic and political power of a dominant class, not the 'decision' in the abstract, but the decision based on socially and historically conditioned interests, not the 'ever-present possibility of conflict', but the ever-present possibility of suspending the rule of law, in order to deal with the internal enemy, which is nothing else than the threat to the capitalist state

Rather than being taken from outside (*ex-capere*), the exception emerges from within the law – it is bound within law because it corresponds to the foundational need of the bourgeois state to reproduce itself in the face of threat. The 'normal' and the 'exceptional' forms correspond to different historical situations, to different levels of intensification socio-economic contradictions, but they both serve the ultimate function of ensuring the reproduction of a regime of power, property and productive relations. The above analysis did not reduce the liberal democratic form of government to the authoritarian one. Rather, it stressed the differences and the reasons behind the differences of the two forms by focusing on the commonalities between them: on the capitalist relations that were reproduced by both as well as on the working-class movement that was obstructed by both, albeit in different ways.

It is perhaps under this prism that Walter Benjamin's 8th thesis on the Concept of History can be better assessed. The 'emergency situation' should be understood from the standpoint of the exploited and the oppressed. This, according to Mark Neocleous, means that:

> if emergency powers have been historically aimed at the oppressed (in advanced capitalist states against the proletariat and its various struggles, in reactionary regimes against genuine politicization of the people, in colonial systems against popular mobilization), then they need to be fought not by demanding a return to the "normal" rule of law, but in what Benjamin calls a real state of emergency.[51]

One could argue then that this 'real state of emergency' corresponds to the 'right of necessity', the 'right of extreme need' that is found in the Hegelian

51 Mark Neocleous, 'The Problem with Normality: Taking Exception to 'Permanent Emergency', (2006) 31 *Alternatives*, no. 2, 191–213.

analysis of the institution of the *Notrecht*. Hegel's *Notrecht* is the 'right of extreme need' of those who risk starving to death; not only do they have the right to steal the bread that will keep them alive, but the 'absolute right' to transgress the one-sided right of property, that legal norm which condemns theft.[52] In the same manner, the exploited and the oppressed can invoke their 'right of need', the 'real state of necessity', to question not only the exceptional form which infringes upon their formal rights, but the validity of the capitalist property regime itself which thwarts the satisfaction of their vital social needs.

52 Domenico Losurdo, *Hegel and the Freedom of the Moderns* (Durham: Duke University Press, 2004), 87.

Chapter 7

'Our Fatherland has found itself on the verge of an abyss'

Poland's 1981 martial law, or the unexpected appearance of the state of exception under actually existing socialism[1]

Rafał Mańko

Introduction

> It is a horrible, monstrous shame for the Party that after 36 years in power it has to be defended by the police. But there is nothing else left ahead of us.
>
> General Wojciech Jaruzelski[2]

'[L]aw ... nourishes itself on [the] exception and is a dead letter without it,'[3] Giorgio Agamben wrote. But does the signifier 'law' refer here to feudal and capitalist law, or also to law in a state-socialist polity? Is the state of exception limited to bourgeois legality and the efforts of its ruling classes to strip the proletariat of the scant legal protections it had won, or is it also possible under conditions of so-called 'socialist legality'? The Polish state of emergency, technically known as 'state of war' (*stan wojenny*), proclaimed on the night of 12–13 December 1981, 'conventionally translated [into English] as 'martial law'[4]

1 I would like to thank Cosmin Cercel, Przemysław Tacik, Gian Giacomo Fusco, Mikhail Antonov and Tormod Otter Johanssen for reading and commenting on earlier versions of this chapter and for sharing with me their insightful ideas. The present chapter presents exclusively my personal views and should not be attributed to any institution.
2 'Protocol No. 18 of PUWP CC Politburo Meeting, December 5, 1981' in Andrzej Paczkowski and Malcolm Byrne (eds), *From Solidarity to Martial Law: The Polish Crisis 1980–1981* (Budapest, New York: Central European University Press. 2007), 443.
3 Giorgio Agamben, *Homo Sacer: Sovereign Power and Bare Life*, Daniel Heller-Roazen transl. (Stanford: Stanford University Press, 1998), 27.
4 Brian Porter-Szűcs, *Poland in the Modern World: Beyond Martyrdom* (Chichester: John Wiley & Sons, 2014) 303. On the terminology, cf. Giorgio Agamben, *State of Exception*, Kevin Attell transl. (Chicago: University of Chicago Press, 2005) 4. Indeed, the translation 'martial law' correctly conveys the link with war present in the Polish term.

is, apparently, a unique example – beside wartime communism[5] – of the use of this ancient legal device[6] in a polity priding itself, even in the Constitution, on being a socialist country where the working class is the sovereign.[7]

The present chapter aims at presenting the juridical nature of the Martial Law[8] in its broader political, economic and social context. That context is different from states of exception in capitalist polities, and therefore, in the next section I will put a strong emphasis on the 'normalcy' of state socialism, including the place of law and fundamental rights in that concrete order. Only against that background can the actual juridical value of the Martial Law be evaluated. The question whether there indeed existed an exceptional situation in December 1981 is a crucial one, as it determines whether the state of exception was justified in the light of the Constitution of the Polish People's Republic, or not. The possibility of a 'fraternal aid' from Poland's Warsaw Pact allies, keen on preserving authoritarian state socialism, is only one aspect of the exceptionality, discussed in the subsequent section. The economic, social but above all internal political situation – with the movement of *Solidarność* (Solidarity) challenging the hegemonic role of the Leninist party (i.e. the Polish United Workers' Party, henceforth the 'Party') – amounted to an exceptional situation, as I will argue. The next section, perhaps the most law-centric one in this chapter, provides a brief overview of the juridical acts introducing martial law – that is, the resolution of the Council of State and the accompanying legislative decrees which, in my view, were all perfectly legal under the state-socialist constitution of the period. Finally, in the last section, I address the question of the nature of General Jaruzelski's *dictatura*, specifically asking about its commissary or sovereign character, and about its role in transforming the Polish polity and building the foundations of the 'rule of law'.

5 Cercel notes that wartime communism 'is and can be regarded as a dictatorship or even more as a state of exception' of a 'transitional character' See Cosmin Cercel, *Towards a Jurisprudence of State Communism: Law and the Failure of Communism* (London: Routledge, 2018), 93.

6 On the other hand, Cercel argues that the Stalinist defence of legality 'was historically consubstantial with a *normalised state of exception* marked by extra-judicial measures, deportations and killings, and (…) was itself a state of exception insofar as it tended to protected both the existing posiitve law and the form of legality' (Cercel, *Towards a Jurisprudence*, 103). However, in the case of Stalinism, the *institution* of the state of exception was not used as such. The state of exception was, arguably, *practised*, but not as a question of legal form, but rather actual functioning of the repressive apparatus of the Soviet state.

7 Article 1 of the Constitution of the Polish People's Republic of 22 July 1952, consolidated version of 16 February 1976, *Dziennik Ustaw PRL* 1976, no 7, item 36.

8 I will use the expression 'Martial Law' in capital letters to denote the Polish martial law declared on 12/13 December 1981 as a unique historical event.

An exception from what? State-socialist 'normalcy'

Any state of emergency is always an exception from a certain 'normal situation', which allows the legal order to 'make sense', as Carl Schmitt wrote.[9] To define this normal situation, I will refer to the concept of state socialism (known also as 'state communism' or 'actually existing socialism') as a unique socio-economic and political formation, distinct from capitalism and feudalism on the one hand, but also from socialism and communism, as envisaged by Marx, Engels or Lenin, on the other.[10] State socialism as a formation was based on what Ken Jowitt conceptualised as the 'Leninist civilisation',[11] a form of organising social life where a key role was played by the Leninist 'party of a new type', a charismatic yet impersonal organisation, convinced of its historical role, combining heroism and arbitrariness with 'sober empirical examination of social change.'[12] In economic terms, state socialism was founded on the state ownership of the key means of production and on central planning.[13] In political terms, the hegemony of the Leninist party, with its system of democratic centralism, was a key element of the system. In legal terms, the system of state-socialism was undoubtedly an authoritarian one.[14]

The legal order was, in itself, dualist: on the one hand there was the *lex scripta* comprising the Constitution, decrees and acts of parliament; on the other hand, the *ius politicum*, often unwritten but partly codified in internal Party documents, enjoyed superiority as the decisive layer of the legal order.[15] It prescribed, in more or less codified forms, the rules of the

9 Carl Schmitt, *Political Theology*, George Schwab transl. (Cambridge, MA: MIT Press, 1985), 3.
10 See especially Jan Sowa, *Inna Rzeczpospolita jest możliwa! Widma przeszłości, wizje przyszłości* [Another Republic is Possible! Specters of the Past, Visions of the Future] (Warszawa: WAB, 2015) 108–109. Cf. idem, 'An Unexpected Twist of Ideology: Neoliberalism and the collapse of the Soviet Bloc' (2012) 5 *Praktyka Teoretyczna* 153, 161–168.
11 Ken Jowitt, *New World Disorder: The Leninist Extinction* (Berkeley: University of California Press, 1992), 1–49.
12 Ibid., 11.
13 Tadeusz Kowalik, *From Solidarity to Sellout: The Restoration of Capitalism in Poland*, transl Eliza Lewandowska (New York: Monthly Review Press, 2011) 26.
14 Cf. Lech Mażewski, *Posttotalitarny autorytaryzm PRL 1956–1989. Analiza ustrojowopolityczna* [Post-Totalitarian Authoritarianism: The Polish People's Republic 1956–1989. An Analysis of the Political Constitution] (Warszawa-Biała Podlaska: Arte, 2010).
15 Cf. Mikhail Antonov, 'Legal Realism in Soviet and Russian Jurisprudence', (2018) 43 *Review of Central and East European Law* 483. My idea of conceptualising the informal, yet empirically binding rules of the *ius politicum* as a layer of the socialist legal system goes against Mikhail Anotonov's understanding, who limits the scope of the signifier 'law' only to what I call here the *lex scripta*. My approach, which I could describe as radically realist, aims to underscore the importance of the Party's internal normative system for the constitutional setup

nomenklatura system, allowing the Party instances to appoint and dismiss key officials in the constitutional system, including not only ministers, directors of enterprises, but also prosecutors, judges, military and police commanders.[16] Of course, this duality was not fully recognised and despite the constitutionalisation of the Party in 1976, it remained partly a taboo.[17] In Lacanian terms, one could say that whereas the *lex scripta* was fully symbolised, the *ius politicum* remained, up till 1989, partly symbolised and partly repressed (as the Real of socialist constitutionalism).

The duality of the legal system reflected the fundamental duality of the party-state political system, conceptualised by Lech Mażewski as the binary structures of the technical and political government.[18] Thus, one could speak of the Politburo as the political government and the Council of Ministers as the technical government. The Council of State was a collective but merely technical head of state, while the First Secretary was the political and actual head of state. Individual ministries were reflected in the structure of the departments of the Central Committee (CC), and each head of department in the CC oversaw his 'technical' counterpart, i.e. a minister. Even Parliament, whose *de iure* constitutional role was supreme, was *de facto* reduced to a technical body charged with rubber-stamping decisions made elsewhere. The actual, political assembly of the country was the Central Committee of the Party[19] which met several times a year and held actual debates among Party factions, enjoyed the power to elect the Politburo, although it was, itself, elected only by Party members, and not by all citizens of the Republic.

Emergency legislation usually provides for the more or less extensive suspension of the rule of law and fundamental rights: this is its constitutional essence. But a state-socialist polity had a rather different approach to these two notions if compared to a bourgeois liberal state. The operation of the juridical was guided by the principle of 'socialist legality', a concept devised

of a state-socialist polity which, without taking into account the *ius politicum*, cannot be properly described only on the basis of the *lex scripta*. For a different, and highly original conceptualisaton in terms of the 'law of the hegemon', see Dawid Bunikowski, 'Hegemoni i ich prawo w czasach polskiego komunizmu. Próba analizy prawnoustrojowej i filozoficzno-prawnej' [Hegemons and their Law in the Times of Polish Communism: An Attempt at a Constitutional and Legal-Philosophical Analysis] (2010) 9 *Roczniki Naukowe Wyższej Szkoły Bankowej w Toruniu* 95.

16 See e.g. Thomas Lowit, 'Y a-t-il des États en Europe de l'Est?' (1979) 20 *Revue française de la sociologie* 431; idem, 'Le Parti polimorphe en Europe de l'Est' (1979) 29 (4–5) *Revue française de science politique* 812.

17 I would like to thank Przemysław Tacik for drawing my attention to this aspect.

18 Mażewski, *Posttotalitarny* 40.

19 Stefan Kisielewski, 'Wywiad ze Stefanem Kisielewskim' [An Interview with Stefan Kisielewski] (1956) 6 *Kultura* 27, at 28 (who even calls the Central Committee a 'parliament').

in the 1930s in the USSR.[20] In short, socialist legality differed from Western liberal rule of law in two fundamental aspects. First, it emphasised the duty of strict observance of the law by citizens and state authorities alike.[21] Hence, it was not so much a shield protecting citizens from government, but rather a sword allowing the government to control citizens. Second, its central tenet was its class character: socialist legality was about the legal form of the will of the ruling class, i.e. theoretically the working people,[22] which, however, expressed its will through the Leninist party.[23] Thus, socialist legality was more about giving legal form to the authoritarian rule of the Party than about protecting citizens from it.

If we look into the question of fundamental rights in a state-socialist polity, it becomes immediately patent that, in contrast to liberal capitalist states, the fundamental economic and social rights are placed at the forefront. They open the constitutional bill of rights and, by and large, they were actually enforced.[24] The state provided heavily subsidised housing, free healthcare, free education even at university level, heavily subsidised access to culture, paid holidays and subsidised holiday facilities, etc. As from 1956, abortion was legal and available for free.[25] In contrast, LGBT rights were not recognised, and in the 1980s members of the LGBT community were even subject to persecutions as part of a project led by the Ministry of the Interior.[26]

As concerns political rights, however, their *prima facie* constitutional formulation did not reflect the reality. One could conceptualise this phenomenon

20 Antonov, 'Legal Realism', 505.

21 See e.g. Article 8(2) of the Constitution of the Polish People's Republic.

22 Se e.g. Jan Ziembiński, 'Zasada praworządności jako metoda realizacji funkcji państwa socjalistycznego' [The Principle of Legality as a Method of Realization of Function of the Socialist State] (1968) 30(2) *Ruch Prawniczy, Ekonomiczny i Socjologiczny* 285, 300. Cf. Antonov, 'Legal Realism' 497. On legal instrumentalism in state-socialist systems see e.g. Alan Uzelac, 'Survival of the Third Legal Tradition?', (2010) 49 *Supreme Court Law Review* 377.

23 Lech Mażewski, *System rządów w PRL 1952–1989* [Constitutional System of the Polish People's Republic, 1952–1989] (Warszawa-Bielsko-Biała: Arte, 2012).

24 See e.g. Oliver MacDonald, 'The Polish Vortex: Solidarity and Socialism' (1983) 139 *New Left Review* 5, 7.

25 Małgorzata Maciejewska, 'Aborcja w PRL-u. Ustawa o warunkach dopuszczalności przerywania ciąży z 1956 r. w kontekście feministycznym' [Abortion in the Polish People's Republic: The Conditions of Permissibility of Pregnancy Termination Act 1956 in a Feminist Context] in Jakub Majmurek and Piotr Szumlewicz (eds.), *PRL bez uprzedzeń* [The Polish People's Republic without Prejudices] (Warszawa: Książka i Prasa, 2010) 167–184; Antoni Rajkiewicz, 'Polityka społeczna w Polsce Ludowej' [Social Policy in People's Poland] in Wiesław Żółtkowski (ed.), Zrozumieć PRL [Understanding the Polish People's Republic] (Warszawa: MUZA SA, 2012) 114.

26 Błażej Warkocki, 'Parametry ukrycia. PRL wobec homoseksualności' [Hiding Parameters: Polish People's Republic and Homosexuality] in Majmurek and Szumlewicz (eds), *Zrozumieć PRL* 197–218; Krzysztof Tomasik, *Gejerel. Mniejszości seksualne w PRL-u* [*Gejerel*: Sexual Minorities in the Polish People's Republic] (Warszawa: Wydawnictwo Krytyki Politycznej, 2012).

either by a very broad abuse of rights doctrine, pointing out that political rights could be exercised only within the framework of the *telos* of the Polish people's Republic and with respect to the hegemonic role of the Leninist party, itself constitutionalised in 1976.[27] Or, one could simply point to the dualist character of the legal system and note that the rights guaranteed by the *lex scripta* were actually trumped by the *ius politicum*. All in all, the political monopoly of the Leninist party excluded the creation of opposition parties (its subjected allies, the Polish People's Faction and the Democratic Faction were called 'factions', not 'parties', to avoid any misunderstanding), or of independent trade unions. The only politically independent organisation in state-socialist Poland was, effectively, the Catholic Church. All these aspects of state-socialist normalcy, and especially the political hegemony of the Leninist party and the command system of the economy, came under unprecedented pressure in 1980/81.

The economic and political crisis preceding the Martial Law

There can be no doubt that, judged against the normalcy of state socialism, Poland's situation in 1981 was profoundly exceptional. This exceptionality manifested itself in three dimensions: economic, socio-political and geopolitical. In economic terms, Poland was going through the deepest economic crisis since the end of World War II. Following a decade of loans-driven development in the 1970s, a radical raise of the interest rates and an unfavourable change in terms of trade meant that Poland, alongside Latin American countries, fell into a deep debt crisis. This had also a political dimension, because the creditors were capitalist states and capitalist banks, meaning that they were extracting capital rent from a state-socialist country and exerting an increasing influence upon its economic life.[28] Loan repayments were taking up a growing share of the GNP, leading to a sovereign debt crisis.[29] At the same time, the internal market was unstable. For political reasons, prices were kept frozen since the 1960s, as attempts to raise them in 1970 and 1976 led to workers' unrest and were essentially withdrawn.[30] At the same time, workers' pay demands were generally met, leading to a market imbalance and a large

27 See Article 3(1) of the Polish Constitution (as of 1976): 'The Polish United Workers' Party is the leading political force of society in the construction of socialism.'

28 MacDonald, 'The Polish Vortex', 9.

29 Janusz Szkodlarski, *Zarys historii gospodarczej Polski* [An Outline of Poland's Economic History] (Warszawa: Wydawnictwo Naukowe PWN, 2007) 483–5; Andrzej Dorosz, 'Zadłużenie zagraniczne PRL' [The Foreign Indebtedness of the Polish People's Republic] in Żółtkowski (ed.), *Zrozumieć PRL* 204–214.

30 Andrzej Leon Sowa, *Historia polityczna Polski 1944–1991* [A Political History of Poland 1944–1991] (Kraków: Wydawnictwo Literackie, 2011), 407–11.

excess of cash in the economy, lacking a backing in goods or services that could be purchased.[31]

All in all, this difficult economic situation led the government to the conclusion that prices and wages have to be finally adjusted in order to restore market stability. A price adjustment operation was planned for July 1980, and targeted meat products, increasingly consumed by the Polish working class. It must be emphasised that the (hidden) price rises of July 1980 were 'a direct consequence of the changed line from Western financial centres made clear to the Polish government in May 1980,'[32] themselves a consequences of Poland's '[i]increasing economic integration with the West'.[33] They caused a massive wave of protests of the working class, leading ultimately to the creation of independent trade unions.

Faced with massive strikes leading to even less market stability (as fewer goods were produced), the outgoing government under the leadership of First Secretary Edward Gierek decided to give in to the workers' demands in exchange for them going back to work. The workers' demands were formulated as a list of 21 points, including the legalisation of independent trade unions, the right to strike, observance of freedom of speech, a broad and inclusive discussion on the economic reform, as well as a rather generous social programme (a significant, flat pay rise for all, coupled with an automatic indexation of salaries for the future, significant reduction of pension age, a five-day working week instead of the six-week one then in force); more political demands were also included, such as abolition of the *nomenklatura* system for management positions or more democratic access to the market (abolition of commercial prices and internal export shops and introduction of vouchers for meat and meat products).[34] The government largely gave in, and the social accord took the form of the August Agreements signed on 31 August 1980 in Gdańsk[35] and in parallel in other places where strikes took place. Most crucially, the government promised to legalise independent trade unions, relax censorship laws, and guarantee the right to strike, as well as to undertake efforts to fulfil most of the other demands.

Following the signature of the August Agreements, the Party leadership, which had accepted them, lost the confidence of the Central Committee.

31 Szkodlarski, *Zarys*, 493–4.
32 Ibid., 9.
33 Ibid.
34 '21 postulatów z 17 sierpnia 1980 roku' [21 Demands of 17 August 1980], available at www.solidarnosc.org.pl/21-postulatow, accessed 23 January 2020.
35 See 'Protokół porozumienia zawartego przez Komisję Rządową i Międzyzakładowy Komitet Strajkowy w dniu 31 sierpnia 1980 roku w Stoczni Gdańskiej' [Minutes of the Agreement Concluded Between the Government Commission and the Inter-Works Strike Committee on 31 August 1980 at the Gdańsk Shipyard], available at www.tysol.pl/a10765–Pelny-tekst-21-postulatow-Porozumienia-Sierpniowe-Zwyciestwo-1980, accessed 5 February 2020.

Edward Gierek and his Politburo were removed and replaced with a new leadership under First Secretary Stanisław Kania. Any attempts by the new government to retreat from the August Agreements met with strikes. Over time, Solidarity was radicalising itself and gaining an ever-broader membership base, ultimately reaching ten million members, compared to three million Party members, in a 35-million population. The movement was definitely massive, and its political ambitions were growing every month. It even sought to reach out to workers in other state-socialist countries, as evidenced by its highly provocative 'Address to the Working People of Eastern Europe', explicitly directed to 'the workers of Albania, Bulgaria, Czechoslovakia, German Democratic Republic, Hungary and of the all the nations of the Soviet Union', in which they wrote that 'contrary to lies propagated in your countries, we are an authentic, ten-million organisation of employees'.[36]

In October 1981, Solidarity adopted its official programme during the 1st Congress of Delegates.[37] Characteristically, the content of this document cannot be found today either on historical websites of Solidarity[38] or on the website of the infamous Institute of National Memory. This is no wonder, as the fifty-page document did not propose to introduce capitalism or even market mechanisms, but rather had an openly anarcho-syndicalist and radically democratic character, demanding the introduction of worker self-management and 'socialised planning' of the economy.[39] Not only the enterprises (thesis 20) but also the media (thesis 32) were to be owned and managed by society, rather than by the state or by the capital.[40] All this allows Jan Sowa to claim that Solidarity 'not only was not an anti-communist movement (…) but also was, in itself, a communist event *par excellence*.'[41] In his view, Solidarity's programme was the embodiment of the 'revolutionary *imaginarium* of

36 'Posłanie I Krajowego Zjazdu Delegatów NSZZ Solidarność do ludzi pracy Europy Wschodniej' [Address of the 1st Congress of Delegates of the Independent and Self-Governing Trade Union Solidarity to the Working People of Eastern Europe] in *Dokumenty I tury zjazdu* [Documents of the 1st Part of the Congress], available at www.solidarnosc.org.pl/wszechnica/wp-content/uploads/2010/10/1-KZD-I-tura-Gdańsk-1981.pdf, accessed 6 February 2020, 94–95.

37 'Program NSZZ "Solidarność" uchwalony przez I Krajowy Zjazd Delegatów', (2010) *Federalista* 83, available at http://ofop.eu/sites/ofop.eu/files/biblioteka-pliki/f1_83-124.pdf, accessed 6 February 2020. The programme is comprised of 37 theses, each of which is explained on 1–2 pages.

38 The programme was initially published as a supplement to the weekly *Solidarność*. However, the online versions available on numerous websites omit the programme.

39 Jan Sowa, *Inna Rzeczpospolita jest możliwa!* [A Different Republic is Possible!] (Warszawa: WAB, 2015), 171.

40 Cf. ibid., 174.

41 Ibid., 177.

the society, which had internalised the ideals of equality and socialisation, foundational to the order introduced in Poland after World War II.'[42]

In this sense, therefore, Solidarity was a part of the broad revisionist current within the communist movement, questioning the practices of state-socialism in the name of what they considered to be an authentic socialisation of the economy and government. As such, Solidarity was a direct and to a large extent *ideologically internal* threat to the concrete order of the Polish People's Republic, based on hegemony of the Party and its domination over the state and of the state over the economy. Solidarity's demands went even beyond what was practised in socialist Yugoslavia and aimed at a total constitutional overhaul. On the other hand, it must be admitted that apart from typically socialist elements of the economic programme, such as full employment (thesis 9), or the right to housing (thesis 17), the Solidarity programme also contained elements inspired by liberal political philosophy, such as political pluralism (thesis 19), judicial and prosecutorial independence (thesis 24), academic freedom (thesis 30) and autonomous local government (thesis 21). Solidarity experts even proposed to introduce direct democracy – referenda as a means of settling conflicts between Solidarity and the Party.[43] Not unsurprisingly, this admixture of anarcho-syndicalism, political liberalism and radical democracy was extremely alarming to the hegemonic Leninist party in power and to Poland's allies in the Warsaw Pact.

In Schmittian terms we can safely say that Solidarity aimed to be a new *pouvoir constituant*, aiming at the abolition of Leninist civilisation in Poland, and its replacement with an anarcho-syndicalist workers' self-government, coupled with pluralism and the rule of law, as outlined in the movement's official programme (which, in itself, could also have been formulated somewhat more moderately and need not have reflected the demands of the more radical activists within Solidarity).

On 3 December 1981 the Presidium of the National Coordination Commission of Solidarity, gathered in the city of Radom, adopted a very tough declaration, approved by the entire Coordination Commission on 12 December 1981. The language was very confrontational, and the Solidarity leadership was wary of the forthcoming legislation on the state of emergency. In the document we read *inter alia* that

> Regardless of whether the law on extraordinary measures will authorize the government to put civilians before a military court, ban gatherings

42 Ibid., 179–180.

43 Stefan Kurowski, Grzegorz Palka, Wacław Adamczak and Zbigniew Karwowski, 'Instytucjonalne zabezpieczenie Programu Ekonomicznego Związku' [Institutional Safeguards for the Economic Programme of the Union] in *Dokumenty I tury zjazdu* 77.

> and restrict traveling, or only to annul the right to strike, it will not be introduced in any other way than through terror. It would amount to an attempt to subdue the society through force. Therefore, the Union will respond to the Sejm's potential passing of the law on extraordinary powers for the government with a 24-hour long universal protest strike in Poland. In case the government takes advantage of the power granted to it by the Sejm to use extraordinary measures, the Union cells and all [workers'] crews should inevitably initiate a general strike.[44]

Radical and very concrete demands were made in categorical language. Solidarity indicated that it was not open to compromise on a number of demands, including a new trade union law following its version, pluralist elections to local councils on all levels and subordination of state administration to such councils, change of economic governance giving Solidarity more powers, and finally access to the media for Solidarity and the Catholic Church.[45] This was the state of mind of Solidarity leadership on 12 December 1981, directly before Martial Law.

Poland's domestic situation was, as from the summer of 1980, a reason of growing concern for its allies in the Warsaw Pact, especially the USSR, GDR and Czechoslovakia.[46] The Soviets created a special commission to oversee Poland, headed by the orthodox Marxist-Leninist Suslov.[47] Large-scale military manoeuvres involving the Soviet Army and other Warsaw Pact armies took place on Polish territory and in the neighbouring countries.[48] A special Soviet command centre was installed nearby Warsaw.[49] Of course, we will never know whether the Soviets were actually intending to repeat the 1953/1956/1968 scenarios or whether it was all mere bluff. As Mark Kramer rightly points out, 'Polish leaders (…) may have genuinely believed that an invasion would occur if a solution "from within" Poland (i.e., martial law) did not materialize. Indeed, Soviet leaders themselves may have wanted to create that impression—even if they did not intend to follow up on it (…).'[50]

What remains important from the point of view of the exceptionality of the situation are two facts. First, that Solidarity intended to build an alternative social *and* political force, competing with the Leninist party and aiming to

44 Solidarity NCC Presidium, 'Position Taken by the Presidium of the National Coordinating Commission and Leaders of the NSZZ. December 3, 1981' in Paczkowski and Byrne (eds), *From Solidarity*, 418.
45 Solidarity NCC Presidium, 'Position Taken….', 418–419.
46 MacDonald, 'Polish Vortex' 23; Sowa, *Historia polityczna*, 463–464.
47 Sowa, *Historia polityczna*, 462
48 Ibid., 471–472.
49 Wojciech Jaruzelski, *Starsi o 30 lat* [30 Years Older] (Toruń: Adam Marszałek, 2011), 112–113.
50 Mark Kramer, 'Jaruzelski, the Soviet Union, and the Imposition of Martial Law in Poland: New Light on the Mystery of December 1981' (1998) 11 *Cold War International History Project Bulletin* 5.

deprive it of its hegemony. Second, that it adopted a radical socio-economic and political programme, incompatible with the concrete order of state socialism. And third, that the Soviets were creating the impression that they might intervene in a military fashion. This impression was, moreover, shared by American intelligence, as reflected in the CIA reports for the US president.[51] If that is how the West perceived the situation, then General Jaruzelski cannot be blamed for evaluating it in the same way. But even leaving aside the *external* dimension of the situation, in purely *internal* terms the exceptionality of what was happening in Poland and the incompatibility of that situation with the state-socialist constitution cannot be put into question.

A December night's decrees

The legal framework of the Martial Law

Unlike the 1921 and 1935 constitutions, the Constitution of the Polish People's Republic of 22 July 1952 did not foresee two distinct types of state of emergency (a state of exception on *internal* grounds and martial law on *external* security grounds) but only one, called 'stan wojenny' (literally, 'war state' or 'martial law'). It could, however, be introduced both for internal and external grounds which allows to assume that this uniform legal institution comprised both forms of the state of emergency in one. The relevant rule on the martial law was located in Article 33(2), sentence 1:

> The Council of State may introduce martial law in a part or on the entire territory of the Polish People's Republic if this is required by reasons of defence or security of the state.

The pre-1939 legislation on the state of exception and martial law, as based on the 1935 constitution, although formally not repealed, was inapplicable by virtue of the principle of *desuetudo*.[52] Poland's post-1944 legal continuity with the pre-1939 legal order was not unconditional: only legislation that was compatible with the new political and economic system was considered to be binding. Therefore, in 1981 Poland found itself in the situation of a legal vacuum[53]: there existed the competence norm of Article 33 of the

51 Douglas J MacEachin, *US Intelligence and the Polish Crisis: 1980–1981* (Washington, DC: Center for the Study of Intelligence, 2000), esp 3, 12–13, 26, 32, 53, 107–108.

52 Paweł Bała 'Stan wojenny 13 grudnia 1981 r. jako zagadnienie prawa ustrojowego. Interpretacja decyzjonistyczna' [The Martial Law of 13 December 1981 as a Question of Constitutional Law: A Decisionist Interpretation] (2013) 21 *Przegląd Sejmowy* no 4, 83, 94 n. 49. Cf. Bunikowski, 'Hegemoni i ich prawo' 108 n. 30.

53 Lech Mażewski, *Problem legalności stanu wojenego z 12–13 grudnia 1981 r. Studium z historii prawa polskiego* [The Question of the Legality of the Martial Law

Constitution empowering the Council of State to introduce martial law, but there was no detailed legislation specifying what changes in the legal regime of the state would occur. Importantly, the competence norm of Article 33 did not specifically refer to any such legislation, which could allow it to be argued that the act introducing the Martial Law (the resolution of the Council of State) could, simultaneously, lay down the legal order of that state for the time of its validity.

This approach, however, was not taken up, and instead the Council of State, gathered during the night of 12/13 December 1981 at an emergency session which started at 1 a.m.,[54] adopted four legislative decrees[55] and a resolution[56] introducing the Martial Law.[57] Formally, the resolution was based on the Constitution 'in conjunction with' the general decree on martial law. To underline this logical order, the resolution was published *after* the decrees, reflecting its subordination to the purported legal basis. However, as all acts were adopted at one and the same sitting of the Council of State, and all were published in the *Journal of Laws* only on 17 December 1981,[58] this technicality can be seen more as the manifestation of some kind of formalist obsession of the government lawyers than any real connection. In substantive legal and political terms, the state of exception was introduced simultaneously with its legal framework.

At the same time, the Military Council of National Salvation was established, a body not only not foreseen by the Constitution but paradoxically not even mentioned in the decrees or the resolution. The Military Council did not have any specific constitutional role or political added value, especially as General Jaruzelski – combining the roles of first secretary, prime minister, and minister of defence – already possessed all the necessary powers to govern the country as its *dictator* (in the Roman and Schmittian sense of the word). As Andrzej Paczkowski argues, it was not the Military Council but the so-called 'Directorate', composed of the

of 12–13 December 1981: A Study in Polish Legal History] (Warszawa: Wydawnictwo von Borowiecki, 2012), 37.

54 Mieczysław F. Rakowski, *Dzienniki polityczne 1981-1983* [Political Diaries 1981-1983] (Warszawa: Iskry, 2004), 135.

55 They will be discussed below.

56 Uchwała Rady Państwa z dnia 12 grudnia 1981 r. w sprawie wprowadzenia stanu wojennego ze względu na bezpieczeństwo państwa [Resolution of the Council of State of 12 December 1981 concerning the introduction of martial law for reasons connected to the security of the state] (Dz.U. 1981 no 29 item 155).

57 This was the *legal* decision. The final *political* decision was taken during the meeting of generals: Jaruzelski, Janiszewski, Kiszczak and Siwicki at 9 a.m. on Saturday, 12 December 1981. Wojciech Jaruzelski *Stan wojenny... dlaczego* [The Martial Law... Why] (Warszawa: BGW, 1992) 412. Cf. Andrzej Paczkowski, *Revolution and Counterrevolution in Poland, 1980-1989: Solidarity, Martial Law, and the End of Communism in Europe* (Rochester: Rochester University Press, 2015), 50.

58 Mażewski, *Problem legalności*, 49.

General's *personnes de confiance*, which assisted him in ruling the country and made 'operative decisions'.[59] Thus, the Military Council was yet another one of those façade[60] bodies and entities that the general had a taste for, such as the Council of National Agreement (proposed in February 1981 but rejected by the opposition),[61] the Patriotic Movement of National Regeneration (1982–1989), or the Social Consultative Council, established in 1986, but boycotted by both the opposition and the Catholic Church.[62] Collective bodies with real power included the Politburo and Secretariat of the Central Committee, on the party side, and the Council of Ministers and the Government Presidium, on the state side.[63]

The legal framework of the martial law was based on a total of four decrees. The first one, the decree on martial law,[64] laid down the substantive provisions. It suspended a number of constitutional rights, including personal inviolability, inviolability of abode and correspondence, rights of association,[65] freedom of speech, print, assembly and demonstration. It foresaw the possibility of introducing curfew and limiting the free movement of persons across the country, it allowed the suspension of associations, suspended the right to strike and introduced the need to request permission to hold assemblies, unless they were religious. Workers' self-government could be suspended,[66] preventive censorship

59 Andrzej Paczkowski, 'Stan wojenny i powojenny stan wojenny: od grudnia 1981 do stycznia 1989' [Martial Law and the Post-War Martial Law: from Decemember 1981 until January 1989] in Krzystof Persak and Paweł Machcewicz (eds), 4 *Polski Wiek XX: PRL od grudnia 1970 do stycznia 1989* [Polish 20th Century: the Polish People's Republic from December 1970 until January 1989] (Warszawa: Bellona, 2011) 211–212; idem, *Revolution* 72-73. Meetings of the 'Directorate' held between 14 December 1981 and 5 May 1982 are described in Rakowski's political diaries (Rakowski, *Dzienniki polityczne 1981-1983*, 136-148, 154-156, 186-187, 190, 272-275).

60 Paczkowski, *Revolution*, 74.

61 See e.g. 'Notatka z konferencji u Wicepremiera Mieczysława F. Rakowskiego na temat koncepcji Rady Porozumienia Narodowego (RPN) w dniu 2.II.1981' [A Note from a Conference hosted by the Deputy Prime Minister Mieczysław F Rakowski concerning the Conception of a Council of National Agreement, held on 2 February 1981] available at www.tygodnikprzeglad.pl/czy-mozliwe-bylo-porozumienie-partia-kosciol-solidarnosc/, accessed 5 February 2020.

62 Kazmierz Z Poznański, *Poland's Protracted Transition: Institutional Change and Economic Growth 1970–1994* (Cambridge: Cambridge University Press, 1996) 148.

63 Paczkowski, *Revolution*, 73-74.

64 Dekret z dnia 12 grudnia 1981 r. o stanie wojennym [Decree of 12 December 1981 on martial law], *Dziennik Ustaw PRL 1981*, no 29, item 154

65 See Zarządzenie nr 51 Prezesa Rady Ministrów 13 grudnia 1981 r. w sprawie zawieszenia działalności związków zawodowych i niektórych organizacji społecznych na czas obowiązywania stanu wojennego [Order no 51 of the Prime Minister of 13 December 1981 concerning the suspension of trade unions and certain other social organisations during the period of the martial law], *Monitor Polski* no 30, item 273.

66 See rozporządzenie Rady Ministrów z dnia 30 grudnia 1981 r. w sprawie zawieszenia działalności samorządu załóg przedsiębiorstw państwowych na czas

formally introduced[67] (it was not a novelty). Individuals and NGOs were prohibited from owning or using printing devices. Correspondence was to be censored and phone calls tapped. Police were authorised to uses emergency measures, including 'chemical incapacitating agents', water cannons and even combat weapons. It made it possible to introduce a duty to work for all above 15 years of age, unless pensioned. Workers could be moved between enterprises and a six-day working week could be introduced. Rationing of foodstuffs and obligatory supplies from farmers were introduced. Transport could be suspended, including the closure of border crossings, and telecom services limited.[68] Administrative detention of individuals was introduced for persons aged above 17, 'in relation to which, for reasons of their hitherto conduct, there is a risk that remaining in liberty they would not conform to the legal order or would undertake an activity threatening the interests of security or defence of the state.'[69] Internment decisions were taken by regional commanders of the police, with the possibility of appealing the decision to the minister of the interior.[70] The decree provided for the creation of 'isolation centres' for those subject to internment, and for the application *mutatis mutandis* on rules on pre-trial detention to those centres.[71,72] Ironically, therefore, state-socialist Poland returned to the authoritarian traditions of pre-1939 capitalist Poland, where administrative detention had been introduced in 1934, following the military coup of 1926.[73]

obowiązywania stanu wojennego [Ordinance of the Council of Ministers of 30 December 1981 suspending the activity of self-government of the crews of state enterprises during the period of martial law], *Dziennik Ustaw* no 32, item 185.

67 See Zarządzenie Prezesa Głównego Urzędu Kontroli Publikacji i Widowisk 12 grudnia 1981 r. w sprawie zasad i trybu udzielania zezwoleń na rozpowszechnianie publikacji i widowisk oraz postępowania przy użytkowaniu zakładów, urządzeń i aparatów poligraficznych w czasie obowiązywania stanu wojennego [Order of the President of the Chief Office for the Control of Publications and Shows of 12 December 1981 concerning the principles and procedures for granting permission to make available publications and shows and procedure concerning the use of poligraphic works, appliances and apparatuses during the period of martial law], *Monitor Polski* no 30, item 278.

68 Detailed rules on telecommunications were laid down in Rozporządzenie Rady Ministrów 12 grudnia 1981 r. w sprawie wykonania przepisów dekretu o stanie wojennym w zakresie łączności [Ordinance of the Council of Ministers of 12 December 1981 concerning the execution of rules of the decree on martial law concerning telecommunication], *Dziennik Ustaw* no 29, item 160.

69 Decree on Martial Law, Article 42.

70 Decree on Martial Law, Articles 43–44.

71 Decree on Martial Law, Article 45.

72 Detailed rules on internment were laid down in rozporządzenie Rady Ministrów 12 grudnia 1981 r. w sprawie zasad postępowania w sprawach o internowanie obywateli polskich [Ordinance of the Council of Ministers of 12 December 1981 regarding the principles of proceeding in cases concerning the internment of Polish nationals], *Dziennik Ustaw* no 29, item 159.

73 See especially Rozporządzenie Prezydenta Rzeczypospolitej z dnia 17 czerwca 1934 r. w sprawie osób zagrażających bezpieczeństwu, spokojowi i porządkowi publicznemu

Finally, a set of new criminal acts was introduced, with penalties ranging from a maximum of three to even ten years in prison.[74] The criminalised acts included *inter alia* the continuing the activity of a suspended organisation, the organisation of strikes or protest actions, acting to the detriment of the interests of state security, or the propagation of fake news. Apart from criminal acts, the decree introduced a number of new misdemeanors,[75] punishable by arrest up to three months or a financial penalty up to 5,000 zlotys – almost half the average monthly salary.[76] These included *inter alia* such acts as participation in a strike or protest action, change of residence without permission, violation of the curfew, presence in a public place without ID, or abstaining from work.

The Decree on Martial Law was accompanied by a decree on special proceedings in cases concerning crimes and petty offences,[77] a decree granting jurisdiction over civilians to military courts,[78] and a decree on amnesty for anti-government acts committed before the Martial Law.[79] The decree on special proceedings allowed for summary trials in a number of crimes already foreseen in the Criminal Code, as well as those introduced in the Decree on Martial Law. The decrees were applied swiftly and effectively with the participation of over 53,000 soldiers.[80] As of 14 December, 3,437 individuals were interned,[81] the figure rising to 3,926 on 16 December,[82] 4,450 on 18 December,[83] 4,612 on 20 December,[84] 5,540

[Decree of the President of the Republic of 17 June 1934 concerning persons threatening security, peace and the public order], *Dziennik Ustaw* no 50, item 473.

74 Decree on Martial Law, Articles 46–51.

75 Decree on Martial Law, Articles 50–51.

76 The average salary in 1981 amounted to 7,689 zlotys, and in 1982–11,631 zlotys. See 'Przeciętne miesięczne wynagrodzenie w latach 1950–2008' available at www.infor.pl/prawo/zarobki/zarobki-w-polsce/686166,Przecietne-miesieczne-wynagrodzenie-w-latach-19502008.html, accessed 26 January 2020.

77 Dekret z dnia 12 grudnia 1981 r. o postępowaniach szczególnych w sprawach o przestępstwa i wykroczenia w czasie obowiązywania stanu wojennego [Decree of 12 December 1981 on special proceedings for crimes and petty offences during martial law] (Dz.U. no 29, item 156).

78 Dekret z dnia 12 grudnia 1981 r. o przekazaniu do właściwości sądów wojskowych spraw o niektóre przestępstwa oraz o zmianie ustroju sądów wojskowych i wojskowych jednostek organizacyjnych Prokuratury PRL w czasie obowiązywania stanu wojennego [Decree of 12 December 1981 on the transfer of jurisdiction concerning certain crimes to courts martial] (Dz.U no 29, item 157).

79 Dekret z dnia 12 grudnia 1981 r. o przebaczeniu i puszczeniu w niepamięć niektórych przestępstw i wykroczeń [Decree of 12 December 1981 on amnesty concerning certain crimes and petty offences], Dz.U. no 29, item 158.

80 Paczkowski, *Revolution*, 94.

81 Rakowski, *Dzienniki*, 136.

82 Ibid., 138.

83 Ibid., 141.

84 Ibid., 143

on 24 December,[85] and 5,817 on 27 December.[86] After that, the figures started falling: as of 27 January 1982, there were 4,893 interned, but 1,356 had been released from internment,[87] and on 5 February 4,394 remained interned, and 2,066 had been released.[88]

During the entire period of the Martial Law (13 December 1981 – 21 July 1983) a total of 7,400 individuals were sentenced for crimes related to the decree on martial law, out of which some 5,700 individuals were sentenced by courts martial.[89] Apart from that, some 208,000 individuals were punished for martial-law related misdemeanours.[90]

On 25 January 1982, Parliament assembled for the first time since the introduction of Martial Law. It adopted an act[91] which formally 'ratified' the Martial Law decrees, stating that 'The Decrees adopted by the Council of State on 12 December 1981 are hereby ratified' (Article 1) and that they remain in force 'until the adoption of an act on martial law' (Article 2). On 18 December 1982 the *Sejm* adopted an act allowing for the suspension of martial law.[92] The next day, the Council of State adopted a resolution suspending martial law as of that day.[93] Following almost seven months of its suspension, the Martial Law was definitely withdrawn by a resolution of the Council of State of 20 July 1983,[94] two days before the main national holiday of 22 July. On 21 July 1984 an amnesty was proclaimed, and *all* 652 political prisoners were released, alongside 25,000 ordinary criminal prisoners.[95]

85 Ibid., 146.
86 Ibid., 148.
87 Ibid., 183.
88 Ibid., 189.
89 Paczkowski, *Revolution* 104. See also detailed statistics as of 12 October 1982 in Rakowski, *Dzienniki polityczne 1981-1983*, 371.
90 Paczkowski, *Revolution*, 109.
91 Ustawa z dnia 25 stycznia 1982 r. o szczególnej regulacji prawnej w okresie stanu wojennego [Act of 25 January 1982 on the special legal regime during the period of martial law], *Dziennik Ustaw* no 3, item 18
92 Ustawa z dnia 18 grudnia 1982 r. o zmianie ustawy o szczególnej regulacji prawnej w okresie stanu wojennego [Act of 18 December 1982 modifying the act on the special legal regime during the period of martial law], *Dziennik Ustaw* no 41, item 272.
93 Uchwała Rady Państwa z dnia 19 grudnia 1982 r. w sprawie zawieszenia stanu wojennego [Resolution of the Council of State of 19 December 1982 regarding the suspension of the martial law], *Dziennik Ustaw* no 42, item 275.
94 Uchwała Rady Państwa z dnia 20 lipca 1983 r. w sprawie zniesienia stanu wojennego [Resolution of the Council of State of 20 July 1983 regarding the abolition of Martial Law], *Dziennik Ustaw* no 39, item 178.
95 Mieczysław F Rakowski, *Dzienniki polityczne 1984-1986* (Warszawa: Iskry, 2005), 106-108; Marceli Kosman, *Wojciech Jaruzelski. Mąż stanu w czasach przełomu* [Wojciech Jaruzelski: Statesman in Times of Breakthrough] (Toruń: Wydawnictwo Adam Marszałek, 2013), 86.

The question of formal legality

Even in the immediate wake of its introduction, the formal legality of the Martial Law was challenged.[96] The most significant elements of the argument are concerned with the competence of the Council of State to issue legislative decrees if the session of the *Sejm* had not been closed, the retroactivity of the decrees given their belated publication in the *Journal of Laws* and the existence of a substantive premiss of the threat to state security justifying the introduction of the Martial Law.[97]

Taking into account the dualist character of the legal system, comprising both the technical *lex scripta* and the political party law, the legality of the introduction of martial law and its legal ramifications need to be analysed not only in line with the written Constitution but also taking account of the Party's will, expressed by its bodies. Specifically, the last meeting of the Politburo before Martial Law gave General Jaruzelski an implicit authorisation to proceed with its proclamation when and how he saw fit.[98] Furthermore, General Jaruzelski, as first secretary, already enjoyed legitimacy within the Party as the country's leader. This, together with the Politburo's preliminary authorisation, makes the Martial Law legal in the light of the *ius politicum* of the Party.

On the side of the written Constitution, as I have pointed out above, the basic law vested state of exception powers in one sole body – the Council of State. This body was the technical head of state, largely a decorative one, and in practice its decisions followed that of the Politburo and the first secretary, the political government and head of state, respectively. But looking only from the perspective of the written Constitution of 1952, the Council of State decision to introduce the Martial Law is perfectly legal – it was based on a competence norm explicitly enshrined in the Constitution. Since no other body's consent was required, it was clear that it was up to the Council of State to determine whether an exceptional situation existed, and if that was the case – introduce martial law as the legal form of the state of exception in the Polish People's Republic.

The session of the Council of State during which the resolution and decrees were adopted lasted from 1 am until 2.30 am on 13 December

96 One of the first academic publications challenging the legality of the Martial Law was Janusz Kochanowski and Tadeusz de Virion, 'Glosa do wyroku SN z 1 marca 1982 r., V KRN 50/82' (1982) 9 *Państwo i Prawo*, 148.

97 See e.g. Bogumiła Lubera and Agnieszka Sikorska, 'Retroaktywność dekretu o stanie wojennym w świetle Konstytucji z 1952 i 1997 r.' [Retroactivity of the Martial Law Decree in the Light of the 1952 and 1997 Constitutions] (2010) 4 *Przegląd Prawa Konstytucyjnego* 125, 131–139; Mażewski, *Problem legalności* 39–65, 131–138.

98 Cf. 'Protocol No. 18' 443–444, where the general presents plans to introduce Martial Law, presumably approved tacitly by the Politburo, as claimed by Mażewski, *Posttotalitarny autorytatyzm*, 104.

1981.[99] Hence, all five acts adopted that night were antedated, as they mention 12 December, and not 13 December, as their date of adoption. Furthermore, the operation of introducing the state of exception started at 11.30 pm on 12 December, i.e. even before the session of the Council of State had begun.[100] The *Journal of Laws* where they were promulgated was dated 14 December, although it became available only on 17 December 1981.[101] However, as the Supreme Court underlined in its judgment of 1 March 1982, the decrees and resolution were well known to citizens as they had been made public in the mass media.[102] The national television informed about the content of the decree, and a communication by the president of the Council of State concerning martial law was made public in poster form.[103] Indeed, taking into account the exceptionality of a state of emergency, it would have rendered the Martial Law inoperative if it had been necessary to wait for its legal effects until the decrees and resolution were correctly published, perhaps even with a *vacatio legis*. Finally, since Poland was a party to the International Covenant of Civic and Political Rights, the ambassador of the Polish People's Republic to the UN informed the secretary general, initially by telephone, and later during an audience.[104] Thus, formal legality was preserved, even on an international level.

Parliamentary scrutiny and judicial proceedings after 1990

Until the end of the Polish People's Republic (1989) the question of the legality of the Martial Law was not questioned by the judiciary, although some scholars already then presented critical views. It was only following Poland's transformation from state socialism to capitalism as a result of the Round Table agreements of 1989 that the question of the Martial Law and its formal legality became an object of heated political debate as well as 'transitional justice' measures. A parliamentary scrutiny committee had worked between 1991 and 1996 on the question, publishing its report in 1996,[105] where it found that the act introducing martial law was legal without any doubt. As to the legislative decrees accompanying it, Parliament noted that technically they should not have been adopted by the Council of State during a session of Parliament, nonetheless it took note of the exceptional situation and the fact that attempts at having them regularly adopted in the Chamber met with fierce opposition from Solidarity, which threatened the government with a

99 Rakowski, *Dzienniki polityczne 1981-1982*, 135; Mażewski, *Problem legalności*, 36.
100 Ibid., 35–36.
101 Ibid., 48–49.
102 Case V KRN 50/82, OSNKW 1982 no 6, item 39.
103 Mażewski, *Problem legalności*, 50.
104 Ibid., 54–55.
105 Ibid., 65–67.

general strike. This led Parliament to consider this form of adoption as a 'justified solution'.

The issue of the formal legality of the Martial Law was also addressed in a number of Supreme Court[106] and Constitutional Court judgments,[107] as well as a criminal case against General Jaruzelski and others, brought in 2007.[108] Characteristically, they all focused on questions of formal legality, such as the proper publication of the decrees, and their retroactivity, or – in the case of the criminal case – on the alleged absence of a clear and present danger of a Soviet intervention,[109] but at the same time failed to address the main constitutional premiss of the Martial Law, i.e. the duty to protect the constitutional system of actually existing socialism against an internal revolution staged by Solidarity.[110] The main legal argument underpinning the act of accusation against General Jaruzelski was that at the moment of adoption of the martial law decrees the session of the *Sejm* had not been formally closed and that the resolution introducing martial law (an act of applying the law) was an *excès de pouvoir* because its aim was to limit citizens' rights, which allegedly was not possible under the Constitution.[111] The silent premiss of the latter head of accusation is based on the absence of any other good reason to introduce the state of exception on the rather controversial assumption that General Jaruzelski and the party-state leadership should have simply given power over to Solidarity, rather than protect the constitutional system under which they held offices. Due to the limits of space I cannot enter here into a fully fledged critique of the act of accusation, but two issues should be

106 Judgment of 20 September 1991, Case II KRN 154/91, OSNKW 1992/1–2/3; Resolution of 11 October 2002, Case SNO 29/02, LEX no 472133; Resolution (Panel of Seven Judges) of 20 December 2007, Case I KZP 37/07, OSNKW 2007/12/86.

107 Judgments: of 27 October 2010, Case K 10/08, OTK-A 2010/8/81; of 16 March 2011, Case K 35/08, OTK-A 2011/2/10.

108 Piotr Piątek, 'Akt oskarżenia przeciwko: 1) Wojciechowi Jaruzelskiemu (…)' [Act of Accusation Against Wojciech Jaruzelski], Case S 101/04/Zk (Katowice, 16 April 2007), available at ipn.gov.pl/download/akt-oskarzenia-S-101–04-Zk2, accessed 18 February 2020.

109 Piątek, 'Akt oskarżenia' 30, 32, 64 (noting that the manoeuvres of the Warsaw Pact armies 'took place in full coordination both with the Polish army command and party leadership, as a means of exerting influence', admitting that in December 1980 an intervention could have taken place, but claiming that in December 1981 there was no such 'risk' (64, 71), but 'General Wojciech Jaruzelski tried to cause such an intervention or at least receive its promise' (64).

110 The act of accusation against General Jaruzelski contains references to such arguments (e.g. Piątek, 'Akt oskarżenia' 75, 81, 83), but does not treat them as a justification of the Martial Law. Piątek even quotes General Jaruzelski's speech at the Politburo meeting on 6 February 1982 where he said: 'The day of 13 December 1981 is an act of defence of socialism, of saving the socialist state (…)' (Piątek, 'Akt oskarżenia' 83).

111 Piątek, 'Akt oskarżenia' 136, 139–141.

underlined: first, the competence to introduce martial law was expressly provided for by the Constitution (Article 33(2)) and, second, the limitation of fundamental rights is, beyond doubt, the very essence of any state of exception even if Article 33 of the Constitution was silent on that issue.

A commissary dictatorship gone sovereign?

Did General Jaruzelski intend to save state socialism, reform it or replace it?

The evaluation of General Jaruzelski's dictatorship – in the precise Schmittian sense of *Diktatur* – depends to a large extent on how one classifies the political system existing before its introduction on the night of 12/13 December 1981. In my depiction of state-socialist 'normalcy' I avoided classifying it – at least on the eve of the Martial Law – as a form of dictatorship. However, if one adopts, along Marxist-Leninist lines, the classification of the Polish People's Republic as a dictatorship of the proletariat,[112] or, along right-wing and conservative lines, as a 'communist dictatorship', then the passage from normal situation to state of exception becomes more problematic. It could then be seen as a passage from dictatorship of the proletariat to military dictatorship, perhaps akin to war communism, or, if the opposite perspective is adopted, a passage from the 'communist dictatorship' of the Party to military dictatorship, executed by a *junta* in the form of the Military Council of National Salvation (WRON). Given the revolutionary origins of the state-socialist form of government, with the sovereign dictatorship at its roots, one could also argue that the constitution of People's Poland was, in fact, an 'ossified sovereign dictatorship', and General Jaruzelski returned to its roots.[113]

However, what needs to be kept in mind is that in its precise Roman meaning later developed by Schmitt, a dictatorship is, by definition, an exceptional political arrangement, rather than a permanent state of a given polity. With this assumption in mind, I wish to enquire whether, in Schmittian terms, General Jaruzelski's dictatorship can be characterised as a commissary or sovereign one.

According to Schmitt's dichotomy, a commissary dictatorship 'suspends the constitution in order to protect it – the very same one – in its concrete form.'[114] A commissary dictatorship, therefore, '*protects* a specific constitution against an attack that threatens to abolish this constitution.'[115] Of course, this entails suspending the constitution which, however, does not cease

112 A characterisation adopted e.g. by law and state theorist Adam Łopatka as late as 1969 – see Adam Łopatka, *Wstęp do prawoznawstwa* [An Introduction to Jurisprudence] (Warszawa: Państwowe Wydawnictwo Naukowe, 1969), 73–74.

113 I would like to thank Dr Przemysław Tacik for suggesting this idea to me.

114 Carl Schmitt, *Dictatorship*, Michael Hoelzl and Graham Ward transl. (Cambridge: Polity, 2014), 118.

115 Ibid. [Emphasis added].

'to be valid, because the suspension only represents a concrete exception.'[116] In contrast, sovereign dictatorship 'does not *suspend* an existing constitution' but rather 'seeks to create conditions in which a constitution (…) is made possible'.[117] For this reason, a sovereign dictatorship 'does not appeal to an existing constitution, but to one that is still to come to power.'[118] Sovereign dictatorship appeals, therefore, to a constituent power (*pouvoir constituant*), i. e. the 'people, the nation (…) which expresses itself in continually new forms' but 'can never constitute itself in terms of constitutional law',[119]*scil.* the existing one. The question is therefore: did General Jaruzelski, by seizing dictatorial powers on the night of 12/13 December, seek to act on behalf of a new *pouvoir constituant*, intending to establish a new constitutional order for Poland, or did he rather act on behalf of the *pouvoir constituée*, seeking to protect the constitutional *status quo*? This question can be addressed in both subjective and objective terms: either a question of the general's intent (analysed through its external manifestations), or as a question of the place of the Martial Law in the existing constitutional system and its actual effects upon the constitutional setup, especially in the short and medium term (until the mid-1980s).

A prime source for analysing the subjective intent of the general is his televised address to the nation[120] in which he explained the reasons for introducing the Martial Law and shared his vision of going out of the crisis. In his speech, the General pointed out the exceptionality of the situation in both economic and political terms. He accused Solidarity of intending to take over power, noting that the recent meetings in Radom and Gdańsk had 'uncovered in their entirety the true intentions of its leadership circles' and its activists, who are openly 'striving towards the total dismantling of Poland's socialist statehood.'[121] More specifically, he referred to the mass demonstrations planned by Solidarity for 17 December 1981 – on the anniversary of the December troubles – pointing out that '[t]hat tragedy may not repeat itself. We cannot, we do not have the right to allow these announced demonstrations to become a spark which can put the entire country on fire.' Concerning the constitutional nature of the state of exception, the general claimed that '[w]e are not heading towards a military coup d'état, towards a military dictatorship' and that the newly established Military Council of National Salvation 'does not replace the constitutional authorities' because

116 Ibid.
117 Ibid. 119 [Emphasis added].
118 Ibid.
119 Carl Schmitt, *Constitutional Theory*, Jeffrey Seitzer transl. (Durham, London: Duke University Press, 2008), 128.
120 Wojciech Jaruzelski, televised address to the nation, broadcast on 13 December 1981, full recording available at www.youtube.com/watch?v=4yUKFzYEFSg, accessed 15 January 2020.
121 Ibid.

'[i]ts only task is the protection of the legal order in the State, the creation of executive guarantees that will enable to restore order and discipline.'[122] Jaruzelski underscored the temporary nature of the dictatorship, promising that the Military Council 'shall be dissolved once rule of law prevails in the country, once conditions appear for the normal functioning of the civil administration and representative bodies.'[123] What is worth underlining in these passages is the absence of Marxist-Leninist ideological tropes and the domination of a state-centrist, rule-of-law rhetoric, quite distant from a revolutionary communist spirit. As a matter of fact, although the General initially wanted to call the emergency body the 'Military Revolutionary Council for the Salvation of the Fatherland' (*Wojskowo-Rewolucyjna Rada Ocalenia Ojczyzny*)[124] – a name consciously evoking the *Revvoyensoviet*[125] – he eventually dropped any allusions to the Revolution, preferring the somewhat nationalist rhetoric of 'national salvation'. As historian Andrzej Paczkowski comments, 'the word "revolution" vanished almost at the last minute, probably because it was reminiscent of the system's roots and ideology, which could have had limited the number of supporters of martial law. It was deemed better to allude to patriotic sentiment and loyalty to the state, embodied by the army (…).'[126]

Concerning the key element of state-socialist constitutionalism – the hegemony of the Leninist party – the general was not so outspoken. In fact, he mentioned the party only in the 13th minute of his televised address, noting that '[d]espite the errors that have been committed and bitter failures, within the process of historical transitions the Party retains an active and creative role.'[127] He even mentioned the party's 'leadership mission', and did not overlook the 'Polish-Soviet alliance' which 'shall remain the cornerstone of the *raison d'état*, the guarantee of the inviolability of our borders',

122 Ibid.
123 Ibid.
124 The name was mentioned by General Florian Siwicki in his talks with the Soviets on 11 December 1981 – see 'Zeszyt roboczy gen. Wiktora Anoszkina' [General Victor Anoshkin's Working Notebook] in Łukasz Kamiński (ed.), 2 *Przed i po 13 grudnia: Państwa bloku wschodniego wobec kryzysu w prl 1980–1982* [Before and After 13 December: States of the East Block Towards the Crisis in the Polish People's Republic 1980–1982] (Warszawa: Instytut Pamięci Narodowej, 2007) 403. See also Stanisław Kwiatkowski, *W stanie wyższej konieczności. Wojsko w sytuacji konfliktu społecznego w Polsce 1981–1983* (Toruń: Wydawnictwo Adam Marszałek, 2011) 120 (who mentions that the adjective 'revolutionary' was to be part of the name of the new body) and Rakowski, *Dzienniki polityczne 1981-1982* 127 (who notes that Jaruzelski mentioned the name 'Military Revolutionary Council' on 7 December 1981).
125 Russian full name: 'Революционный Военный Совет', the supreme military command body of Soviet Russia, existing between 1918 and 1934.
126 Paczkowski, *Revolution*, 51.
127 Ibid.

promising that Poland would remain a 'reliable member of the socialist community of nations.'

During the last meeting of the Politburo prior to the introduction of martial law– a meeting which was obviously secret – General Jaruzelski clearly indicated that he intends to protect the hegemony of the Leninist party.[128] It seems, therefore, that Jaruzelski aimed at presenting his dictatorship as a commissary one, and his intention was also perceived in these terms in Moscow. The Soviet Politburo noted that in Jaruzelski's address 'the emphasis was properly placed on fundamental issues', especially 'the leading role' of the Party and the 'fidelity of the [Polish People's Republic] to its alliance obligations'.[129]

On the other hand, in Jaruzelski's own memoirs, written after 1989, he did not emphasise the desire to protect state socialism, but rather pointed to two other aspects. First, the threat of an intervention of Warsaw Pact forces in defence of state socialism, and second, the will to pacify the country and prepare it for transformation at a later point. The general, obviously writing in hindsight, claimed that 'the Martial Law cleared the path towards dialogue, towards agreement' and that it 'froze the socio-political setup', 'brought it forward to a different historical time and to a different geopolitical dimension', underlining that the Round Table agreements of 1989 were 'essentially a repetition of the idea of the Council of National Agreement' he had 'put forward in the autumn of 1981.'[130] He presented the 'care for Polish statehood – even defective, even limited' as 'one of the key elements which impacted upon [his] thinking and [his] decisions in the dramatic months towards the end of 1981.'[131]

There are strong objective arguments in favour of claiming that the Martial Law was, in fact, a sovereign dictatorship. Lech Mażewski underscored that Jaruzelski 'did not intend to suspend the force of some socialist constitutional arrangements with the aim of protecting them', because his true aim was to 'preserve the monopoly of the political power of the security apparatus' and to introduce, at the same time, 'changes leading to a more effective functioning of the economy and make further steps towards the construction of the foundations of the rule of law.'[132] In his view, the Martial Law led to the 'dethronement of the Politburo (…) as the "political"

128 'Protocol no 18' 443. Cf. Rakowski, *Dzienniki polityczne 1981-1983*, 125-126.

129 'Protocol no 40 of the CPSU CC Politburo Meeting' (13 December 1981), in Paczkowski and Byrne (eds), *From Solidarity*, 473.

130 Wojciech Jaruzelski *Stan wojenny*, 412.

131 Jaruzelski, *Stan wojenny*, 276.

132 Lech Mażewski, 'O sposobie prawniczej interpretacji stanu wojennego z 13 grudnia 1981 r. i jego następstw. Nie Carl Schmitt, a Jerzy Stembrowicz' [On the Method of Juristic Interpretation of the Martial Law of 13 December 1981 and Its Consequences: Not Carl Schmitt but Jerzy Stembrowicz] (2013) 21 *Przegląd Sejmowy* (4) 103, 108.

government.'[133] Paweł Bała, in turn, claimed that Jaruzelski's initial intent was to protect the existing order (i.e. to introduce a commissary dictatorship), but that nonetheless he abolished it and ended up being a sovereign dictator.[134] Indeed, Bała's claim resonates with Mażewski's view that the Martial Law effectively ended the leading role of the Party, reducing it to an 'empty shell'.[135] Following this line of reasoning, the Martial Law would be a sovereign dictatorship which replaced the original state-socialist constitution providing for the hegemony of the Leninist party, with an interim constitution based on the power of the formal governmental bodies and backed by the political police, which, towards the end of the decade, opened the process of transformation towards capitalism.[136] This interpretation finds some corroboration from the construction of the rule of law, which I discuss in the next section.

The path towards transformation

The introduction of martial law coincided, paradoxically, with a series of legal and economic reforms which could be introduced without much discussion with the now silenced opposition. Although the first building block of the rule of law – the creation of judicial review of administrative action – was already laid down in 1980, the construction of the Polish *Rechtsstaat* speeded up following the Martial Law.[137] On the one hand, the constitutional *lex scripta* gained authority at the expense of the *ius politicum*: the Council of Ministers, hitherto only a technical government overshadowed by the Politburo and the Secretariat of the Central Committee, gained real decision-making powers;[138] also, Parliament, hitherto a rather decorative body, was strengthened and its legislative authority expanded, making parliamentary debates more lively and publicly accessible.[139] This was accompanied by an increasing juridification of life, as General Jaruzelski 'decided to stress the need for legalism in state-citizen relations in order to both reduce the level of social dissatisfaction and depoliticize it.'[140] The

133 Mażewski, *Posttotalitarny*, 105.
134 Paweł Bała 'Stan wojenny 13 grudnia 1981 r. jako zagadnienie prawa ustrojowego. Interpretacja decyzjonistyczna' [The Martial Law of 13 December 1981 as a Question of Constitutional Law: A Decisionist Interpretation], (2013) 21 *Przegląd Sejmowy*, (4) 83, 99.
135 Mażewski, *Posttotalitarny*, 108.
136 In ideological terms, one can speak of a depletion of the Marxist-Leninist ideology already progressing from the 1970s, when it came under pressure of consumerism and technocratism, before being replaced with nationalist rhetoric in the early 1980s. This paved the way towards the neoliberal and nationalist ideological hegemony after 1989.
137 Lech Mażewski, 'O sposobie', 108.
138 Poznański, *Poland's Protracted*, 144.
139 Ibid. 144–145.
140 Ibid. 148.

'construction of the rule of law in the Polish People's Republic became clearly accelerated.'[141] The 1982 constitutional amendment created a constitutional court[142] and a tribunal of state, the latter body tasked with judging ministers and other holders of high public office. The Constitutional Court started to function in 1986, and although it had a relatively weak mandate – its judgments could be rejected by Parliament – nonetheless it was a second important element of the *Rechtsstaat*, following the Chief Administrative Court, functioning since 1980. The two courts were joined in 1987 by a third liberal institution, the Commissioner for Citizens' Rights (ombudsman), with consumer lawyer Professor Ewa Łętowska being the first incumbent. Legal reforms were also accompanied by radical economic reforms, such as the adjustment of prices (by as much as 400%), a reduction of real wages (by 25%) and the introduction of elements of a market economy (prices of many goods were no longer regulated).[143]

Conclusions

In 1980, the fundamental pillars of the Leninist model of Poland's state-socialist constitution came under direct challenge from the *Solidarność* movement, which emerged in the midst of the country's deepest economic crisis since World War II. *Solidarność* increasingly openly challenged the Leninist party's leadership position and Poland's strategic alliance with the Soviet Union – to the dismay of Poland's allies in the Warsaw Pact, who created a commonly perceived impression of their readiness to intervene in order do defend the authoritarian state-socialist system, just as they had done in 1953, 1956 and 1968 in other countries of the bloc. The decision to introduce martial law on 12/13 December 1981 was aimed, in particular, at blocking the further activity of *Solidarność*, subjecting its chief activists to administrative detention without trial, outlawing strikes and introducing a temporary military control of the state apparatus and the economy. On an ideological level, the Martial Law was yet a further step in the decomposition of Marxist-Leninist ideological hegemony in Poland. While in the 1970s, under the rule of Edward Gierek, a rhetoric of technocracy and consumerism had been introduced,[144] the Martial Law signalled a language of 'national salvation' even in the most basic, biological sense. The presence of the military in many positions of responsibility, starting from the first secretary and prime minister, certainly contributed to the ideological shift.

141 Mażewski, *Posttotalitarny*, 115.
142 On the origins of the Court see e.g. Adam Sulikowski, 'Government of Judges and Neoliberal Ideology: the Polish Case' in Rafał Mańko, Cosmin Cercel and Adam Sulikowski (eds), *Law and Critique in Central Europe: Questioning the Past, Resisting the Present* (Oxford: Counterpress, 2016).
143 Poznański, *Poland's Protracted*, 85.
144 Cf. Sulikowski, 'Government of Judges', 35.

From its inception, the formal legality of the Martial Law has been subject to debate. The main arguments of its opponents include the lack of a substantive legal basis for its introduction (lack of security threat), the alleged retroactivity of the legislative decrees on the emergent legal regime and of the introduction of martial law, and finally the fact that the decrees were adopted without first closing the session of the *Sejm* (the Council of State was allowed to issue decrees only between sessions). Against the backdrop of this critique, I have argued that the act of introduction of martial law was beyond doubt formally legal, keeping in mind that the decision that an exceptional situation is at stake is, in its very essence, a political decision and is not susceptible to juridical evaluation.[145] Concerning the legislative decrees, issued despite the formally ongoing session of Parliament, I noted that any prior debate on the emergency legislation would have undermined the effectiveness of the state of exception, voiding this constitutional institution of its purpose. In any event, in January 1982 Parliament ratified the decrees in the form of an act of parliament.[146]

Looking at General Jaruzelski's dictatorship through the lens of Schmitt's dichotomy of sovereign vs. commissary dictatorship, one should keep in mind that the state-socialist order, revolutionary in its origin, preserved, to a certain extent, the essence of a sovereign dictatorship, even if ossified.[147] The general's act of introducing the Martial Law, however, was presented at the time as a commissary dictatorship, aimed at protecting the status quo threatened by *Solidarność*. Nonetheless, objective factors indicate that already in 1982 the General commenced the construction of elements of the liberal rule of law, as well as implemented far-reaching economic reforms which, on the one hand, created an effective workers' self-government in state enterprises but on the other hand also broadened capitalist elements in the economy. However, despite a temporary transfer of power to the military, as early as 1985 the general withdrew from the position of prime minister, and retained the role of first secretary. The party-state system of dualist governance, based on the *nomenklatura* system, was once again in place. Despite the Party's relatively weakened position, the general refused to dissolve it, prolonging its existence up to January 1990, even if as an 'empty shell'.[148] My radically realist approach to state-socialist constitutionalism, taking into account not only what was presented as 'law' (the *lex scripta*) but also what de facto operated *qua* law (the *ius politicum*) has been instrumental to conceptualising the real significance of General Jaruzelski's act of introducing the Martial Law: on the level of the *lex scripta* it was merely commissary, but if we take the

145 Mażewski, *Problem legalności*, 71.
146 Ibid., 57–63.
147 I would like to thank Przemysław Tacik for suggesting this idea to me.
148 Mażewski, *Posttotalitarny*, 108.

constitution as a whole, in its substantive and not only formal sense, it had clear elements of a sovereign dictatorship.

A final question that begs for an answer is the place and role of the working class in the historical process. After all, in a state-socialist polity the working class is, in a constitutional sense, the sovereign, even if organised and expressing its will through the channels of the Party. The emergence of Solidarity as a working-class movement with a generous social programme and more or less concealed political ambitions challenged the Party's role as the *porte-parole* of the working class. The direct effects of the Martial Law were the outlawing of strikes and protest actions, the suspension of Solidarity and the internment of its chief activists, many of them workers. In that sense, the Polish state of exception is no exception: it was directed against the working class. On the other hand, however, reforms introduced under Martial Law created, for the first time in Polish history, an effective workers' self-government in state enterprises (though many were exempt from it), making an unprecedented move towards the Yugoslav model of socialisation of the economy, rather than its *etatisation*.[149] But in the long run workers were the losers as it was them who were asked to pay the bill of transformation to capitalism in 1989.[150] The 21 proposals of August 1980 or the 1981 programme of a 'Self-Governing Republic' were deliberately forgotten.[151] The Party elites joined the opposition elites, leaving the working class behind.[152] The Martial Law was a success in preserving the role of the *nomenklatura* and allowing it survive until more favourable geopolitical circumstances, when they could engage in the infamous '*nomenklatura* privatisation'.[153] It destroyed Solidarity as a workers' movement which would have most probably fiercely opposed the later neoliberal transformation.[154] The working class, the *de nomine* sovereign in the Polish People's Republic, was the ultimate loser.[155]

149 Poznański, *Poland's Protracted*, 154.
150 See e.g. David Ost, *The Defeat of Solidarity* (Ithaca, London: Cornell University Press, 2005); Jane Hardy, *Poland's New Capitalism* (London, New York: Pluto Press, 2009).
151 Kowalik, *From Solidarity*, 33–49.
152 Sowa, *Inna Rzeczpospolita*, 168.
153 Hardy, *Poland's New Capitalism*, 24–25; Kowalik, *From Solidarity*, 50–54; Sowa, *Inna Rzeczpospolita*, 183–184.
154 Sowa, *Inna Rzeczpospolita*, 181–183.
155 For a poignant anthropological case study see Elizabeth C Dunn, *Privatizing Poland: Baby Food, Big Business and the Remaking of Labor* (Ithaca, London: Cornell University Press, 2004).

Chapter 8

A state in anomie

An analysis of modern Turkey's states of exception

Ceylan Begüm Yıldız

Introduction

> [T]he norm functions precisely by way of managing the prospect of its undoing, an undoing that inheres in its doings.[1]

It is late January 2016; a group of people are trapped in the basement of an apartment building in Cizre, a town in Şırnak, Turkey.[2] This event, which would go on to monopolize Turkey's politics until 1 February, was not the result of unfortunate circumstances or a natural disaster, rather it was caused by ongoing round-the-clock curfews and military operations which had begun to dominate the life of Kurdish-populated cities in Turkey's south-eastern regions, where Cizre/Şırnak is located.[3] The declaration of curfews, followed by intensive military operations, had caused those injured to seek shelter in a basement, where they waited, trapped, for an ambulance that would never arrive. On 1 February, communication with those trapped in the basement was lost for good.[4] According to reports from local and international human rights organisations, a similar accident happened in at

1 Judith Butler *Frames of War: When is Life Grievable?* (London: Verso, 2010), 12.
2 'Urgent Action: Injured, Stranded, in Need of Emergency Care', *Amnesty International*, 26 January 2016, available at www.amnesty.org/download/Documents/EUR4433222016ENGLISH.pdf, accessed 13 February 2019.
3 For the latest figures on the curfews, see the Human Rights Foundation of Turkey report: *Curfews in Turkey between the Dates 16 August 2015–1 January 2019* (2019b), available at http://en.tihv.org.tr/curfews-in-turkey-between-the-dates-16-august-2015-1-january-2019/, accessed 13 February 2019.
4 According to MPs from the People's Democratic Party (Halkların Demokratik Partisi – HDP), through whom communication was carried out, people trapped in the basement were left under the debris after the building they were in was hit by bombs. 'Latest reports from wounded in Cizre: We're under debris', *Bianet*, 1 February 2016, available at http://bianet.org/english/human-rights/171692-latest-reports-from-wounded-in-cizre-we-re-under-debris, accessed 13 February 2019.

least two more basements in Cizre around the same time,[5] with at least 130 people losing their lives.[6]

The story of those who were trapped and died in that basement is just a drop in the ocean of Turkey's juridico-political history of deadly exceptional measures. After the demise of the one-party regime in 1945, Turkey experienced a series of military coups in 1960, 1971 and 1980. In 1982, after the 1980 coup, Turkey's military regime drafted a new constitution, under the authority of the ruling military group. The 1980 coup was followed by a dual regime of state of emergency rule and counter-terror law that dominated political, as well social and economic, life in the 1990s. Since the summer of 2015, the infamous tight control seen in the 1990s has been extended further still to include round-the-clock curfews and a nationwide state of emergency. During the final state of emergency in 2016–2018,[7] Turkey went through a parliamentary regime change after a constitutional referendum. The state-form change – from a parliamentary system to a strong presidential one – took place de facto through executive decrees (KHK –*Kanun Hükmünde Kararname*) issued during the state of emergency, which were later formalised via the constitutional referendum of April 2017.[8] The new system was presented by the ruling Justice and Development Party (AKP) as a Turkish-style presidency.[9] While some scholars referred to it as hyper-presidentialism, emphasising the 'strong single executive power with very little or no

5 The Human Rights Foundation of Turkey's Cizre field report located three shelter basements, which had been destroyed by military forces. Although some of the bodies were identified and buried hastily, either by the families or by local government authorities, the whereabouts of the other bodies is still unknown. The field report mentions human remains scattered all over the city and witness testimonies mention some human remains thrown in the Tigris River. Human Rights Foundation of Turkey, *76-Day Curfew: Cizre Field Report*, 2016, available at http://en.tihv.org.tr/79-day-curfew-cizre-field-report/, accessed 26 February 2019.

6 Amnesty International reports that the number of people who sought shelter in various other basements in Cizre amounts to 130. Amnesty International, *Amnesty International Report 2016/17: The state of the world's human rights* (2017), available at www.amnesty.org/download/Documents/POL1048002017ENGLISH.PDF, accessed 26 February 2019.

7 A nationwide state of emergency was declared on 21 July 2016 after the failed coup attempt by the followers of Fetullah Gülen. The AKP government used this opportunity to eliminate all opposition with mass purges in governmental posts including civil service and the military. For an overview of events, see (Amnesty International 2017: 367–371). For figures of two years of emergency measures, see 'OHAL sona erdi: İki yıllık sürecin bilançosu', *BBC Türkçe*, 19 July 2018, available at www.bbc.com/turkce/haberler-turkiye-44799489, accessed 26 February 2019.

8 Sinan Erensü and Ayça Alemdaroğlu, 'Dialectics of reform and repression: Unpacking Turkey's authoritarian "turn"', (2018) 52(1) *Review of Middle East Studies* 16.

9 For political context on this Turkish style of presidency, see Ersin Kalaycioğlu, 'The challenge of à la Turca presidentialism in Turkey', *Global Turkey in Europe*, 2014, available at www.iai.it/sites/default/files/gte_c_18.pdf, accessed 23 July 2019.

constitutional constraints',[10] others presented the reform as a part of the ongoing process of weakening political institutions.[11]

Despite these various readings, it is common to analyse the current state of Turkey as a sudden 'authoritarian turn', which became apparent after the 2013 Gezi protests, accelerated after the 2016 failed coup attempt and, finally, was legalised by the presidential regime change.[12] While an authoritarian turn is often related to a 'democracy in crisis',[13] or even considered a betrayal of democracy,[14] some suggest the recent political and legal change in Turkey 'signals a transition to a more "exceptional" paradigm of security'.[15] However, neither authoritarian tendencies nor exceptional measures are new trends in Turkey's political and legal climate.

In this chapter I would like to consider the transformation of the exceptional measures from a historical perspective, with the aim of exposing the evolutionary pattern of the states of exceptions in modern Turkey. In order to do so, I will consider the round-the-clock curfews as a signpost. Even though Turkey is living proof of exception being the norm, I suggest that the round-the-clock curfews expose a pattern of anomie within the paradigm of exception; that is to say, that some exceptional measures are even more exceptional than others are. Although Giorgio Agamben demonstrates in the book *State of Exception* that exceptional measures are necessarily neither internal nor external to law[16] – in other words, situated in a zone of indistinction – Turkey's states of exception show nuances due to its subject target. Hence, this chapter follows Agamben's lead in investigating Turkey as an anomic state,

10 Şule Özsoy Boyunsuz, 'The AKP's proposal for a "Turkish type of presidentialism" in comparative context', (2016) 17(1) *Turkish Studies.*

11 Canan Aslan Akman and Pınar Akçalı, 'Changing the system through instrumentalising weak political institutions: The quest for a presidential system in Turkey in historical and comparative perspective', (2017) 18(4) *Turkish Studies* 577.

12 In addition to those cited within the text, there are special issue journals focusing on the matter of authoritarian turn in Turkey, see: Kerem Öktem and Karabekir Akkoyunlu (eds.), 'Exit from Democracy: Illiberal governance in Turkey and beyond', (2016) 16(4) *Southeast European and Black Sea Studies* 469. Cemal Burak Tansel, 'Decoding the Repertoires of Authoritarian Neoliberalism in Turkey', (2018) 23(2) *South European Society and Politics* 197. Kumru F. Toktamiş, and Isabel David, eds. 'Critical Crossroads: Erdogan and the transformation of Turkey' (2018) 29(3) *Mediterranean Quarterly* 1.

13 Ziya Öniş, 'Monopolising the Centre: The AKP and the uncertain path of Turkish democracy', (2015) 50(2) *International Spectator.*

14 Kumru F. Toktamiş and Isabel David, 'Introduction: Democratization betrayed: Erdogan's New Turkey' (2018) 29(3) *Mediterranean Quarterly.*

15 Özlem Kaygusuz, 'Authoritarian neoliberalism and regime security in Turkey: Moving to an 'exceptional state' under AKP', (2018) 23(2) *South European Society and Politics* 281.

16 Giorgio Agamben, *State of Exception*. Kevin Attell transl. (Chicago: University of Chicago Press, 2005).

while introducing a subject-oriented perspective to bring to light the particular pattern of states of exception on which the Turkish nation state was built (and continues to live in).

Turkey: a state in anomie

Exceptional measures suspend the juridical order for its restoration or defence. As Agamben stresses, those measures are

> neither external or internal to juridical order, and the problem of defining it concerns precisely a threshold, or a zone of indifference, where inside and outside do not exclude each other but rather blur with each other. The suspension of the norm does not mean its abolition, and the zone of anomie that it establishes is not (or at least it claims to be) unrelated to the juridical order.[17]

In other words, exceptional measures indicate a state of anomie, where legal boundaries and definitions of inside and outside blur. With this definition in mind, I propose to analyse Turkey as a state in anomie where the inside and outside of the juridical order blurs.

'A state in anomie' bears a double meaning. In their discussion on the nation state, Judith Butler and Gayatri C. Spivak remind the readers of the double meaning of the word 'state'.[18] The first meaning is the juridico-political construct, that 'signifies the legal and institutional structures that delimit a certain territory', while the other refers to the 'conditions in which we find ourselves'.[19] These two meanings collide, especially in exceptional times. As the boundaries between the juridical and political order blur, so does the distinction between those two meanings of state as the state manifests its force on subject-bodies. During states of exception, the state claims to restore or defend its juridical order by leaving subjects in a certain "state", such as being trapped in a basement sheltering from military operations conducted by the state of which you are a citizen. At this point, it is crucial to unearth the relationship between the state in juridico-political terms and the subjects left in a determinate state. In order to understand the relationship between the Turkish state and the state of those subjects trapped in the basement to die, it is necessary to recall the foundational state of the Republic of Turkey, or in other words its foundational state of war.

After the establishment of the Turkish Republic in 1923, the first exceptional measure issued was against a Kurdish rebellion known as the

17 Ibid., 23.
18 Judith Butler and Gayatri Chakravorty Spivak, *Who Sings the Nation-State?* (London, New York and Calcutta: Seagull Books, 2010).
19 Ibid., 3.

Sheikh Said Rebellion of 1925. The government ordered mobilisation only in certain areas where the revolt took place and established martial courts (*İstiklâl Mahkemeleri*) in Turkey's new capital, Ankara, and in the de facto capital of the Kurdish region, Diyarbakır, where Kurdish community leaders, including Sheikh Said, were hanged.[20] Additionally, the government adopted the Law for Maintenance of Order *(Takrîr-i Sükûn Kânunu,* no. 578),[21] which ended the multi-party regime and replaced it with single-party rule, embellished with extraordinary powers, which lasted until the end of World War II.[22] During this period yet another Kurdish uprising – the *Dersim* rebellion of 1937 – was supressed by heavy military operations, which again concluded with hanging the leader, Seyit Rıza, his sons and five other followers.[23]

Although in the interwar period exceptional measures were quite common among nations across the continents,[24] it is worth noting that in Turkey's case what triggered the single-party regime was not an outside threat but rather an inside one.[25] However, prior to the establishment of the martial courts and the Law for Maintenance of Order, two other legal measures were adopted, just a couple of months after the official foundation of the Republic of Turkey in 1923. The first one is a law called *Izale-i Şekavet* (no. 356), translating as 'elimination of bandits',[26] which declared that the killing of those labelled bandits was not a crime.[27] This was followed by another decree (no. 372),[28] which gave amnesty to all possible criminal actions carried out while

20 'Bir Halki Yargılamak: Türkiye'de Ulus-Devlet ve Kürt Meselesi', *Toplum ve Kuram* (2012), 6–7, 13–27.

21 Law for Maintenance of Order (Takrîr-i Sükûn Kânunu), 4 March 1925, no. 578.

22 Erik J. Zürcher, *Turkey a Modern History* (London: I. B. Tauris, 2017).

23 Nicole Watts, 'Relocating Dersim: Turkish State-Building and Kurdish Resistance, 1931–1938', (2000) 23 *New Perspectives on Turkey* 5.

24 After emphasising the role of World War I in generalising the exceptional measures, Agamben provides a brief history of the exceptional measures taken during the world wars. Agamben, *State of Exception*, 11–22.

25 For a detailed analysis of exceptional measures of the interwar period, see: Joakim Parslow, 'Theories of Exceptional Executive Powers in Turkey, 1933–1945', (2016) 55 *New Perspectives on Turkey.*

26 İzale-i Şekavet was adopted when the Rumi calander was still in use, hence in the official documents the year of the law is 1339. Elimination of Bandits (İzale-i Şekavet). 18 October 1923, no. 356. The İzalei Şekavet law was terminated in 1962. In a report prepared by the Ministry of Justice it was noted that the law was in breach of the Constitution and also that it was no longer needed since there were provisions to punish bandits under criminal law, police conduct law and gendarme conduct law. Draft Law to Abolish Law on Elimination of Bandits and Reports from Ministry of Interior and Justice (İzalei Şekavet Kanununun yürürlükten kaldırılmasına dair kanun tasarısı ve İçiŞleri ve Adalet komisyonları raporları (1/191)), *TBMM*, 27 April 1962, No. 255.

27 Selin Esen, *KarŞılaŞtırmalı Hukukta ve Türkiye'de Olağanüstü Hal Rejimi* (Ankara: Adalet Yayınları, 2008).

28 Degree no. 372, 19 November 1923.

defending the country between the years 1918 and 1923.[29] It appears that this decree was enacted in response to the Ottoman war criminals tribunal, which aimed to prosecute the military elites of the independence war – such as Enver, Cemal and Talaat Pashas, who later became political leaders of the Turkish Republic – for offenses against Greeks and Armenians.[30] As Taner Akçam's detailed account of crimes committed within those years discloses, 'Christians were to be eliminated by expulsion or massacre. Non-Turkish Muslims, such as the Kurds, Arabs, and Balkan migrants (refugees from Christian persecution), were relocated and dispersed among the Turkish majority to be assimilated into the dominant culture.'[31] In other words, the *Izale-i Şekavet* (no. 356) and the decree no. 372 pardoned any criminal acts carried out in supressing Greek, Armenian and Kurdish minorities to prevent their possible alliance with the occupying forces.[32] These two legal measures cannot be dismissed as exceptional measures taken during exceptional times of crisis; rather, they indicate the pattern of exceptional norms in which modern Turkey's juridico-political system operates. Even in this brief history of exceptional measures taken during the foundation of the Republic of Turkey, it is possible to spot the difference in terms of 'who was left in what state', which serves as a pattern for upcoming states of emergency.[33] The answer lies in what type of state of exception was granted to different subjects; in other words, who was killed and who was granted amnesty for their killings.

In his inquest on the state of exception, Agamben unearths an interesting relationship between mourning, feast and anomie.[34] He considers mourning in terms of public mourning, and specifically in the case of a sovereign's

29 Esen, 146.

30 The offences subject to the war crimes tribunals were the expulsion of Greeks and Armenian Genocide. The articles 2216–230 of the Treaty of Sévres, which is a peace treaty signed between the Ottoman state and the Allied forces (the European opponents in the First World War) in 1920 but later on replaced by the Lausanne Peace Treaty with the foundation of the Turkish Republic in 1923, were concerned with prosecution of Ottoman war criminals. Taner Akçam, *From Empire to Republic: Turkish Nationalism and The Armenian Genocide* (London: Zeb Books, 2004), 180–207.

31 Taner Akçam, *The Young Turks' Crime Against Humanity: The Armenian Genocide and Ethnic Cleansing in the Ottoman Empire* (Princeton: Princeton University Press, 2012), xv–xvi.

32 The Treaty of Sévres aimed to partition Anatolia to establish Armenian and Kurdish nation states and included partitioning Thrace to Greeks (ibid.).

33 It is hard to spot such an obvious pattern in the late Ottoman period, which suggests that the pattern has to do with the foundation of Turkey as a nation state. For an analysis of exceptional measures taken during the Ottoman period, see: Noémi Lévy-Aksu, 'An Ottoman variation on the state of siege: The invention of the idare-i örfiyye during the first constitutional period', (2016) 54 *New Perspectives on Turkey* 1.

34 Agamben, *State of Exception*, 65–73.

funeral and its potential to create public chaos. He writes: '[t]he correspondence between anomie and mourning becomes comprehensible only in the light of the correspondence between the death of the sovereign and the state of exception'.[35] Agamben considers public mourning a ritualised form of the state of exception that is declared to prevent chaos. The other point he makes is related to the periodic feasts 'that are characterised by unbridled license and the suspension and overturning of normal legal and social hierarchies [when] criminal behaviour is considered licit or, in any case, not punishable'.[36] Although Agamben's reading of mourning and feast are quite specific, I believe his exposure of the relationship between mourning, feast and anomie enables us to comprehend the workings of two parallel regimes of states of exception embedded within the foundation of the Republic of Turkey.

At this point I would like to bring a contemporary account of mourning in relation to a state of exception to the discussion. Just after the 2015 bombings in Paris, which were followed by a two-year state of emergency,[37] Judith Butler wrote a short commentary unpacking this intrinsic relationship between public mourning and exception.[38] Referencing Gillian Rose, Butler titles her commentary 'Mourning Becomes the Law'. Although Butler does not openly refer to Agamben's work, she elaborates in a similar vein:

> 'Hollande announced three days of mourning as he tightened security controls [...] Are we grieving or are we submitting to increasingly militarized state power and suspended democracy? How does the latter work more easily when it is sold as the former?'[39]

35 Ibid., 68.
36 Ibid., 71.
37 A state of emergency was declared in France following the November 2015 attacks, which expired in November 2017. The state of emergency served as grounds for legitimising the AKP government's grip on power through the emergency measures. Similar to the executive power grab of AKP through a referendum, France ended its state of emergency by introducing a counter terrorism bill, which was criticised for normalising the state of emergency. 'France declares end to state of emergency almost two years after Paris terror attacks', *Independent*, 31 October 2017, available at www.independent.co.uk/news/world/europe/france-state-of-emergency-end-terror-attacks-paris-isis-terrorism-alerts-warning-risk-reduced-a8029311.html, accessed 26 February 2019.
38 Judith Butler, 'Mourning becomes the law: Judith Butler from Paris', *Verso*, 2015, available at www.versobooks.com/blogs/2337-mourning-becomes-the-law-judith-butler-from-paris. The text appears to be taken down from the website, however it can be reached from: Judith Butler, 'Mourning becomes the law: Judith Butler from Paris', *Instituro 25 de Mayo para la Democracia*, 2015, available at https://instituto25m.info/mourning-becomes-the-law-judith-butler-from-paris/, accessed 28 February 2019.
39 Ibid., 2.

What Butler suggests is that the state of public mourning had become an excuse for the state of exception. This contemporary example can help us relate Agamben's analysis on mourning and exception to today, and to see that their relationship is not only a casual one, but rather, they overlap and blur into one another. In other words, the state of mourning is not only a part of the apparatus of exception but at times it appears as a form of a state of exception that paralyses and captures subjects in a constant state of mourning.

These two parallel states of exception operated within the foundational years of modern Turkey – one issuing a state of mourning (*Takrîr-i Sükûn Kânunu)* and the other a state of feast (*Izale-i Şekavet* and *decree no. 372).* They constitute a frame for what is inside and what is outside of the Turkish nation state. Here I am referring to the Butlerian concept of 'frame' which is defined as follows: 'to call the frame into question is to show that the frame never quite contained the scene it was meant to limn, that something was already outside, which made the very sense of the inside possible, recognisable'.[40] Considering the framing of the Turkish nation state enables us to approach its inside/outside features, free from the limitations of territorial nation state borders. The last point is crucial to help us unpack Turkey's anomic state characterised by the territorial nation state borders of Turkey (known as *misak-i milli*) containing both those left in the state of mourning and those granted the state of feast (or amnesty). The exceptional measure of issuing an amnesty for criminal acts only makes sense if there is an exceptional criminal activity that would not be accepted in normal times on recognised subjects. Hence, the double form of states of exception, mourning and feast, sets the frame of the Turkish nation state, which indicates a group of subjects placed out of the frame regardless of their citizenship status. However, there is a catch; it is this outside that makes the inside possible and recognisable.

Regardless of its ethnic diversity, the Republic of Turkey is commonly referred to as the Turkish state (*Türk milleti*) rather than the state of Turkey. This choice of words is not random; it refers back to the nation state building process in Turkey.[41] Since its foundation, all other ethnicities, other than those recognised non-Muslim minorities, have been forced to unite under one national identity.[42] In other words, the Turkish state is the 'frame' of the

40 Butler, *Frames of War*, 9.

41 Barış Ünlü in his work on the social contract of the Turkish nation state suggests that the contract of being a Turk is built on being Muslim. In this way, only non-Muslims are recognised as minorities while other Muslim ethic groups were assimilated under the identity of Turkishness. Barış Ünlü, *Türklük Sözleşmesi: OluŞumu, İşleyişi ve Krizi* (Ankara: Dipnot Yayınları, 2018).

42 The Lausanne Peace Treaty was signed after the conclusion of the First World War in July 1923 between Turkey and the allied forces. According to Section III 'Protection of Minorities', the Republic of Turkey recognised only non-Muslims

Republic of Turkey, not only as a separation from a territorial outside (enemy) but more so, from the inside, through which other identities have been placed out of the frame. As Butler reminds us the inside of the frame is only recognisable by its outside. Thus, what is left out of the frame becomes the condition for the existence of the Turkish state.

Furthermore, as Butler remarks, there is yet another meaning to the word 'frame'; that is 'to frame' in the sense of falsely accusing someone of a crime or wrongdoing. This blurring of the division of the outside and inside of the Turkish state relates to the perpetual framing of Kurdish subjects as bandits, or to put it in modern terms, as terrorists. In this regard, Butler's deliberation on the frame of recognition, that is, recognising the inside through its outside, is to ask the question: when is a life 'grievable', or to be more precise, whose life is 'grievable'. She mentions 'specific exploitation of targeted populations' and that '[...] when such lives are lost they are not grievable, since, in the twisted logic that rationalizes their death, the loss of such populations is deemed necessary to protect the lives of "the living"'.[43] Butler suggests that the lives ended to secure other lives are the ones who are considered 'ungrievable'. However, the case of Turkey demonstrates that the issue of grievability is more complex than that general statement. Not only is there always someone to grieve – in other words, to mourn after the lost ones – but in relation to the frame of recognition there is the question of who is grieving and whether the shared (public) grief or mourning of a targeted population is recognised by the rest. Different from the state of exception resulting from public mourning, the frame of the Turkish state constitutes a line of separation: one person's mourning is the other person's feast. Thus, Turkey is an anomic state and at the same time, in a state of anomie.

The threshold of lawfulness/lawlessness

Turkey's pattern of states of exception is reflected on the legal form of such measures. Theoretically speaking, the characteristic of the state of exception is the blend of executive, juridical and legislative powers – which are claimed to be clearly separate from one another in a democratic state – producing a zone of anomie. In *Homo Sacer*, Agamben highlights that life becoming a target of a political decision allows an uninterrupted shift from democracy to totalitarian (absolute state) and totalitarian regimes to democracies.[44] This is one of the main collateral factors for exceptional measures

as minorities and granted only non-Muslims with minority rights. The rest of the population is recognised as Turkish by the allied forces. 'Lausanne Peace Treaty', 24 July 1923, *Republic of Turkey Ministry of Foreign Affairs*, available at www.mfa.gov.tr/lausanne-peace-treaty.en.mfa, accessed 28 February 2019.

43 Butler, *Frames of War*, 31.

44 Giorgio Agamben, *Homo Sacer: Sovereign Power and Bare Life*, Daniel Heller-Roazen transl. (Stanford: Stanford University Press, 1998) 72.

transformed into a paradigm of governance. By declaring exceptional measures, nation states do not lose the legitimacy that comes with them being 'democratic', since the suspension of the juridical order for its restoration or defence does not mean the abolition of the entire juridical system. Rather, adopting exceptional measures results in a dual system in which both the juridical order and its exception co-exist. Agreeing with this broad description of the state of exception, I would like to highlight a pattern evident in Turkey's states of exception; that is, a dual regime of exception. While one covers completely the juridico-political territory of Turkey, the other is specific to the Kurdish-majority provinces of eastern and south-eastern Turkey, an area even more legally arbitrary and militarily fortified than the former. This pattern is related to the discussion of 'who is left in what state', and at the same time unearths the threshold of lawfulness and lawlessness within Turkey's anomic state.

In the aftermath of Turkey's founding years, in 1951 some amendments were made to articles 141 and 142 of the Turkish Penal Code (no. 5844)[45] in response to the Cold War that added communism as a threat. Article 141 criminalised any acts to abolish a social class, establish the rule of one social class above others or change economic and state structures, while article 142 criminalised the making of 'propaganda' in favour of those crimes listed in the previous article, including writing about them. After the military coups of 1960, 1971 and 1980, a separate emergency law was added to the new constitution, commonly known as OHAL (*Olağanüstü Hal Kanunu,* no. 2935),[46] in spite of already having an article on the state of siege in the previous 1961 constitution.[47] OHAL was implemented immediately, with a similar scope to the round-the-clock curfews of 2015, mainly covering the Kurdish majority in southern and south-eastern provinces of Turkey. While the juridico-political territory of Turkey was governed by exceptional

45 Amendments to Article 141 and 142 of Turkish Penal Code, 3 December 1951, No. 5844.

46 OHAL (Olağanüstü Hal Kanunu), 25 October 1983, No. 2935.

47 The state of exception (OHAL) was split from the state of siege by the 1982 Constitution. The Constitution, amended after the Constitutional Referendum of April 2017, combined the two back again under the responsibilities of the National Security Council, although the president alone can declare a state of emergency. As article 119 says: 'In the event of war, the emergence of a situation necessitating war, mobilization, an uprising, strong rebellious actions against the motherland and the Republic, widespread acts of violence of internal or external origin threatening the indivisibility of the country and the nation, emergence of widespread acts of violence aimed at the destruction of the Constitutional order or of fundamental rights and freedoms, serious deterioration of public order because of acts of violence, occurrence of natural disasters, outbreak of dangerous epidemic diseases or emergence of a serious economic crisis; the President of the Republic may declare state of emergency in one region or nationwide for a period not exceeding six months'. Amendments to the Constitution of the Republic of Turkey, 16 April 2017, No. 6771.

measures, the Kurdish-majority provinces were governed under a double regime of exception that was established by the combination of the anti-communist articles of the Turkish Penal Code and OHAL emergency measures. In 1991, while OHAL in the Kurdish provinces continued, Turkey adopted its first version of the counter-terror law (no. 3713). This was presented as a more comprehensive version of the anti-communist articles of the Turkish Penal Code, which were due to be abolished after the passing of the counter-terror law. The 1990s, which saw the intensified regime of exceptional governance through the combination of OHAL and the counter-terror law, are renowned as among the deadliest times in the Kurdish regions. Unlike the state of emergency declared according to the Constitution, the curfews and military operations were based on the Provincial Administration Law (*İl İdaresi Kanunu*, no. 5442),[48] which originated a debate about its legality.[49] The declaration of the round-the-clock curfews accompanied by military operations were based on provisions relating to governors' and sub-governors' responsibility to take the 'necessary measures to prevent crimes from being committed and to protect public order and security' and 'to secure peace and security, personal immunity, safety of private property, public well-being and the authority of preventive law enforcement'.[50] The European Commission for Democracy through Law, known as the Venice Commission, issued a detailed report on the legal framework of the curfews.[51] The Commission concluded that 'the curfews imposed since August 2015 have not been based on the constitutional and legislative framework which specifically governs the use of exceptional measures in Turkey, including curfew'.[52]

The case of Turkey shows, therefore, that there are different standards in the exceptionality of exceptional measures. Grounding the curfews and military operations within the Provincial Administration Law without declaring a state of emergency exposes a double standard according to which the Turkish state's understanding of the rule of law differs depending on the targeted subject. Furthermore, the arbitrariness of the curfews exposes, once more, the pattern of Turkey's states of exception as being nothing other than a never-ending civil war with its Kurdish citizens.

48 Provincial Administration Law (İl İdaresi Kanunu), 10 June 1949, no. 5442.
49 Erkan Şenses, 'OHAL'siz OHAL Sokağa Çıkma Yasakları!' (2016) 145 *Güncel Hukuk Dergisi*.
50 Article 11(a) and (c) of Provincial Administration Law.
51 European Commission for Democracy through Law, *Opinion on the Legal Framework Governing Curfews*, 2016, available at www.venice.coe.int/webforms/documents/?pdf=CDL-AD(2016)010-e, accessed 25 November 2019.
52 Ibid., 20.

Uncovering stasis*: round-the-clock curfews*

Agamben adds a note at the very end of his elaboration on the concept of civil war (*stasis*): '[t]he form that civil war has acquired today in world history is terrorism'.[53] And immediately after, he repeats an argument already advanced in book *Homo Sacer* in relation to *stasis*. He writes:

> [i]t is no coincidence that the 'terror' should coincide with the moment in which life as such – the nation (which is to say, birth) – became the principle of sovereignty. The sole form in which life as such can be politicised is its unconditioned exposure to death – that is, bare life'.[54]

By taking this note as a point of departure, I suggest that Turkey has been in a never-ending state of civil war since its foundational war of independence in 1923, which served as a condition for the continuity of the Turkish nation state and, hence, for its sovereignty.

As argued above, throughout its history the Turkish state has governed the Kurdish region through exceptional measures while legitimising those measures through the rhetoric of the 'war on terror', nearly a decade prior to its global use. Those exceptional measures against the Kurdish population were legitimised with the historic accusation of terrorism, and they enabled the threshold to be pushed further still and the anomie to be extended even further. Today's post-referendum question of 'what went wrong'[55] concerning Turkey's *de jure* dictatorship has its answers in this gradual expansion of anomie through the ultra-exceptional measures issued on the Kurdish population. During the most violent times of the curfews, this point was raised by a large group of Turkey-affiliated academics, known by the name *Academics for Peace*, who wrote in a statement that Turkey has been systematically killing its own Kurdish citizens.[56] This is civil war and the current situation of de

53 Giorgio Agamben, *Stasis: Civil War as a Political Paradigm*, Nicholas Heron transl. (Edinburgh: Edinburgh University Press, 2015), 18.

54 Agamben, *Homo Sacer*, 18.

55 At the 'Law and Politics in Turkey: Reform, Authority and Emergency' conference that took place on 26–28 October 2017 at Northwestern University, the question of 'what went wrong?' dominated the debate. To follow up the conference debate, see: Saygun Gölarıksel and Z. Umut Türem, 'The banality of exception? Law and politics in "post-coup" Turkey' (2019) 118(1) *South Atlantic Quarterly* 175.

56 Academics who signed this petition statement have been facing mass purges and state prosecution. For the full statement by the Academics for Peace, see: 'We will not be a party to this crime', *Academics for Peace*, 10 January 2016, available at https://barisicinakademisyenler.net/node/63, accessed 18 February 2019. For a detailed report focusing on the aftermath of the peace petition see; Human Rights Foundation of Turkey, *Academics for Peace: A Brief History*, 2019, available at www.tihvakademi.org/wp-content/uploads/2019/03/AcademicsforPeace-ABriefHistory.pdf, accessed 17 July 2019.

jure dictatorship is a simple outcome of a state of a civil war extended nationwide.

To investigate further the state of Turkish civil war it is worth looking at the first part of Agamben's volume *Stasis*, which is a response to Nicole Loraux's series of articles on this theme. By studying the concept and the practice of *stasis* in ancient Greece she concludes that civil war is 'war within the family'.[57] Agamben, although relying heavily on Loraux's detailed study, objects to this idea and suggests placing *stasis* exactly in between family and the city; indeed, '*stasis* does not have its place within the household but constitutes a threshold of indifference between the *oikos* and the *polis*, between blood kinship and citizenship'.[58] Like Agamben's other propositions on anomie, *stasis* is a blurred space in which the apolitical life of kinship becomes politically charged, and the politically charged citizenship is depoliticised.[59] Despite the problematic assumption of bare life that is presupposed by Agamben in general, Turkey's anomic state confirms in a way his theory of *stasis* as a threshold between kinship and citizenship.

If the Turkish nation state was a family, in the eyes of the state Kurdish citizens are considered the unreliable sibling who is likely to betray the family, if they have not already done so. The troubled relationship between kinship and citizenship was at its peak during the peace negotiations, which were carried out between the Turkish state and the Kurdish Worker's Party (PKK – *Partiya Karkerên Kurdistanê*) between 2009 and 2015.[60] During this time 'my Kurdish sibling' became a common phrase, which was often used by the then prime minister and now president R. T. Erdoğan, and by the rest of the Turkish state officials, to emphasise the period of reconciliation after a decade-long blood feud.[61] However, peaceful times did not last long and the Turkish state officials who were carrying out the negotiations once again accused their Kurdish siblings of backstabbing, to which the Turkish state responded with round-the-clock curfews and military operations.[62] As

57 Agamben, *Stasis*, 3–8.
58 Ibid., 11.
59 Ibid., 14.
60 Mesut Yeğen, 'The Kurdish peace process in Turkey: Genesis, evolution, and prospects', *Global Turkey in Europe*, 2015, available at www.iai.it/sites/default/files/gte_wp_11.pdf, accessed 19 February 2019.
61 'Benim Kürt kardeŞlerim' in Turkish. On 5 March 2019 at a rally Erdoğan repeated his gesture of calling Kurds his siblings while asking for the Kurdish votes for the upcoming March 2019 local elections. 'Erdoğan Kürtlere seslendi: Bak size 'kardeŞlerim' diyorum!', *Cumhuriyet*, 5 March 2019, available at www.cumhuriyet.com.tr/haber/siyaset/1278526/Erdogan_Kurtlere_seslendi__Bak_size__kardeslerim__diyorum_.html, accessed 5 March 2019.
62 This chapter does not intend to debate the events, which are arguably the cause of the failed peace process, nor the events prior to the curfew, but rather aims to demonstrate the specific exceptional measures issued to the Kurdish region, within the framing of the Turkish state.

argued above, this has its roots in the foundational war of the Republic of Turkey and its nation state framing process.[63] The exceptional measures that followed, and which had been implemented within the Kurdish regions since the foundation of the republic, demonstrate the evolution of the founding war of the Turkish state into a continuous state of civil war that has been kept as a possibility within the anomic state of Turkey from the start. Thus, the Kurdish population have always been perceived by the Turkish state as potential terrorists, and the Kurdish majority provinces have always been considered the headquarters of terrorism to keep *stasis* a waiting possibility. Indeed, as Agamben claims, *stasis* 'must remain always possible in the city, yet … nonetheless must not be remembered through trials and resentments'.[64]

For *stasis* to remain a possibility in a state, the times of feast and mourning should be left unpunished. This has been the case in Turkey since the first amnesty of 1923. The Turkish state neither accepted responsibility for the systematic violence imposed on the Kurdish region nor punished those responsible for the extra-judicial killings, which took place during the double regime of OHAL and the counter-terror law of the 1990s.[65] Relatives of those who were forcibly disappeared during those times, known as the Saturday Mothers (*Cumartesi Anneleri*), have been gathering in Istanbul at Galatasaray Square every Saturday since 27 March 1995. The Saturday Mothers not only demonstrate the transitiveness of kinship and citizenship but also contribute to the argument raised above regarding Turkey's anomic state, leaving the Kurdish subjects in a constant state of public mourning.

Finally, the last aspect that is exposed by the round-the clock curfews is the economy of Turkey's anomic state, which is yet to be explored in the literature. Agamben briefly mentions the economic aspect of *stasis* when he writes; 'civil war marks the threshold through which the unpolitical is politicised and the political is "economised"'.[66] The Turkish government issued 'emergency expropriation' orders in the areas under the curfew. According to Amnesty International's report on displacements during the curfews, 'in the city of Cizre, a total of 22 plots of land were expropriated across three neighbourhoods',[67] and this

63 While Turkey's founding war, commonly referred to as the independence war, is glorified by Turkish nationalists as a victory against occupying colonial powers, it is also remembered as a time of public mourning by its minorities.
64 Agamben, *Stasis*, 16.
65 During the peace negotiations, as a sign of reconciliation the state accepted the existence of hundreds of mass graves located across Turkey's Kurdish region. According to the Human Rights Association's special report of 2014 on mass graves, 49 mass graves were estimated in Diyarbakır alone, of which only eight have been opened. These contained remains belonging to 77 individuals. Human Rights Association, *Türkiye'de Toplu Mezarlar Raporu* (2014), available at www.ihddiyarbakir.org/Content/uploads/28148ca9-d128-4b4c-afde-87cec90eef89.pdf, accessed 11 July 2017.
66 Agamben, *Stasis*, 17.
67 Amnesty International, *Displaced and Dispossessed: Sur Resident's Right to Return Home,* (2016), available at www.amnesty.org/download/Documents/EUR4452132016ENGLISH.PDF, accessed 28 February 2019.

number goes up to 60% of land in the historical Sur district of Diyarbakır. The report concludes that this was a systematic plan to displace its Kurdish residents.[68]

At this point, I would like to recall Agamben's critique of Michel Foucault's genealogy of biopolitics in which Foucault suggests that the sovereign power's interest in the economy of life began with liberalism.[69] In *Kingdom and the Glory*, Agamben argues that every primary target of the sovereign power requires calculation, writing: '[e]very act of government aims at a primary target, yet, precisely for this reason, it can lead to "collateral damage" which can be expected or unexpected in their specifics, but are in any case taken for granted'.[70] Surely, Agamben has a point here, that the Turkish forces consider the people trapped and killed in the basement as no more than collateral damage, and their deaths require no further investigation or punishment. However, I believe the economy of emergency can be considered in broader terms, either in the Foucauldian sense of *homo economicus* (biopolitics in the sense of economy of life) or in terms of neoliberal war economies.[71] Over the last decade, Turkey's economic growth has been heavily based on the construction sector.[72] In this sense, curfews reveal the economic aspect of the state of exception; that the destruction of cities and the deaths of their inhabitants were coordinated in order to facilitate rebuilding – to generate growth not only through rebuilding infrastructure but also through the rebuilding, or rather re-branding, of Kurdish cities that are to be consumed by 'the other'; such as for tourism.[73] In other words, in neoliberal times of crises, economic projections become the driving force behind the implementation of states of exception.

68 On the relationship between curfews and the government's gentrification plans as a form of cleansing at the Kurdish cities, see; Ceylan Begüm Yıldız, 'Diyarbakır's objects of memory: "Restoration" of the Kurdish city into a biblokent' (2016) 2 *London Journal of Critical Thought*.

69 Michel Foucault, *The Birth of Biopolitics: Lectures at the Collège de France, 1978–79*, Graham Burchell transl. (New York: Palgrave Macmillan, 2008).

70 Giorgio Agamben, *The Kingdom and the Glory: For a Theological Genealogy of Economy and Government*, Lorenzo Chiesa and Matteo Mandarini transl. (Stanford: Stanford University Press, 2011 [2007], 119.

71 It is not possible to further discuss this within this chapter due to space limitations. However, to clarify, my emphasis is on the necessity to merge subject oriented questions – such as who constitutes collateral damage; or in other words, who is consumed, and who are the consumers – with neoliberal analysis while considering the economy of exceptional measures.

72 On Turkey's economic transformation from being a neoliberal success story to civil war economy see: Yahya M. Madra and S Yılmaz, 'Turkey's decline into (civil) war economy: From neoliberal populism to corporate nationalism' (2019) 118(1) *South Atlantic Quarterly* 41.

73 Regarding the government's plans to make Kurdish cities desirable for tourists after the curfews, see: Yıldız, 2016.

Conclusion

Although Agamben exposes the crucial placement of *stasis* within the modern juridico-political systems, he provides little explanation as to how the active state of *stasis* is calmed or concluded only to be evoked again in the future. Surely, this is partly due to Agamben's general argument of exception being an everyday paradigm of government; hence, *stasis* never calms down. However, as the case of Turkey demonstrates, it changes form; and at this point it is possible to direct a criticism at Agamben's lack of differentiation between different forms of states of exception.[74] As the case of Turkey exhibits, although exception is the norm, there are different forms of exception, which leave targeted subjects in different, and at times opposing, states. Furthermore, target-oriented exceptional measures, such as granting one group an amnesty while another is left in mourning, are the motor that keeps *stasis* as a constant possibility within the state. Hence, in order to keep an active state of *stasis* as a possibility, there must be passive form(s) of *stasis* when the active state of civil war seems to be concluded. As a way of conclusion, I would like to recall the state of those trapped in the basement.

On 26 January 2015, one of the trapped people in Cizre lost his life while waiting for an ambulance to arrive, and while waiting for the European Court of Human Rights' (ECtHR) decision on the request for an interlocutory injunction due to interim measures.[75] He was the sixth person to die in that basement. The next day three MPs began a hunger strike to raise awareness of those trapped, calling for ambulances not to be stopped at military checkpoints.[76] This should have created a commotion in parliament, but the hunger strikers were MPs from the People's Democratic Party (Halkların Demokratik Partisi – HDP), the Kurdish Party-led leftist coalition party which was accused of conspiring against the Turkish government. They were quickly labelled as terrorists by the government,[77] and on the third day of their hunger strike, the Turkish Constitutional Court denied their application for

74 Agamben's theory of state of exception provides a very helpful lens, however as a result of its broadness fails to guide any detailed analysis. As in the case of Turkey, his lack of differentiation between state of emergency and counter terror laws proved to be problematic.

75 'Selami Yılmaz dies while waiting for ambulance in Cizre', *Bianet*, 26 January 2016, available at http://bianet.org/english/human-rights/171502-selami-yilmaz-dead-while-waiting-for-ambulance-in-cizre, accessed 28 February 2019.

76 '3 HDP MPs on hunger strike for ambulance to reach injured', *Bianet*, 27 January 2016, available at http://bianet.org/english/human-rights/171554-3-hdp-mps-on-hunger-strike-for-ambulance-to-reach-injured, accessed 28 February 2019.

77 'MPs on hunger strike call government to pull their weight', *Bianet*, 28 January 2016, available at http://bianet.org/english/human-rights/171585-mps-on-hunger-strike-call-government-to-pull-their-weight, accessed 28 February 2019. 'MPs on hunger strike: Don't hinder ambulances', *Bianet*, 29 January 2016, available at http://bianet.org/english/human-rights/171626-mps-on-hunger-strike-don-t-hinder-ambulances, accessed 28 February 2019.

an injunction.[78] While a group of 132 public figures issued a statement that they were ready to save those trapped in the basement, it was already too late. On 1 February, the hunger-striking MPs declared that they had lost communication with the people in the basement. They added that in their final contact they had heard explosions and those in the basement said they were trapped under debris.[79] Both national and international human rights organisations reported that the basements were destroyed by heavy weaponry, if not specifically targeted by the Turkish forces. The Human Rights Foundation of Turkey's Cizre field report says that basements were burnt and that human remains were spotted in the neighbourhoods where basements were located, with some said to have been thrown in the Tigris River. An active *stasis* transformed into a passive one when one side wins; when one side feasts on the other's mourning; when the memory of *stasis* is erased through destruction. Whether it is a gravestone or a land; when everything belonging to the losing side becomes the property of the other.

78 'AYM Cizre'de Ambulans Talebini Reddetti', *Bianet*, 29 January 2016, available at http://bianet.org/bianet/insan-haklari/171640-aym-cizre-de-ambulans-talebini-reddetti accessed 28 February 2019.

79 'Latest reports from wounded in Cizre: We're under debris', *Bianet*, 1 February 2016, available at http://bianet.org/english/human-rights/171692-latest-reports-from-wounded-in-cizre-we-re-under-debris, accessed 28 February 2019.

Chapter 9

Beyond 'the most serious suspension of rights' of Genoa

Violence, anomie and force (of law)

Sara Raimondi

Introduction

The language of the exception has increasingly been used in academic literature to denote a wide range of phenomena proliferating globally in the last decades, particularly in the wake of the global war on terror and the recent migration 'crises'. Prisons and refugee camps, extraordinary renditions, counter-terrorist legislation and the increased focus on border controls are just some of the examples that are often listed as instances of exception. Much less attention, however, tends to be paid to the weight that similar circumstances play at the domestic level and in the putatively liberal-democratic life of states. The chapter intervenes in this debate by offering a novel analysis of the case of acute violence and police brutality that occurred in the context of the 2001 Genoa G8 summit, which for gravity and scope has been described as the 'most serious suspension of democratic rights in a Western Democracy after WWII'.[1] The analysis departs from existent attempts to investigate the case through the lens of studies of popular protests or brutal police behaviour. It argues that the framework drawn from Carl Schmitt, Walter Benjamin and Giorgio Agamben, which defines the exception as an anomie produced by a specific triangulation of power, law and life, provides an original and unexplored reading of the case. By applying the framework of the exception to the case of Genoa, the aim of the enquiry is twofold. First, it demonstrates that the taxonomy of the exception stretches beyond the instances commonly found in the literature on the topic and to which the term is often reduced. Second, it opens up the question as to the function of exceptional measures within the context of contemporary democracies.

In this regard, the analysis highlights how, across multiple contexts, exception operates at the intersection and blurring point of the juridical and the political, right and violence, inside and outside, legal and physical status of those who are victims of exceptional practices, of citizenship and bare life. In

1 Amnesty International Annual Report, 'Italy: G8 Genoa Policing Operation of July 2001. A Summary of Concerns', November 2001.

so doing, the chapter aims at suggesting an enlargement of the current use of the concept of the exception and intimates that the applications and instances of the measure are in fact more complex, nuanced and blurred than the current literature accommodates. The case of abuses and law suspension of Genoa may offer an example of exception beyond its factual declaring, and demonstrates that exceptional instances are used by states also in the context of democratic life, and, potentially, against their own citizens whenever state institutions feel threatened. In this light, the study here conducted raises the question of the historical continuity and geographical circulation of models of exception and suspension of rights and the function that these have in securing power in domestic state life.

Between law and politics: the framework of the exception

In modern juridical and political literature, the concept of the 'state of exception' has been used to designate an extra-ordinary measure applied by states in situations of perceived emergency or potential or actual crisis. The flourishing of theories around the phenomenon is historically linked to the inter-war period and the collapse of European democracies in the first half of the 20th century.[2] In that scenario, the figures of Carl Schmitt and Walter Benjamin contributed to framing the debate, reaching different and mutually responsive reflections. More recently, the concept has been revitalised by Giorgio Agamben, whose contribution has been central in informing the reception of the measure today. The works of the three authors can be used to conceptualise the framework along which instances of exception can be examined, by looking at the configuration that the exception produces between political power, legal order and life. It is here suggested that the constitutive criteria to recognise the measure can be identified with the following: a factual suspension of the existent legal or normative order, the presence of a sovereign power that performs such an action and the limiting and downgrading effect that the legal suspension produces on subjects' lives.

Historically, the idea of the exception has been used to identify the conferment of exceptional powers in periods of superior external or internal threat to the life of states, resulting in the suspension of the rule of law and in the expansion of executive powers.[3] At the beginning of the 20th century, Carl Schmitt brought the concept to attention by applying it to his contemporary historical scenario. Taking issue with the positivist legal approach of authors like Hans Kelsen,[4] Schmitt articulates a decisionist position that puts the

2 Giorgio Agamben, *State of Exception*, Kevin Attell transl. (Chicago: University of Chicago Press, 2005 [2003]), 6.

3 Jef Huysmans, 'The Jargon of Exception: On Schmitt, Agamben and the Absence of Political Society', (2008) 2(2) *International Political Sociology* 165, 183.

4 Hans Kelsen, 'The Pure Theory of Law: Its Methods and Its Fundamental Concept', (1934) 50 *Law Quarterly Review* 474, 498.

focus on the mechanism of institution of the measure. Against claims arguing for the self-sufficiency of the law, Schmitt ties the origin of the exception to the figure of the sovereign, defined as 'he who decides on the state of exception'.[5] The reference to the sovereign becomes key to classifying the measure: the decision upon the exception highlights the existence of an agent, or agency, that is in fact superior to the norm and that can, at any time, transcend it. Exception denotes 'the decision in absolute purity',[6] which overcomes any legal order and mediation. A formal legal power is then opposed to the actual, empirical power that can at any time bypass the legal order, revealing the constitutively political character of the action that precedes and transcends the law. Hence, whereas the rule of law safeguards the regular performance of domestic affairs, the exception effects a superior political decision, which can suspend the law and act above the legal system. By connecting the notion of the exception to sovereignty, Schmitt makes clear the controversial nature of the exception, which stands as 'ambiguous, uncertain, borderline fringe, at the intersection of the legal and the political'.[7] If the exception is enforced as a juridical measure – a bracketing of the ordinary rule of law – it only gains significance because of a *political* decision that turns the measure into actual practice.

It should also be noted that the sovereign authority that produces an exception does not need to coincide with the top of institutional state structures. William Rasch makes this clear when, commenting on Schmitt, he highlights that the sovereign must be figured 'as an autonomous entity, an agent, or at least an agency, which has the authority to make decisions. That agent may be a monarch, a dictator, a ruling body, or any of a variety of other decision-making mechanism'.[8] The crucial element for an exception can thus be identified with the factual suspension of the law by the contingent authority that can, in a specific situation, surpass the norm and impose a legal void.

Interestingly, the role of state institutions and the scope for action and decision left to them with regard to the legal order is touched on by Walter Benjamin in his *Critique of Violence*.[9] As the author announces, the essay investigates the relationship between violence and justice and thus, the space

5 Carl Schmitt, *Political Theology*, George Schwab transl. (Cambridge, MA: MIT Press, 1985 [1933]), 5.
6 Carl Schmitt, *Political Theology*, 7; also in Georg Schwab, *The Challenge of the Exception: An Introduction to the Political Ideas of Carl Schmitt between 1921 and 1936* (Westport: Greenwood Press, 1989).
7 Alessandro Fontana, 'Du Droit de Résistance au Devoir d'Insurrection', in Jean-Claude Zancarini (ed.) *Le Droit de Résistance, XIIe-XXe Siècle*, 15–33, (Paris: ENS, 2001), 16.
8 William Rasch, 'Conflict as a Vocation: Carl Schmitt and the Possibility of Politics', (2000) 17(1) *Theory, Culture and Society* 8.
9 Walter Benjamin, 'Critique of Violence' in Marcus Bullock and Michael W. Jennings (eds.), *Walter Benjamin: Selected Writings. Vol. 1, 1913–1926* (Cambridge: Harvard University Press, 1996 [1921]).

for violence in relation to the law. In this regard, the author distinguishes between forms of institutionalised violence that can either create the law (law-making) or maintain it (law-preserving) and that are part of the functioning of the modern state.[10] In this classification, he defines the function of the police in particular as a 'spectral mixture' that sits astride the two forms of institutional (legal) violence and but is emancipated from both: in the author's words, 'this (of the police) is violence for legal ends, but with the simultaneous authority to decide these ends itself within wide limits (in the right to decree)'.[11] While operating within the mythical function of the law, the police, as an authority of the modern state, also have the power to decide their own ends, thus enabling a hybrid and, for Benjamin, ignominious, form of violence. To continue with the author: 'the police intervenes "for security reasons" in countless cases where no legal situation exists',[12] thus creating a mismatch between their own ends and the ends of the general law. For Benjamin, therefore, the figure of the police is chiefly well positioned to perform a type of violence where no clear legal situation exists, by acting in a factual legal void where decision-making institutions are able to define their own ends. The result is a contingent action by the police that can act simultaneously within and beyond the law. I maintain that, although not openly defined as such, the role of the police reproduces a configuration analogous to an exception by filling a situation of legal anomie with an action that bears no essential relation to the law. Therefore, it can potentially transgress and transcend the ordinary legal order in its actual conduct.

In addition, the analysis of Benjamin's work allows us to shift attention beyond the moment of the suspension of the law onto the dynamics produced *within* the legal vacuum: the factual bracketing of the law – produced by the police's deciding upon their own ends – questions the nature of the acts committed under the anomie, which escape any legal classification. For Benjamin, an authority like the police, or, in fact, following Rasch, any decision-making agency of the modern state, can enact a form of violence whose aims are not identical to and, potentially, even disconnected from, those of the general law. By doing so, they create a potential source of exceptional

10 In fact, Benjamin introduces another category of violence, which he calls 'pure' or 'divine'. In contrast to legal violence, pure violence is the only form of (revolutionary) violence that has existence outside the legal order, by reaffirming the subjective power to act in the name of justice and against the coercive power of the law (Benjamin, *Critique of Violence*, 282). Although the alleged matter of contention between Schmitt and Benjamin at the time chiefly concerned this category of sovereign action, the focus of the chapter is on the question of the space for violence within the institutionalised structures of the state in maintaining – or bypassing – the legal order. I thus do not engage further with the yet many central ideas discussed by Benjamin in the essay.

11 Benjamin, *Critique of Violence*, 286.

12 Ibid.

violence that, going beyond that of law-making or law-preserving, has no essential relationship with the law at all.

By creating a space for violence within the institutions of the state, moreover, an action similar to the one performed by the police implies a shift of level, from the normative dimension of the rule to that of the instantaneous decision – that is, to the sphere of contingent and immediate *fact*. This develops further and even potentially moves beyond Schmitt in classifying the instituting of the measure and the relation to sovereignty. Jacques Rancière voices this when, criticising the situation of a-political subjects in modernity, he notes that the effect of the exceptional action beyond the law is 'the erasure of the boundary between law and fact, law and lawlessness'.[13] Under legal anomies, the decision no longer follows a norm, but is rather left to the immediacy of the *praxis*. This inversion has a related impact on the definition of sovereignty: sovereign power does not require a formal instituting; rather, it is affirmed in the very moment of the decision over the suspension and transcending of the law. The divide between the formal declaration and the actualisation of power that derives from a factual exception is highlighted clearly by Judith Butler, who notices:

> it is not, literally speaking, that a sovereign power suspends the rule of the law, but that the rule of the law, in the act of being suspended, *produces* sovereignty in its action and its effect. This inverse relation to law produces the 'unaccountability' of this operation of sovereignty.[14]

Closing the circle of what has been presented above, the action of institutions like the police can thus be defined as sovereign, since, by acting beyond the law, they are produced in such a capacity. As Benjamin also specifies,[15] this is more true (and, in fact, for him, more devastating) in regimes like democracies, where the modern conditions of rule of law and separation between legislative and executive are active, than in cases like an absolute monarchy, where the two powers are already united in the figure of the king. It is thus democracies that can bear witness 'to the greatest conceivable degeneration of violence.'[16]

The unfettered power enabled by the situation of legal indefiniteness, therefore, discloses the arbitrariness with which sovereign power can be exercised: the exception effects the possibility of a sovereign action, which is not accountable to the regulations, or constraints of the general law. Any ruling or executive act can be performed without justification of the reasons that

13 Jacques Rancière, 'Who is the Subject of the Rights of Man?', (2004) 103(2/3) *The South Atlantic Quarterly* 306.
14 Judith Butler, *Precarious Life: The Powers of Mourning and Violence* (London: Verso, 2004), 66 [emphasis added].
15 Benjamin, *Critique of Violence*, 286.
16 Ibid.

make the action possible, and that bear nothing essential in their ends and aims, if not renewing their position of sovereignty. Agamben describes this dynamic when he notices that

> In order to apply a norm it is ultimately necessary to suspend its application, to produce an exception. In every case, the state of exception marks a threshold at which *logic* and *praxis* blur with each other and pure violence without *logos* claims to realize an enunciation without any real reference.[17]

The justification of rational *logos* is separated from the task of governing so that any action is disconnected from any declared end. The undefined, and even paradoxical, character of the exception lies therefore in this controversy: a power different from the rule establishes itself by altering the rule and actualising its suspension. While still dependent on the legal order, it replaces the function of the legal apparatus and imposes itself as the new sovereign voice. By overcoming the law, thus, the political decision upon an exception obtains an immediate access to the target that is protected through the legal order, that is, subjects' life. Life that can be subject to a sovereign decision emerges thus as a further logical element implied by the enactment of an exception. It is in particular with the formulation given by Giorgio Agamben that the dimension of 'life' is incorporated into the conceptual edifice of the state of exception.

The notion of life is introduced by the author when defining the measure. In his view:

> the state of exception is the device that must ultimately articulate and hold together the two aspects of the juridical-political machine by instituting a threshold of undecidability between anomie and *nomos*, between life and law [...]. It is founded on the essential fiction according to which anomie in the form of *auctoritas*, living law or force of law, is still related to the juridical order, and the power to suspend the norm has an *immediate hold on life*.[18]

Besides the legal dimension, the exception enables a direct reach to the lives of the subjects involved. In particular, the challenge of the exception consists in opening an area of 'undecidability', where a pure decision disconnected from the regular legal ends (and the violence ensuing from it) may occur. The divide between law and sovereign decision, between norm and fact in the

17 Giorgio Agamben, *State of Exception*, Kevin Attell transl. (Chicago: University of Chicago Press, 2005 [2003]), 40.
18 Ibid., 86 [emphasis added].

exception, is paralleled by a correspondent blurring of the threshold between 'human' and 'non-human', between 'meaningful' and 'bare' life.[19]

The roots of this division may be found already in the work of Hannah Arendt, who stresses such distinction when analysing the condition of refugees in *The Origins of Totalitarianism*.[20] Here, Arendt insists on the controversial relationship of both the link and the opposition between nature and politics, between bare and qualified life, that establishes different degrees of existence. Significantly, the same concepts also appear in Rancière's work expanding on the same topic: a bare conception of life is opposed to the fully human condition, a form of being appraised by the inscription in a political structure that grants rights to life: only then does life gain meaning and become entitled to preservation and protection.[21] This core distinction, therefore, provides the demarcation between a life that 'deserves' to be safeguarded and a simple being without purpose, on which, consequently, everything is permitted.

The possibility of an existence denied of importance provides the logical counterpart of the unfettered decision that was pointed out with regard to the establishment of the exception: if the authority that acts as sovereign holds the power to act beyond the law that protects subjects, then the legal suspension downplays simultaneously the life valued by those rights. Consequently, any form of behaviour, even that which is violent and degrading, becomes possible in the exception, since the sovereign does not obey any rule. The behaviour of the authority is thus a pure decision over a naked and unqualified existence: under the exception, subjects are neither full citizens nor human and are potentially exposed to any form of conduct, even that which is annihilating and humiliating.

It appears thus evident why Agamben reintroduced the notion primarily to describe the condition of men in camps under totalitarianism: the sovereign decision undermines the consideration of subjects' existence as properly *human*. The implications of this are clearly presented by Rancière:

> what is correlated with the exceptionality of sovereign power is the exception of life. It is life as bare and naked life, which means life captured in a zone of indiscernibility, of indistinction between *zoe* and *bios*, between natural and human.[22]

The dynamic active in the moment of the exception is then a declassification, a return to a bare acceptation of being. Hence, to actualise an exception, the

19 Giorgio Agamben, *Homo Sacer: Sovereign Power and Bare Life*, Daniel Heller-Roazen transl. (Stanford: Stanford University Press, 1998 [1995]).
20 Hannah Arendt, *Origins of Totalitarianism* (New York: Harvest Books & Harcourt, 1985 [1951]).
21 Jacques Rancière, 'Who is the Subject of the Rights of Man?'.
22 Ibid., 306.

authority must consider subjects' lives as having no meaning, since potentially this deprives them of any recognition and safeguard. By denying their existence the protection of the law, any action on them becomes conceivable (and applicable). Quoting Thanos Zartaloudis, what characterises the exception is a 'zone of indistinction between bare life and qualified life, it is the understanding of this relation [...] that binds and at the same time abandons the living being to a law without a content'.[23] The element of the arbitrariness of the decision then returns: through the exception, the sovereign obtains a direct access on life, and decides over it by transcending the legal mediator that prevents abuses. The idea of a devalued and naked life is thus introduced to the conceptual matrix of the notion, and suggests that only when qualified as political – that is, entitled to protection – can life be considered as fully human.

The main elements pointed out in the analysis so far – a contingent authority that transcends the law, the factual enacting of an exception beyond any formal declaration and the downgrading of subjects' lives – can be deployed as a framework to read instances of the exception. The analysis just conducted defined the exception as a complex measure that shares both a legal and a political nature. If it implies an action in the juridical sphere – by a factual suspension of the rule of law – the decision upon the exception is in fact a political act by which the sovereign regains direct access to life. Ultimately, the exception realises a condition of lawlessness, wherein any contingent authority can exercise a sovereign power and devalue subjects' lives.

Anomies in practice: the 'exceptional' reading of the case of Genoa

In the following section, I want to demonstrate that the conceptual heuristic just outlined can provide an alternative framework to read through and identify circumstances of exception, particularly in opposition to the vast literature that uses the concept in critical IR studies, and in the context of the politics of security in particular, where the notion has been widely adopted.[24] With this aim, I set out to apply the framework of the exception just analysed to a case that would seem to escape the common taxonomy of the concept.

The series of protests and demonstrations that accompanied the International G8 Summit held in Genoa in July 2001 was an emblematic case

23 Thanos Zartaloudis, *Giorgio Agamben: Power, Law and the Uses of Criticism* (Abingdon, UK; New York: Routledge, 2010), 160.

24 See for instance Mitchell Dean, *Governmentality: Power and Rule in Modern Society* (London: Sage, 1999); Vivienne Jabri, *Discourses on Violence* (Manchester; New York: Manchester University Press, 1996); Andrew Neal, 'Foucault in Guantanamo: Towards an Archeology of Exception', (2006) 37(1) *Security Dialogue* 31, 46; Jef Huysmans, 'The Jargon of Exception' 183.

brought to the attention of public opinion, media and scholars. The diverse literature on the topic tends to point out the extraordinary intensity of the violence deployed in the policing operations surrounding the event. The pervasiveness of repressive tactics by police and security forces resulted from a pre-emptive regime of control which, according to Naomi Klein, was enforced around the city even a month before the summit took place.[25] Nevertheless, the peculiarity of the circumstances witnessed in Genoa was a use of force beyond the limited situations of protests, which was manifested in moments exceeding regular policing tasks on the streets.[26]

The spread layer of abusive facts perpetrated by law enforcement authorities emerges clearly in a study conducted by Michael Boyle[27]: his analysis of the experience of groups of activists during the protests shows how Genoa was characterised by a set of incidents of patrolling all the areas of the event, culminating in degrading treatment and curtailment of rights against the subjects involved. I maintain that the events witnessed in Genoa were not only a case of accidental brutality in enforcing policing duties. Rather, the exceptionality of facts turned into systematic conduct that can be classified as an instance of exception according to the criteria highlighted above: there, a police body acting as sovereign created a legal anomie where the law was de facto suspended and subjects' rights were downgraded to the point of dehumanisation. These dynamics ascribe a particular interest to the events occurred and distinguish them from a simple case of deployment of brutal force by the police. Before approaching the analysis, it is useful to briefly describe the episodes in more detail.

Among the widespread examples of ill-treatment and excessive measures deployed across the whole set of events in Genoa, two specific cases stand out as relevant for the analysis. On the night of the 21 July 2001, the second day of the protests, a squad of police national forces attacked the Diaz-Pertini

25 Naomi Klein, 'Getting Used to Violence: How Years of Police Brutality Culminated in the Death of the Italian Protester Carlo Giuliani' in Klein, *Fences and Windows: The Front Lines of the Globalization Debate* (New York: Flamingo, 2002), 149.

26 Notably, the protests culminated with the killing of one of the demonstrators (see Klein, 'Getting Used to Violence: How Years of Police Brutality Culminated in the Death of the Italian Protester Carlo Giuliani', or Rory Carroll, 'Italian Police Framed G8 Protesters', *The Guardian*, 22 June 2002. For the International regulation around the use of force by enforcement officers in situations of protest, see the UN legislation around protest policing; in particular, the UN Code of Conduct for Law Enforcement Officials (Art. 3) and the UN Basic Principles on the Use of Force and Firearms by Law Enforcements Officials (Pt. 4–10, 14; also in Amnesty International Annual Report, 'Italy: G8 Genoa Policing Operation of July 2001. A Summary of Concerns').

27 Michael Boyle, 'The Criminalization of Dissent: Protest Violence, Activist Performance, and the Curious Case of the VolxTheaterKarawane in Genoa', (2011) 55(4) *The Drama Review* 113, 127.

High School building in one of the town districts. It had been transformed into a temporary centre for the Genoa Social Forum[28] and the broadcast organisation Indymedia, both collecting national and non-national demonstrators, journalists and lawyers involved in the event. The raid by the police, initially explained as a check against the carrying of weapons and damaging acts allegedly carried out by the group of 93 activists, turned later into a prolonged assault, with systematic beatings, ill-treatment and injuring of the provisional detainees. The subjects' status within the detention has been described in the statements of the victims, which denounced the 'special kind of discipline' that the police performed by incarcerating victims in 'a detention centre that became a place of dark terror'.[29] Beatings were accompanied by further abuses, mutilations, physical violations and the enforced simulation of animal behaviours.

A similar situation was later replicated at the police point of the nearby Bolzaneto facility, which had been reassigned as a detention structure for protesters before they were moved to formal imprisonment. Here, the same regime of cruel and inhuman tactics was deployed against the over two hundred detainees, with repeated beatings, verbal abuse, needs deprivation and humiliating physical and psychological mistreatment by both law enforcement officers and medical staff during the days of confinement. Again in reports: 'Prisoners described their feeling of being cut off from the rest of the world, in a place where there were *no laws* and *no rules.* Indeed, the police forced their captives to sign statements waiving all their legal rights.'[30] The downgrading of political and human rights was therefore a remarkable feature pertaining to the whole experience and imposed by the officers involved in the event.[31]

The incommensurability of violence deployed has been significantly captured by the words of one of the policemen involved, who later defined the beating at the Diaz as a 'Mexican butcher's shop',[32] signalling the inhuman and degrading character of the abuse. What is relevant for the argument, however, is primarily the judgment that came from the international community, which intervened to define the event as 'the most serious suspension of democratic rights in a Western country after the Second World War', stressing

28 A counter-globalisation organisation made up of political movements and parties and civil society.

29 Nick Davies, 'The Bloody Battle of Genoa', *The Guardian*, 17 July 2008.

30 Ibid. [emphasis added].

31 The description of the facts is here derived from secondary sources; for a more detailed description of the events and testimonies released in the aftermath, see the reports Nick Davies, 'The Bloody Battle of Genoa' and Amnesty International Annual Report, 'Italy: G8 Genoa Policing Operation of July 2001. A Summary of Concerns'; the latter was eventually also used in the legal trials.

32 Declaration by the police commissioner Michelangelo Fourier during the trial, 2007.

the disproportion and uniqueness of the facts witnessed in Genoa.[33] Eventually, judicial and parliamentary inquiries sanctioned Bolzaneto as a case of torture, referring to the systematic curtailment and downplay of rights perpetrated in the facility.[34]

I argue that the events of Genoa can be productively captured by the conceptual elements outlined in the framework of the exception suggested above – that is, a transcending of the legal order, a contingent authority exercising sovereign power and the effects of this action on subjects' lives. The situation of anomie and suspension of rights is a common feature cited in the literature on the issue: as has been described, the reclusion of provisional detainees turned into a 'lawless limbo', and unrestricted action could be applied to the subjects involved.[35] The source of the legal openness pertaining to the detainment of Genoa derived, first, from the role played by the police responsible for deciding on the events: through 'their special kind of discipline',[36] the police enforced a new order transcending the regular application of the rule in the contingent moment of the confinement and abuses. The police acted as the sovereign voice and actualised a suspension of the ordinary rule of law and of the ensuing rights. The establishment of an exception can here be recognised: the police could contingently exercise the sovereign power of suspending the law and behaving as an agent superior to it; a condition of exception was thus enforced, and the police even created a physical space where the legal anomie could take place.

Moreover, as argued above, the subversion of the regular legal order did not require a formal instituting; rather, it was enacted at the level of concrete *facts* established in the particular and contingent moment. In this, the point that was derived from Rasch becomes fully clear: an exception can be enacted by any agency that has decision-making force. By exercising this sort of decisional power, enforcement officers in Genoa were able to suspend any legal order and condemn victims to a status where, in detainees' own testimony, 'there were no law and no rule'.[37] As has been powerfully described by Benjamin, despite maintaining their structure and organisation, the police

33 Amnesty International Annual Report, 'Italy: G8 Genoa Policing Operation of July 2001. A Summary of Concerns'.

34 To present briefly the legal events that followed: though hundreds of policemen were declared involved, a restricted number were finally convicted, and none served the full application of the sentence. For a full consideration of juridical procedures in the aftermath of Genoa and the ensuing charges, see the series of 'Parliamentary Commission Acts' produced during the trials until the final sentences on 12 July 2012 (Diaz) and 14 June 2013 (Bolzaneto). (Parliament of Italy, 'Commissioni Parlamentari di Inchiesta', 2001–2013).

35 Paul Kennedy, 'One Deadly Summit (The Italian Collective Documentary Project about G8 in Genoa and the Concomitant Protest Movement)', (2001) 11 *Sight and Sound* 28.

36 Davies, 'The Bloody Battle of Genoa'.

37 Ibid.

were able to create a space for an action independent from and unconnected to the regular functioning of the law. The police thus became the vehicle through which the exception was realised, acting as a sovereign power with the ultimate decision-making authority in the situation.

The dual role of the police and the fine line between policing duties and arbitrariness of behaviour may not only be contingent to the case, but rather a feature substantially embedded in the figure of the police. As seen in Benjamin, in the function of enforcing public order, police authority is constitutively placed on the threshold between the legitimacy of the action and the discretionary application of legal measures. Agamben further restates this point when, in an essay titled 'Sovereign Police', he notes that 'contrary to public opinion', in performing their task the police are

> not merely an administrative function of law enforcement; rather, the police are perhaps the place where the proximity and almost constitutive exchange between *violence* and *right* that characterizes the figure of the sovereign is shown more nakedly and clearly than anywhere else. [...] If sovereign, in fact, is the one who marks the point of indistinction between violence and right by proclaiming the state of exception and suspending the validity of the law, the police are always operating within a similar state of exception. Their rationale [...] defines an area of indistinction between violence and right that is exactly symmetrical to that of sovereignty.[38]

The indefinite detentions of Diaz and Bolzaneto may thus be considered as points in which the sovereign role constitutively belonging to the police was expressed and realised in its highest manifestation, activating an exceptional vacuum where sovereign action could constantly turn into violence. The sovereign role of the police in these cases could be described as the kind of violence defined by Benjamin, implied by and simultaneously transcending the duty of enforcing the law and setting ends outside those of the general legislation. For this reason, the action of the police in Genoa cannot simply be reduced to the (more straightforward and declared) need to maintain public order; rather, it can be considered as an even higher degeneration of violence, since it maintains no essential link to the regular ends of the law. A further point for classifying Genoa as exception derives therefore from its disclosing a pure exercise of sovereign power, by which the threshold between right and abuse may constantly blur without any justification.

38 Giorgio Agamben, *Means without Ends: Notes on Politics*, Vincenzo Binetti and Cesare Cesarino transl. (Minneapolis: University of Minnesota Press, 2000 [1996]), 103.

In addition, if sovereign action addresses primarily the domain of the law, the further dimension that is involved in the exception is the parallel effect on targets' lives. The same challenge to individuals' lives may now be applied to the context considered, where power is embodied by the sovereign figure of the police and the subjects are the provisional detainees deprived of their rights. In particular, the tipping point here is not only the threat to the political rights of the individuals involved, but the curtailment of even physical rights at all levels. The notably degrading ill-treatment perpetrated against the subjects signals the (dis)qualification of the lives involved: by the 'lawless' action taken, existence is affirmed as unqualified, naked life – that is, a life lacking any value. Thus, the exceptionality of the circumstance lies not only in performing an action that lies beyond any legal end but also in the form of existence that is produced: subjects are no longer political entities or bearers of rights, but reduced to merely physical, bare existence. Resorting to Agamben's most famous definition,[39] subjects are reduced to *homines sacri*.

Central for understanding this point is the annihilating and degrading treatment perpetrated, in which the subjects were forced to act like animals. The characteristics highlighted in the first section are therefore realised in the case and complete the meaning of the 'indefinite' detentions pointed out by Boyle[40]: the indefiniteness of the case pertains both to the legal openness created by the factual suspension of the law and, connectedly, to the suspension of the humanity of the subjects involved. The triangulation between power, law and life is reactivated and meaningfully confirmed in the cases analysed: in the comment of Giuseppe D'Avanzo: 'Diaz and Bolzaneto appear as places "outside the law", wherein *rules* as well as *humanity* are suspended and in which only the civic sense of the police would be ultimately held accountable'.[41] A condition of exception is thus created here in the relation between a normless power of the sovereign police and the naked life of provisional targets left at the mercy of the contingent authority acting in the circumstance.

Hence, with the disclosure of the concept of inhumanity in the form of bare existence, the second side of the relation between power and life pertaining to the exception also re-emerges: in its extreme manifestation, the figure of naked, unqualified life brings back to the image of the man in the 'camp', in relation to which the modern idea of the exception was forged. The analogy is confirmed when Monica Jansen notices that the case of Bolzaneto in particular has been often linked to the humiliating conditions within the Nazi camps, as political aggression aimed at affecting life and bodies – in this case,

39 Agamben, *Homo Sacer,* 47–52.

40 Boyle, 'The Criminalization of Dissent. Protest Violence, Activist Performance, and the Curious Case of the VolxTheaterKarawane in Genoa'.

41 Giuseppe D`Avanzo, 'Prefazione', in Massimo Calandri, *Bolzaneto: La Mattanza della Democrazia* (Roma: DeriveApprodi, 2008), 10 [author's translation; emphasis added].

those of the protesters involved.[42] The presence of an unqualified life deprived of any form suggests a connection with the array of examples in which the paradigm of the exception has been moulded and formulated, both in their more immediate understanding (concentration camps) and in their modern articulations (detention places, provisional confinements or places of 'indefinite' justice where no clear law applies): in all situations, a devaluation of life is replicated, and a sovereign act – here coinciding with the police – may turn the status of political subjects into unqualified, non-political and, thus, inhuman existence. All these reasons prevent us from considering Genoa as just an example of police brutality and suggest instead that we define it as a peculiar condition of exception.

Existent analyses of the case might include the example in the overall series of violent events occurred around the summit. Following Donatella della Porta and Lorenzo Zamponi,[43] it is certainly true that the spread of violence of the protests resulted from the reciprocal interactions between demonstrators and authorities, which were determinant in structuring the confrontation. Nevertheless, my interest lies in the deliberate perpetration of exceptional measures rather than the degeneration of actions during the actual moments of the demonstrations. In my argument, the specificity of the experiences of Diaz and Bolzaneto consists in the 'indefinite detainment' created there[44] as lawless situations in which even abuse and torture became possible. Departing from the mainstream literature that links the facts to the comprehensive context of protests, the episodes described should be considered in their autonomy, and identified as circumstances where an exception has been materialised: scholars, protesters and even enforcement officers involved suggested that the police in Genoa created 'zones of indistinction', drawing from Agamben's famous definition.[45] This clarification is useful in order to distinguish the reading suggested here from other approaches found in the literature: mainstream analyses associate the case of Genoa with the anti-globalisation movement and with the trends peculiar to the phenomenon.[46]

42 Monica Jansen, 'Narrare le Forze dell'Ordine dopo Genova 2001', (2010) 65(3) *Italian Studies* 418.

43 Donatella della Porta and Lorenzo Zamponi, 'Protest and Policing on October 15th, Global Day of Action: The Italian Case', (2013) 23(1) *Policing and Society: An International Journal of Research and Policy* 65, 80.

44 Boyle, 'The Criminalization of Dissent: Protest Violence, Activist Performance, and the Curious Case of the VolxTheaterKarawane in Genoa', 114.

45 Agamben, *State of Exception*, 4.

46 See for instance Donatella della Porta and Herbert Reiter, *La Protesta e il Controllo: Movimenti e Forze dell'Ordinenell'Era della Globalizzazione* (Milano: Altraeconomia/Piacenza: Berti, 2004); Luis Fernandez, *Policing Dissent: Social Control and the Anti-Globalization Movement* (New Brunswick, NJ: Rutgers University Press, 2008); John Noakes and Patrick Gillham, 'Aspects of the "New Penology" in the Police Response to Major Political Protests in the United States, 1999–2000', in Donatella della Porta, Abby Peterson and Herbert Reiter (eds),

Alternatively, some research focuses on structural features of protests and demonstrations, referring to the composition of groups involved,[47] tactics and strategies deployed,[48] or surrounding discourses of criminalisation of dissent.[49] Finally, other works explain the dynamics that occurred as a legacy of the fascist culture embedded in the Italian police, re-emerging in response to the events of 2001.[50] All these readings may contribute to defining the wider framework, but they do not cover the specific object of study that has been highlighted here, which may add a new perspective to the application of states of exception.

The example can also be distinguished from other cases of exception. The remarkable denouncing of the case by Amnesty International (AI) as 'the most serious suspension of rights' in the Western world for over half a century indicates the depth, magnitude and distinctiveness of the facts and their extraordinary character. In AI's statement, two fundamental aspects in particular can be highlighted. First, the statement underlines the link between the case and the current life of a democracy, with the only antecedent going back to the period of the Second World War. The link to the circumstance of conflict – and the War in particular – suggests a comparison with the unique political events of that time: the instauration of totalitarian regimes and the experience of the concentration camps. As we have seen, the literature has already made the connection in the case analysed here, pointing out the analogy with the political conduct of totalitarianism and the practices of the Nazi regime.[51]

AI's sentence also highlights that the fact pertains to the realm of a Western liberal-democracy. The challenge for theoretical investigation is thus that of justifying similar occurrences in the context of liberal-democratic countries, where the endowment and achievement of basic rights is taken for granted. An instance that proves the contrary questions the relation between formal recognition of democratic principles and their concrete implementation. In this sense, the argument may go further than existent studies on the subject and enlarge the array of modern exceptions: if the measure has already been

Policing Transnational Protest: In the Aftermath of the 'Battle of Seattle' (Aldershot: Ashgate, 2006).

47 Peter Hajnal, 'Civil Society at the 2001 Genoa G8 Summit', (2001) 58(1) *International Journal* 13, 15; Jeffrey, Juris, 'Violence Performed and Imagined: Militant Action, the Black Bloc and the Mass Media in Genoa', (2005) 25(4) *Critique of Anthropology* 413, 32.

48 Donatella della Porta and Lorenzo Zamponi, 'Protest and Policing on October 15th, Global Day of Action: The Italian Case'.

49 Boyle, 'The Criminalization of Dissent. Protest Violence, Activist Performance, and the Curious Case of the VolxTheaterKarawane in Genoa'.

50 John Allen, 'Fascism's Face in Genoa', *The Nation*, 20 August, 2001; Melody Niwot, 'Narrating Genoa: Documentaries of the Italian G8 Protests of 2001 and the Persistence and Politics of Memory', (2011) 23(2) *History & Memory* 66, 89.

51 Jansen, 'Narrare le forze dell'ordine dopo Genova 2001'.

applied in contemporary contexts (in the highest exemplification of Guantanamo Bay dealt with by Agamben[52]) and with regard to other 'lawless' subjects, such as refugees, migrants, provisional detainees,[53] the aim is now to extend discussion to its embedding and presence within domestic state life.

Beyond Genoa: enlarging the taxonomy of the camp

At first, Genoa may appear a contingent case of rights curtailment produced by an accidental degeneration in police behaviour during the circumstance of the protests. The analysis of the inner dynamics, however, allowed for a reading of the case as an example of a state of exception, enforced by the police acting as sovereign and producing the consequent dehumanising treatment against the subjects involved. By replicating these mechanisms, the case can be compared to the wider set of occurrences gathered under the concept of the exception, which can now be further explicated.

The identification of instances of exception has been often linked analytically to the image of the 'camp' to denote a locus that undergoes an autonomous logic of governing: the camp designates a space of juridical void, where no difference between rule and fact holds.[54] The connection with the exception is thus close: by physically realising the suspension of the norm, the camp formalises the decision upon an exception and creates the material conditions for locating the anomie. The rule of law is totally subverted within the dimension of the camp, and the actual power is transferred to the hands of the contingent authority that acts as sovereign.

It is important to notice that, if historical experiences of camps during the totalitarian regimes contributed to the formulation of the image, the theoretical figure of the camp must be taken as an independent analytical concept that denotes the peculiar structure effecting an exception. Treating the notion of the camp as explanatory category rather than as 'mere' historical occurrence helps enlarge its application and allows us to export the model beyond its literal meaning: the camp defines all instances where a legal suspension and curtailment of rights is replicated. As a consequence, subjects that 'inhabit' these various forms of camp are equally part of the same classification since, missing a defined juridical status, they are liable to a fully arbitrary rule: refugees, provisional detainees, illegal immigrants become the subjects of modern exceptions, given their condition of juridical indefiniteness.[55] By taking the camp as physical locus of the exception, it is then possible to fulfil the connection and enlarge the array to also include the case studied: if the

52 Agamben, *State of Exception*, 4.

53 Vivienne Jabri, 'War, Security and the Liberal State', (2006) 37(1) *Security Dialogue* 47; Rancière, 'Who is the Subject of the Rights of Man?'.

54 Agamben, *Homo Sacer: Sovereign Power and Bare Life.*

55 Giorgio Agamben, *State of Exception*; Jabri. 'War, Security and the Liberal State'; Rancière, 'Who is the Subject of the Rights of Man?'.

camp represents the space where law and fact blur and sovereignty accesses bare life, then the case of torture and abuses of Genoa provides an example of the same form of 'camp': legal norms are totally abandoned and the situation is left in the hands of authorities that exercise an unfettered power over subjects' lives. As expressively explicated by Agamben:

> If this is true, if the essence of the camp consists in the materialization of the state of exception and in the creation of a space in which bare life and juridical rule enter into a threshold of indistinction, then we find ourselves virtually in the presence of a camp every time such a structure is created, independent of the kinds of crime that are committed there and whatever its denomination and specific topography. [...], an apparently innocuous space delimits a context in which the normal order is suspended and in which whether atrocities are committed depends not on the law but on the civility and ethical sense of the authority that temporarily acts as sovereign.[56]

The already known areas where German authorities gathered 'illegal' subjects under the Nazi regime, the prisons for suspects where police deploy counter-terrorist measures, the structures for immigrants along the borders of Western countries and, we can now add, the temporary facilities where officers keep demonstrators before an official trial can all be considered *camps*: they all provide the material condition to locate an exception and degrade individuals to the level of an unqualified existence. Reading the exception as a juridical-political category realised empirically by the camp helps us connect the case of Genoa to the comprehensive range of modern exceptions and reconsider the pervasiveness of the measure in the political life of current modern states: all cases open a space of juridical anomie wherein any sorts of behaviour, even violent and inhuman, become possible.

Moreover, with the extension just reached, the case that was presented may even go further than previous examples: if, so far, the concept has been ascribed to subjects with uncertain legal status – refugees, immigrants or individuals placed at the margins of the juridical order – Genoa shows that it is possible to direct such mechanisms towards the same citizens that the state is responsible for protecting. The measure of the exception, then, gives consistency to a single comprehensive process: if restricted to well-defined situations in the past, the exception gradually turns into a targeted measure and, finally, appears possible in episodes addressed potentially to any subject. In all cases, a degrading, abusive and dehumanising action is performed, independently of the specific circumstances and context of application. The argument thus achieves a double result: on the one hand it suggests that Genoa is not an accidental occurrence but partakes to a precise analytical category; on the

56 Agamben, *Homo Sacer*, 174.

other, it tests that practices of exception are more pervasive than their standard definition and are present within current democracies.

A final clarification may be added: in discussing the exception in today's domestic contexts, many authors, and Agamben himself, critically extend the measure to an encompassing reading of the modern political condition. They draw from Foucault's biopolitical approach[57] and take life as the core objective of politics. In these readings, the aim of state power is to achieve a totalising control over its citizens by also disciplining the natural, (apparently) non-political existence. The practice of the exception is thus seen as overwhelming, up to the point of interpreting the camp as the 'fundamental biopolitical paradigm of the West'.[58] Moreover, today's use of Foucauldian governmentality[59] tends to connect the topic to the 'exceptional' measures adopted in discourses of security in the West after 9/11: provisions such as monitoring communications, borders checks and all the operations enforced as internal defence are included in the same range of exceptional practices.

The analysis of the case of Genoa using the framework of the state of exception can be seen as opening up an additional dimension that cuts across the trends and mainstream approaches identified in the literature. On the one hand it distances itself from the language of security studies that tend to mainly apply the analysis of the exception to the societal trends supported by the discourse of the 'war on terror' and the structuring of the social field with exceptional practices. On the other hand it also moves beyond the more easily recognisable cases of dehumanisation and ill-treatment. If cases like Guantanamo Bay or Abu Ghraib have become emblematic of the application of the 'no man's land' that the exception produces, and of the 'inclusive exclusion'[60] through which bare life is incorporated in the very order and legitimation of modern politics, Genoa demonstrates that cases of exception are even more pervasive and hidden in the context of democratic life and can also be enforced by states against their own citizens. More than as a paradigmatic example, therefore, the analysis of the case provided here wishes to open up an additional avenue of enquiry to the approaches usually emphasised in the literature in relation to the exception. Even more, the case examined here invites treating the concept of the exception as more blurred and 'messier' than many categorisations in the literature would have it. The analysis performed highlights how, across multiple contexts, exceptions require the co-presence of only apparently opposite terms of analysis: the juridical and the political; right and violence; the legal status and the physicality of those who

57 Michel Foucault, *Discipline and Punish* (London: Penguin, 1977); Michel Foucault, *Society Must be Defended: Lectures at the Collège de France*, 1975–76 (London: Penguin, 2004).
58 Agamben, *Homo Sacer,* 181.
59 Jabri, 'War, Security and the Liberal State'; Neal, 'Foucault in Guantanamo: Towards an Archeology of Exception'.
60 Agamben, *Homo Sacer,* 22.

are victims of exceptional practices; citizens and bare life. Beyond the cases usually analysed, then, the exception can become a privileged point of observation for a reflective diagnosis of the life of modern states. More than interrogating the changing nature of politics in the age of globalisation that the literature on exceptionalism often tends to highlight,[61] the analysis conducted here opens up new questions around the function of exceptional measures within the context of contemporary democracies, their historical continuity and geographical circulation, and asks what exception reveals about the complex relationship between the legal, political and social dimension (also) of domestic state life.

61 Huysmans, 'The Jargon of Exception, 165-83.

Afterword: Emergencies, exceptions, legalities

David Fraser

Pessimism of the intellect, optimism of the will.

– Antonio Gramsci

I write this afterword in the middle of the Covid-19 pandemic. We live day to day in compulsory social isolation. We are citizens and subjects of the state of emergency and of states of exception. While some have argued that the pandemic is exaggerated and being deployed for nefarious purposes, the death tolls are not fictional.[1] The legal and political possibilities of the virus, its potential to serve as a fundamental disruption to the constituted order remain real, but are perhaps overwrought in relation to other 'normal' states of legal exception.[2] The chapters of this book are now more than theoretical, jurisprudential, historical, socio-legal interrogations of the state of exception; they are part of the explanation of our quotidian reality and an examination of our existential and jurisprudential state of being.[3] The law and politics of the state of exception are no longer the outliers of our existence.

Of course, as the contributors make clear, governments do not need a pandemic to institute emergencies or states of exception. Before Covid-19, Myanmar committed genocide against the Rohingya, whose very juridical existence they deny.[4] China placed tens of thousands of Uighers in re-education camps to teach them authentic Chinese values, before, during, and no

1 Lukas van den Berge, 'Biopolitics and the coronavirus: Foucault, Agamben, Žižek', (2020) 49(1) *Netherlands Journal of Legal Philosophy* 3-6. Available at SSRN: https://ssrn.com/abstract=3566072 SSRN 3566072.

2 Cristiano Paixão and Juliano Zaiden Benvindo, '"Constitutional dismemberment" and strategic deconstitutionalization in times of crisis: Beyond emergency powers," Int'l J. Const. l. Blog, 24 April 2020, available at http://iconnectblog.com/2020/04/constitutional-dismemberment-and-strategic-deconstitutionalization-in-times-of-crisis-betond-emergency-powers/.

3 Simon Western, "Covid-19: An intrusion of the Real. The unconscious unleashes its truth", Academia.edu, available at https://birkbeck.academia.edu/SimonWestern.

4 Application of the Convention on the Prevention and Punishment of the Crime of Genocide (The Gambia v. Myanmar), Order, 23 January 2020, International Court of Justice, General List, no. 178.

doubt after the coronavirus.[5] India attempted to reconfigure its laws to exclude citizenship for many Muslims.[6] Dingong Duterte in the Philippines cured himself of being gay by being surrounded by beautiful women, urges regulatory simplification to aid his economic supporters and allies, and gives official approval to the killing of drug dealers as enemies of the state.[7] In Brazil, Bolsonaro destroys indigenous populations in the name of economic progress and allows the coronavirus free reign in the favelas.[8] In the United States, Trump used the invasion of "bad hombres" from the south to take military funding to build his wall.[9] He asserted ordinary executive powers to exclude travellers from Muslim countries.[10] Detention camps for migrants from Australia to the Balkans to Italy are a commonplace of normal governmental practice.[11] The camp is no longer, if it ever was, a place of exception or emergency. Attacks on Roma in every country in the European Union, where their status as *gens du voyage* poses a threat to sovereignty of the nation state and the pan-European polity at one and the same time, continue unabated.[12]

The pandemic simply gives an excuse, and a broader power and authority to governments who wish to use it, to institute long-term anti-democratic reforms that will persist after the exception. This is the fear, and the reality, of Orban's Hungary, but that country is perhaps only the exception to the exception.[13] History teaches us that the processes of states of emergency and exception are constituted by complex matrices of power and resistance. The most effective tools of ideology, politics, and law have always involved the invocation of the

5 Darren Byler, "Violent paternalism: On the banality of Uyghur unfreedom", (2018) 16 (24–4) *The Asia-Pacific Journal: Japan Focus*, available at https://apjjf.org/2018/24/Byler.html, 15 December 2018.
6 "'Muslims are foreigners': Inside India's campaign to decide who is a citizen", *New York Times*, 4 April 2020.
7 "Duterte says he "cured" himself from being gay", *New York Times*, 3 June 2019; Hannah Ellis-Petersen, "Rodrigo Duterte's drug war is 'large-scale murdering enterprise,' says Amnesty," *Guardian*, 8 July 2019.
8 'What Brazil's President, Jair Bolsonaro, has said about Brazil's Indigenous Peoples', *Survival* at www.survivalinternational.org/articles/3540-Bolsonaro; "Lula: Bolsonaro leading Brazil 'to slaughterhouse' over Covid-19", *Guardian*, 17 April 2020.
9 Maggie Haberman and Zolan Kanno-Youngs, 'Trump plans to divert additional $7.2 billion from military to wall', New York Times (1 January 2020); 'Donald Trump's contempt for democracy', New York Times (20 October 2016); 'Donald Trump: Deport "bad hombres"', New York Times (20 October 2016).
10 *John Doe et al v Donald Trump et al.*, Stipulated Dismissal, Case 2:17-cv-00178-JLR, Document 205, 10 February 2020, United States District Court, Western District of Washington, Seattle.
11 Irit Katz, "Between *Bare Life* and *Everyday Life*: Spatializing Europe's migrant camps", (2017) 12(2) *Architecture Media Politics Society* 1, DOI:10.14324/111.444.amps.2017v12i2.001.
12 "EU to delay human and minority rights initiatives due to Covid-19", *EURACTIV*, 16 April 2020, available at www.euractiv.com/section/eu-priorities-2020/news.
13 "Hungary's emergency law 'incompatible with being in EU', say MEPs group", *Guardian*, 31 March 2020.

need to protect, to immunize, the body politic from a foreign threat. The pandemic has merely allowed the invocation of these signifiers in a blatant and overt way, bringing to light already present prejudices and hatreds. The figurative virus of history has become the literal virus of the present.

For Donald Trump, Covid-19 is a new "Yellow Peril," a Chinese virus.[14] Exceptional measures inside and at the border continue in a slightly magnified, and more legally plausible, form. In India, anti-Muslim violence, already widespread under Modi's proto-fascist attempts to change the citizenship laws, has morphed into the creation of a Muslim virus, spread perniciously by the Other among true (Hindu) Indians.[15] In Israel, ultra-Orthodox Jews protest against the secular authorities of the Jewish state and their attempt to identify and isolate them for what they experience, or classify for their own political ends, as discriminatory, anti-religious purposes.[16] In the United States, Canada, and throughout Europe there has been a rise in anti-Asian violence against the Chinese virus and its embodied enemy carriers.[17] At the same time, the Jew as virus, the signifying apparatus of law and politics so popular among the Nazis, has simply been reconstituted by today's antisemites.[18] Historical "fact" gives way to a reconstituted historical present as new/old tropes and signifiers are deployed by the opponents of the "deep state" and "fake news." Anti-lockdown demonstrators invoke Holocaust imagery, introduce tropes signifying and constructing modern liberal government as a Nazi regime in disguise, controlled by the Jews Soros and the Rothschilds. The idea of a Nazi Jewish regime is deployed with no apparent ironic, and certainly no historical, self-understanding. The protesters create a self-signification as the real victims of Hiterlite/Jewish oppression.[19] They demand a return to normal constitutional order, an order which for many requires the deconstruction of the state itself. Those on the far right have found a danger to true democracy in the invocation of the state of exception by authorities they consider antithetical to "authentic" values. As Elie Mystal has concluded, this is a new embodied form of constitutional unpatriotism.

14 "'Not racist at all': Donald Trump defends calling coronavirus the 'Chinese virus'", *Guardian,* 18 March 2020.

15 "Coronavirus conspiracy theories targeting Muslims spread in India", *Guardian*, 13 April 2020.

16 *Loewenthal, Adv. et al v. Prime Minister*, HCJ 2435/20.

17 "Targeting Asians and Asian Americans will make it harder to stop Covid-19", *Washington Post*, 2 April 2020.

18 Marcy Oster, "Anti-lockdown protests spawn more anti-Semitic conspiracy theories, Holocaust imagery", *The Forward,* 20 April 2020; Lev Topor, "Covid-19: Blaming the Jews for the Plague, again", *Fathom*, March 2020.

19 Frank Hornstein, "Holocaust trivialization at protests isn't just offensive. It threatens democracy", *The Forward,* 20 April 2020; "Dutch-Muslim politician tweets Jewish yellow star to protest coronavirus surveillance plan", *Jewish Telegraphic Agency*, 20 April 2020.

Solidarity is for them a demand from the deep state that must be resisted in the name of liberty.[20] The battles of resistance to the power of the state of exception can and do take on forms sometimes as dangerous as the emergency itself.

In the anti-lockdown protests against public health measures we can uncover the real nature of the exception and its juridical apparatus. When those on the left voice their fears of a surreptitious attack on civil liberties and on broad understandings of the appropriate place for social solidarity in modern democracies, when Orban and Modi use the virus to deepen their power and authorise violence against the enemy, and far-right protesters invoke a Jewish plot to control true citizens and profit from the cure for the "fake" or manufactured pandemic, the law and politics of emergencies come into the light in a much clearer fashion. The state of exception is never simply about the "state" in the exception, but more centrally focuses on deeper iterations of the nation and its others. Everywhere the idea of the nation, of an authentic identity combatting pretenders, including the state, the "deep state," and real Other, becomes the true ideological, political, and legal point of contention in the different, but always recognizable, states of exception.

Before Covid-19, as Fusco (chapter 1) and Cercel (chapter 2) highlight, France lived under a state of emergency for significant periods of Fifth Republic democracy. From "Muslim terrorism" to the *gilets jaunes* and pension reform protests, the constitution and a supplementary legislative framework establish the legal context for the exception that is not one.[21] Before the pandemic, in eastern and central Europe, conservative, populist, nationalist governments turned back democratic reforms and reconfigured institutional arrangements in the name of national identity and sovereignty, with gutless non-reactions from their neighbours and the European Union.[22] All that was and is needed in each of these cases, and others studied by the contributors to this volume, is an identified enemy and law.

As Fusco (chapter 1) argues, the creation of the enemy, of the threat to the state, or the nation, of the war that demands and indeed creates the exception, is largely an ideological device. Rhetoric and propaganda, assertions by executive and legislative branches of a public emergency, demanding exceptional measures, are left unchallenged or merely confirmed by the judicial branch of liberal democracies. The "historical"

20 "These people aren't freedom fighters – they're virus-spreading sociopaths", *The Nation*, 21 April 2020.

21 Bruno Latour and Nikolaj Schultz, "*Gilets Jaunes* as an occasion to restart politics", *Dagbladet Information*, 15 December 2018; French Constitution, Article 16, Article 36, Loi no 55–385 du 3 avril 1955, relative à l'état d'urgence.

22 Wojciech Sadurski, "Poland's ruling party just made its anti-democratic agenda radically clear", *Washington Post*, 13 September 2019; Martina Klicperová and Jaroslav Koštál, "European Sociopolitical Mentalities: identifying Pro-and Anti-democratic Tendencies", (2015) 17 *European Societies* 301.

requirement for the factual existence of a state of war or revolution is now replaced, or more accurately reversed, by the jurisprudential demand that the factual conform to the legal. The state of exception, like law itself for legal positivists, which has much to answer for here, determines the conditions of its own existence. The exception as fiction becomes the exception as juridical and political reality.

As Cercel reminds us (chapter 2), the Kelsenian *Grundnorm* and the apparently cruder (or perhaps more honest?) Schmittian project of politicizing law can lead and have each led us to the state of exception. No jurisprudential understanding or device can save law from itself, particularly when law does not wish to be saved from its true self. Both Kelsen and Schmitt have laid the intellectual groundwork for those who followed a path of constitutional legitimation and strict legality within and underneath the state of exception.[23] Non-normative positivism of the Hartian variety, the great *différend* of the Anglosphere, most clearly underscores the position of law as the determinant of its own existence at the core of legalized atrocity.[24] Normative theories of Marxism, as the great jurisprudential challenger to liberal and anti-liberal legal theory, offer no solace. As Cercel highlights, law was never absent from a Stalinist state of exception in the USSR or the "satellite" jurisdictions of central and eastern Europe. At the intersection of political theory and the practical invocation and implementation of the state of exception we always find law.

We likewise find law at the intersection of the state and the individual, the citizen, the patriot, who can be transformed with little effort into the *homo sacer*. As Tacik illustrates (chapter 3), an appropriately nuanced and critical account of the concept of sovereignty as articulated in international law theory, but especially practice, leads us, perhaps inevitably, to a place of the lawful exception. History, as both Tacik and Cercel demonstrate, places us in a state of exception that can only be law-full. Emergencies are legal fictions with real world consequences as the repressive and ideological state apparatuses find their best and most appropriate, and perhaps, "natural," iteration in the identification of the war, the emergency, the enemy, the *Homo sacer*, the exception, as a juridical reality.[25]

Lavis (chapter 5) elucidates the jurisprudential analysis that places law at the centre of the exception with a careful study of the jurisprudential history of the Schmittian exception as deployed by Agamben and attacked by his critics. In the context of the Nazi state, he rightfully situates the Schmitt/Agamben position in the context of Fraenkel's emplotment of the "Dual

23 Or Bassok, "The Schmitelsen Court: The question of legitimacy", (2020) 21 *German Law Journal* 131.

24 HLA Hart, "Positivism and the separation of law and morals", (1958) 71 *Harvard Law Review* 593.

25 Louis Althusser, "Idéologie et appareils idéologiques de'État", (1976) *Positions (1964–1975)*, (Paris: Les Éditions sociales, 1976), 67.

State."[26] Law and the Nazi state were in a constant position of self-contented juxtaposition and mutual reflection throughout the 1933–1945 period. Any argument that this was not the case must confront the historical and constitutional realities set out and analyzed by Lavis. As Kivotidis (chapter 6) also makes clear, the insights of Schmitt and Agamben into the core law/exception nexus are not marginal to our endeavors. We have known, or should have known, for some time that "law is politics." To dismiss Schmitt is to dismiss the central reality of law as a political phenomenon in either its "normal" or its "exceptional" manifestations. There is never, nor can there be, any kind of fundamental normative or taxonomical change from the Schmittian consolidating conflict between friend and foe within a state of exception. The politics of the exception are always political, and the law of the exception is always law.

Kai Ambos in his recent work has established and carefully analysed the close and intractable links and continuities between Nazi criminal law, the immediate pre-Nazi period, the 1933–1945 "*caesura*," and the post-Nazi period.[27] The time has come to move beyond any debate that Nazi law was not law, or that the National Socialist period was marked by some kind of pure exceptionality devoid of law. An appropriately nuanced "rediscovery" of Schmitt is a step in the right direction. The normativity and legality of the exception are core elements of any confrontation with the emergencies that constitute our lived realities. This does not mean, as the writers in this volume make clear in a variety of historical and geo-political contexts, that we must resign ourselves politically to a Schmittian right-wing political dictatorship. The dynamics and outcomes of power/resistance are not written in jurisprudential or political stone. We simply need to become comfortable with a legal philosophical place where the actual nature of the form and content of Nazi law, the position of exceptionality within its normative structures, and the ideas of a truly constitutive "exceptionalism" are placed at the centre of our historical and philosophical inquiries. When, as a jurisprudential matter, the Nazi state is understood as a legal state, the exception as a lawful constitutional moment, true critical engagement can begin. When we arrive at this constitutional and constitutive realization, Trump, Orban, Modi, Bolsonaro, Duterte, *et al.*, for all the necessary contextual differences, occupy a similar and comparable jurisprudential space.

The political and philosophical critique of our current legal/political regimes and the place of the "exception" within that social and juridical order are at the heart of all the contributions to this volume. From French constitutional normativity to the historical events and jurisprudential

26 Jens Meierhenrich, *The Remnants of the Rechtsstaat: An Ethnography of Nazi Law* (Oxford: Oxford University Press, 2018).

27 Kai Ambos, *National Socialist Criminal Law: Continuity and Radicalization* (Nomos/Hart: Baden-Baden/Oxford, 2019).

developments of natural law and legal positivism in European and English legal theory and legal history, the different forms of the law/exception nexus are clear. As Kivotidis sets out, our existential position can only be properly situated, and forms of possible resistance identified, if we understand the centrality of Schmittian jurisprudence to the historical realities of the constitutive orders of norm and exception from Weimar to National Socialism, from the new Europe of "rights" to normal and ordinary exceptional regimes around the world.

The current situation must also be placed in another set of institutional and jurisprudential frames that operated, and operate today, in Europe. As Cercel (chapter 2), Johansen (chapter 4), and Mańko (chapter 7) elucidate in different circumstances and in the context of multiple legal/political ideologies, the state of emergency, the exceptional rules of law under "extraordinary" circumstances, are not known only to "westernized" natural law or legal positivism, from Kelsen to Hart. The state of exception, in different but related guises, was never unknown to socialist/Marxist legality. Law has not disappeared as the state withered away; the commodity form has not been superseded by a non-legal reconfiguration of social relations. The dialectical oppositions of actually existing socialism and its exceptions were always presented in political and juridical guises. The current state of right-wing, anti-democratic populist governmentality and law in Poland has its historical, special, political, and jurisprudential roots in the martial law regime in that socialist country from 1981.

Issues of exception, emergency, constitutional order, and re-ordering are at the heart of the modern legal history of Europe. The moves from capitalism to the dictatorship of the proletariat, (through the vanguard of the revolution, the Party), from democracy and the Weimar crisis to "Nazi dictatorship," and from Communist "dictatorship" to democracy post-1989, are less characterized by "transition" or transitional justice, than by the substitution of one form of the legal exception by another, equally lawful, state of emergency. Law, it would seem, in all its guises, democratic capitalist, National Socialist, Marxist Leninist, has always found, and has had to find, space in its own normative and institutional structures for the state of exception.

Yildiz (chapter 8) moves the geographical frame to Europe's legally constituted formal borders, but the legal history echoes the same ideological structures and state juridical practice. From democratic regimes, to military rule, to Erdogan's populist, quasi-Islamizationist AKP, the laws of emergency have been invoked over and over again to protect the nation. The nation and its others situate legality and the exception wherever they are found as foundationally juridical phenomena necessary to safeguarding, preserving, and constituting, legally and politically, the real Turkey.

The Schmittian enemy remains a constant of our political and legal realities. Kurdish nationalists, democrats, *gilets jaunes*, Muslim terrorists, or just Muslims, striking shipyard workers, Jews, Nazis, communists, the "deep state"—the identity of the enemy matters little. Every state, every nation concretized inside or outside, or even in opposition to, formal nation state structures has complex or crude mechanisms for identifying the internal or external enemy and for dealing with the threat through the state of the exception. The taxonomies deployed are always, despite local, national particularities and specificities, reducible to a juridified enemy who must be eliminated. As Raimondi (chapter 9) sets out, liberal democracy, the rule of law, the *Rechtsstaat*, are no shield. In Italy, this enemy, foreign and domestic, in the form of G8 protesters, can be identified, singled out, "exceptionalized," and as the *Homo sacer*, beaten and killed by the forces of a legitimate democratic European legality. The new European order, the Europe of human rights, a Europe allegedly constructed on the premise of a post-1933–1945 legalized "never again," confirms the state's right to kill within some regime of undefined, but apparently murderous, legal proportionality.[28] There is, as there has always been, a legal frame in which the state of exception permits the execution of its will through the execution of its enemy.

Johansen (chapter 4) offers a somewhat more optimistic (but still always realistic) argument that the condition of law/emergency is perhaps not permanent. He seeks to place law in a minor key, reduced in power and significance, by social and political actions of reorganization and re-ordering. The dynamics and possibilities of resistance to emergency power can be identified. The process of a new, diminished legality and the questions of social practices as moments of resistance to law, of the reconfiguration of a knowledge/power juridical and political dynamic, of norm and exception, are however still decided within a legalized frame that appears to be dominated by law and lawful exceptions. The identification of spaces available for a Johansenian resistance appears from this perspective to be one of practising deconstructive politics, of identifying the necessary lacuna, the signifying break in the chain of social meaning through political endeavor. The deconstruction occurs in a moment or in a place, in a spatio-temporal site, a point of weakness into which a new politics might make some form of disruptive incursion. The problem, the legalized exception as resistance to counterpower, may or indeed must always nonetheless remain. Writing law under some form of political erasure still requires both the original writing of law and the irreducibility of the law that remains, even when deconstructed. The dynamic relationship between that which is written (law) and that which is erased (law) must still, as Johansen recognizes, as do the other contributors to the volume, operate in the new relationship and dynamic of the written that is resistance. Law has yet to wither away or to be replaced in any meaningful fashion by some still ill-defined and barely recognizable set of social practices that would eliminate, or even significantly reduce, the omnipresence of a

28 Stephen Skinner, *Lethal Force: The Right to Life and the ECHR* (Oxford: Hart, 2019), 92, 139.

looming state of legalized emergency. The enemy is always present because the enemy is the fictionalized *sine qua non* of the conditions of law's exceptional existence.

Instead of glorifying the rule of law or the *Rechtsstaat* that can kill when "necessary" and "proportional," hardly criteria meant to instil confidence on the question of which side of the line we might fall, every entrance to every law faculty and court house should carry Dante's inscription, "Abandon hope all ye who enter here." Nonetheless, as we despair, we continue to get out of bed every day. We remain socially isolated, Covid-19 or no Covid-19. We are full and free democratic citizens, socially distant, confined, living in a world of the commodity form and commodity fetishism. We inhabit and are inhabited by the emerging rule of data. We are always already more consumers than citizens, more data points to be exploited than free subjects of law imbued with transcendent and inherent "rights." We may no longer need emergencies and exceptions when we can simply consent to whatever cookies we encounter. As jurists, whether we like it or not, whatever our practices and moments of resistance may be, writing chapters in a book about the state(s) of exception, we incrementally strengthen the enemy, law, as we fight against it. There is no anti-law vaccine.

David Fraser, FAcSS
Professor of Law and Social Theory
University of Nottingham

Index

For Product Safety Concerns and Information please contact our EU representative GPSR@taylorandfrancis.com
Taylor & Francis Verlag GmbH, Kaufingerstraße 24, 80331 München, Germany

www.ingramcontent.com/pod-product-compliance
Ingram Content Group UK Ltd.
Pitfield, Milton Keynes, MK11 3LW, UK
UKHW020201200926
475702UK00004B/554
* 9 7 8 0 3 6 7 0 7 7 1 6 7 *